THE
MALBIM HAGGADAH

THE
MALBIM HAGGADAH

Translated, Adapted & Annotated
by
Jonathan Taub & Yisroel Shaw

Targum / Feldheim

First published 1993
Copyright © 1993 by J. Taub & Y. Shaw
ISBN 1-56871-007-0

Portions of this Haggadah have been reprinted from *The Hirsh Haggadah* with permission of Feldheim Publishers

Phototypeset at Targum Press
Printing plates produced by Frank, Jerusalem

Published by:
Targum Press Inc.
22700 W. Eleven Mile Rd.
Southfield, Mich. 48034
in conjunction with:
Mishnas Rishonim

Distributed by:
Feldheim Publishers
200 Airport Executive Park
Spring Valley, N.Y. 10977

Distributed in Israel by:
Targum Ltd.
POB 43170
Jerusalem 91430

Printed in Israel

Rabbi CHAIM P. SCHEINBERG

Rosh Hayeshiva "TORAH-ORE"

and Morah Hora'ah of Kiryat Mattersdorf

הרב חיים פינחס שיינברג

ראש ישיבת "תורה-אור"

ומורה הוראה דקרית מטרסדורף

בס"ד

הנה באו לפני הר"ר יונתן טאוב נ"י מגיד שיעור בישיבות אור ירושלים ומרכז התורה פה

עיה"ק ירושלים והבחור המוכשר ר' ישראל שאו נ"י

אשר רחש לבם דבר טוב לתרגם לשפת האנגלית ההגדה של פסח עם הפירוש מדרש הגדה

המיוחס להגאון המלבי"ם זצ"ל והוסיפו מראה מקומות והערות מאירות. הן אמנם שהאברכים

הנ"ל כתבו מאמר מחקרי יסודי להוכיח שסבר להניח שמחבר הפירוש הנ"ל אינו הגאון

המלבי"ם זצ"ל אך עכ"ז חשוב מאד להו"ל הפירוש הנ"ל בשפת האנגלית מפאת חשיבותו

העומד בפני עצמו. הלא המחבר של הפירוש מדרש הגדה הלך בעקבות הגאון המלבי"ם זצ"ל

לפרש ולבאר כל מאמרי חז"ל בהלכה ובאגדה ולהוכיח שדברי חז"ל נמצאים בתוך הלשון

והסגנון של תורה שבכתב להראות בפני עם ועדה שתושבע"פ ותושב"כ יחידה אחת הם.

ב"ה שזכינו בדור הזה להתגברות דרישת ה' ועתו ע"י תרגום הרבה ספרי קודש לשפת האנגלית

וע"י הוצאה לאור של הפירוש הנ"ל יתגבר בין דוברי האנגלית האמונה בעיקר העיקרים של

תורה אחת היא תורה שבכתב ותורה שבע"פ. אשר ע"כ יתכן עם האברכים הנ"ל ואמינא

לפעלם טבא ואיישר חילם לאורייתא להגדיל תורה ולהאדירה ולהוסיף זכות הרבים בעוד

ספרי יסוד בשפת האנגלית המועילים כספר הזה.

הכו"ח לכבוד התורה ולומדיה

חיים פנחס שיינברג

פה עיה"ק ירושלים

רחוב פנים מאירות 2, ירושלים, ת. ד. 6979, טל. 371513-(02), ישראל

2, Panim Meirot St., Jerusalem, P.O.B. 6979, Tel (02)-371513, Israel

בס"ד

MOSHE AND RIVKA FINK TORAH INSTITUTE • ישיבת רבינו חיים כהן רפאפורט
MERCAZ HATORAH

הנה האברכים החשובים ר' יונתן טאוב
ור' ישראל שאו נ"י תרגמו את הגדה של
פסח המיוחס להמלבי"ם לשפה אנגלית,
אומר, שאינני מומחה בשפה האנגלית - בכל זאת
מתוך שבאתי נוכחתי לדעת שעשו
מלאכתם באמונה, והתוכן מאד מאד הבל כולו,
והכל ששמעתי עדי בין כותלי ישיבתנו
הן בהתמדה והן במוסר - ור' יונתן טאוב
שהוא ממניני שיעור ב' בישיבתנו והוא משמש
שנים וזכה להעמיד תלמידים,
ויהי רצון שספרו יתקבל בין דוברי אנגלית
וישבו אמונה,
ממני המוקירם,
חיים קמיל וויטה

Tax exempt name:
AMERICAN FRIENDS OF MERCAZ HATORAH INC.
NEW YORK OFFICE: 84-12 115th St., Kew Gardens, N. Y. 11418, Tel. 718-805-1885
JERUSALEM OFFICE: Ein Tzurim 17, Talpiot, Jerusalem, P. O. Box 10067, Tel. 712 866 or 711 100

Translators' Foreword

The *Malbim* — for those acquainted with it, the name evokes a sense of clarity and simplicity in understanding the words of the Torah. The *Malbim's* classic commentary on *Chumash*, as well as on the rest of *Tanach*, is distinguished by its pertinent questions and elegant explanations of the most basic (and most important) level of understanding the text. One who is familiar with the style of the *Malbim* can easily imagine how welcome a *Malbim* commentary on the Haggadah would be, for the Haggadah — the most widely read Jewish text after the Bible — is also one of the least understood.

Although the Haggadah stands at the center of the Seder, and although every Jew is obligated to participate in its recitation, to a great extent it remains obscure and confusing. As a story, the text seems incoherent, the chrononology awry; certain events are inexplicably placed out of order, while others are repeated without any apparent reason. As a halachic guide, the text is similarly unintelligible; fragments of halachic discourse are scattered throughout, seemingly at random, leaving a bizarre mosaic that cries out for explanation, but at the same time seems to defy it.

In his brilliant analysis of the *p'shat*, or the simple, straight-forward meaning of the text, the author of *Medrash Haggadah*, the formal title of the *Malbim Haggadah*, reveals the Divine

inspiration underlying the words of our Sages which, along with the relevant verses from the Torah, comprise the Haggadah. He raises the questions that perplex the intelligent reader, and then offers lucid explanations rooted in a sensitive analysis of the text. His explanations demonstrate that the allusions the Sages derived from the verses are not merely man's arbitrary assignments of meaning to God's word, but are the genuine intent of His word.

A little known edition of this famous commentary, printed in 5654 (1894) and only recently rediscovered, includes a remarkable essay that reveals the secret of the structure of the Haggadah, a puzzle which has challenged generations of scholars. This essay, entitled *Maamar Yesod Mosad — A Statement of the Fundamental Principle [of the Haggadah]* — has been translated and adapted as the *Overview*.

Our English translation of the *Malbim Haggadah* follows the question-explanation style of the original Hebrew commentary. We have also included source references that were lacking in the original. Parts of the author's commentary that we felt were not essential to understanding the Haggadah are included as footnotes. In addition, our own comments on the commentary are included in footnotes marked by "(Eds.)." Although not included in the original *Malbim Haggadah*, we have translated and included the *Malbim*'s commentary on Tehillim for the second part of Hallel.

Although this commentary on the Haggadah has been known for many years as the *Malbim Haggadah*, recently doubts have arisen concerning the authorship of the commentary. We have researched the question and have included our

findings in an intriguing essay that we hope sheds light on this mystery.

We are grateful to many individuals whose helpfulness contributed to this translation, including Rabbi Yitzchok Lebovits (New York), Rabbi Label Lopiansky (Jerusalem), Rabbi Joseph Pearlman (author of *HaMeir Sidrah Sheets*, London), Mrs. Corinne Fishman (New York), Yechezkal Anis, Yechiel Greenbaum, Avraham Rosenblatt, David Silber, Daniel Taub, Ian Yaegar (Jerusalem), and each member of the Targum Press team. We also express our thanks to Feldheim Publishers for permission to use parts of the Haggadah text of the *Hirsch Haggadah*. This translation has been adapted to suit the *Malbim* commentary.

We are privileged to present the *Malbim Haggadah* to the English-speaking public for the first time since its appearance in Hebrew one hundred years ago. We offer our humble expression of gratitude to the Almighty for granting us this privilege, and we pray that this commentary assist the reader in the quest for a deeper understanding of the Haggadah, a heightened appreciation of the Pesach Seder, and a greater reverence for the words of our Sages and, ultimately, for the word of God.

Overview

"מה לתשובה אם אין שאלה"

"There can be no answer without a question."

(Introduction to *Medrash Haggadah*)

Some Questions

1) The compiler of the Haggadah should have placed the paragraph עבדים היינו לפרעה במצרים, *We were slaves unto Pharaoh in Egypt, after* the paragraph מתחלה עובדי עבודה זרה, היו אבותינו *At first our fathers were idol worshippers*, according to the chronological order of events. The second paragraph refers to Terach, Avraham's father, who died two hundred years before Avraham's children descended to Egypt and became slaves, the topic of the first paragraph.

This question is strengthened when we look at the conclusion of the second paragraph, מתחלה עובדי עבודה זרה: *and Yaakov and his children went down to Egypt.* These words would have served as an ideal transition to the paragraph עבדים היינו, *We were slaves unto Pharaoh in Egypt*, had the compiler of the Haggadah placed the paragraphs in chronological order.

2) The opening paragraph of the Haggadah, from עבדים היינו to ואפילו כלנו חכמים, *Therefore, even if we were all wise,*

v

is unnecessary. The narrative which עבדים היינו briefly relates is expounded in extensive detail later in the Haggadah in the paragraphs beginning with צא ולמד, *Go and learn*. There, each detail of the descent to Egypt, the servitude, the affliction, and the miracles of the Exodus are described and explained at length. What does עבדים היינו at the beginning of the Haggadah add to the lengthy narration that comes later?

3) What is the reason for the injunction, ואפילו כלנו חכמים, *Therefore, even if we were all wise... we would nevertheless be obligated to recount the story of the departure from Egypt?* What purpose does relating the story serve for those who already know it?

4) What is the reason for the word "and" in the phrase ואפילו כלנו חכמים, *And even if we were all wise?* The word "and" denotes an addition to a previous idea. For example, had the Haggadah previously mentioned that every person is required to recount the story of the Exodus, then the phrase "and even if we were all wise..." would have been appropriate. However, this phrase is the first mention of any obligation! The statement should instead read: *Even if we were all wise*, without the unnecessary conjunction "and".[1]

5) Many commentators have questioned the insertion of the paragraph אמר רבי אלעזר בן עזריה, *Said Rabbi Elazar ben Azaryah*, in the Haggadah. Rabbi Elazar ben Azaryah said, in the name of Ben Zoma, that the daily obligation for every Jew to mention the Exodus from Egypt applies at nighttime as well

---

1. The addition of the word "and" is not insignificant. *Tosafos* in *Menachos* 40b, *s.v. Techeles*, infers significant Halachic ramifications from the addition of the word "and" in a similar phrase "and even...".

as daytime (his opinion is the law, and we fulfill this law every night when we recite the Shema). Obviously, this dictum applies to every night of the year, not just the night of Pesach. Why, then, is it included in the Haggadah? What relevance does it have to Pesach more than any other night?[2]

6) Why did the compiler of the Haggadah insert the paragraph יכול מראש חדש, *One might think that the obligation to recount the story of the departure from Egypt begins from the first day of the month of Nissan*, between the paragraphs כנגד ארבעה בנים (the Four Sons) and מתחלה עובדי עבודה זרה?

The paragraph יכול מראש חדש expounds the reason for the timing of the obligation to recount in detail the story of the Exodus on Pesach night and not earlier. This discussion has no connection with either the preceding or following paragraphs.

7) Why did the compiler of the Haggadah place the paragraph רבן גמליאל היה אומר, *Rabban Gamliel used to say*, between the paragraphs כמה מעלות טובות and בכל דור ודור? The statement of Rabban Gamliel, that one must recite specific statements about the Pesach offering, matzah, and maror, has

---

2. The commentators have suggested that Pesach night indeed differs from all other nights, for on Pesach there is an additional mitzvah to *elaborate* upon the story of the Exodus. Their suggestion, however, does not answer the question. The mitzvah to elaborate is not an obligation, but merely a meritorious deed. The Haggadah itself states that this elaboration — one of the unique features of Pesach night — is only a commendable addition to the year-round obligation to *mention* the Exodus at night. The obligation to recount the story of the Exodus remains the same on Pesach night as on every other night. Therefore, the question remains, how does the night of Pesach differ from all other nights with regard to the obligation to mention the Exodus?

no connection with either the preceding or following paragraphs.

Moreover, it would have been appropriate after the paragraph יכול מראש חדש, which concludes with the words, *...at such a time when the matzah and the maror are in front of you*, for these are two of the three features which Rabban Gamliel instructs us to discuss.

8) Rabban Gamliel says that *whoever does not explain the following three things at the Pesach festival has not fulfilled his obligation, namely: Pesach, matzah, and maror.* From where does Rabban Gamliel learn his rule?[3]

---

3. *Tosafos* in *Pesachim 116a, s.v. V'amartem*, suggests that Rabban Gamliel derives his directive from the verse, *And you shall say, "This is the Pesach offering to God..."* (Exodus 12:27), which implies an obligation to verbally declare the reason for the Pesach offering. Rabban Gamliel, says *Tosafos*, derives the obligation to similarly declare the reasons for matzah and maror from their association (היקש) with the word "Pesach" in other verses. This answer for the source of Rabban Gamliel's law is very problematic.

First, how can Rabban Gamliel derive an obligation to recite specific phrases on Pesach night from a verse which has nothing to do with Pesach night? The verse, *And you shall say,* is the response to the question of the son who asks, "What is this service to you?" It does not mention Pesach. Nor does it mention any obligation to recite the response if the son does not ask, as Rabban Gamliel requires. Nor does it say that one who does not recite this statement about the Pesach offering has not fulfilled his obligation of relating the story of the Exodus, as Rabban Gamliel states.

Second, this verse is not even the source for the obligation to relate the story of the Exodus on Passover. Rather, the source for that is the verse, והגדת לבנך ביום ההוא לאמר, *And you shall relate to your child on that day saying...* (Exodus 13:8). But in that verse, there is no command to recite the phrases of Pesach, matzah, and maror.

Third, even if Rabban Gamliel does derive his principle from the verse, *And you shall say,* it would suffice to recite, *The Matzah which we eat...,* without

9) Why did the compiler of the Haggadah place the paragraph בכל דור ודור, *In every single generation*, after the paragraph רבן גמליאל היה אומר, *Rabban Gamliel used to say?* One paragraph has no connection with the other. בכל דור ודור discusses the obligation for every person to consider himself as if he personally left Egypt, whereas רבן גמליאל היה אומר discusses the obligation to recite the three specific phrases of Pesach, matzah, and maror.

Furthermore, the compiler of the Haggadah should have placed בכל דור ודור *before* רבן גמליאל היה אומר, because the paragraphs which precede רבן גמליאל היה אומר list the abundant acts of kindness God performed for the Jewish people, and they mention the obligation to praise and thank God for His benevolence. Therefore, it would have been appropriate to place בכל דור ודור — which discusses the obligation for every person to view himself as if he personally received God's acts of kindness — immediately after the list of those acts!

10) The above-mentioned paragraph states, בכל דור ודור, In every single generation one is obligated to look upon himself as if he personally had gone forth out of Egypt. The

---

the specific word "this": *This matzah which we eat...* Why does Rabban Gamliel require the word "this" in each of the three phrases about Pesach, matzah, and maror?

Fourth, again assuming that Rabban Gamliel derives his principle from the verse, *And you shall say*, he should only require that the Pesach offering be explained, for that is the only feature mentioned in this verse; matzah and maror are not mentioned. Although *Tosafos* asserts that these two are derived from their association with the word "Pesach" elsewhere, this needs explanation. Furthermore, even if they are derived from "Pesach", there should be no obligation to recite them at a time when there is no Pesach offering.

problem is that this concept has already been presented at the beginning of the Haggadah! In the paragraph עבדים היינו we read, *And if the Holy One, Blessed be He, had not taken our fathers out of Egypt, then we, our children, and our children's children would still have been subjugated to Pharaoh in Egypt.*

Why is this concept stated twice, and why is there such a lengthy interruption between the two statements?[4]

11) Why did the compiler of the Haggadah place Hallel, the verses of praise and thanksgiving to God, after the paragraph בכל דור ודור? Is there any reason behind the proximity of these paragraphs?

12) Why is this book called the *Haggadah*?

The word הגדה, *Haggadah*, comes from the verb להגיד, which means *to tell*. A more appropriate verb would have been לספר, *to relate* or *to recount*, which appears in many places, such as in the verse, *In order that you relate* (תספר) *in the ears of your children* (Exodus 10:2), as well as in the Haggadah itself, *We would nevertheless be obligated to recount* (לספר)... and, *They were relating* (מספרים) *the story of the departure from Egypt....*

Therefore, this book should have been named סיפור, *Sippur*, and not הגדה, *Haggadah*.

These questions — and many others — paint the picture of a jumbled text compiled in no meaningful order, a clutter

---

4. If the Haggadah repeats this concept in order to cite the verses which verify the source for this obligation (Shemos 13:8 and Devarim 6:23), then the compiler of the Haggadah should have quoted them earlier in the Haggadah the first time this concept appears. On the other hand, if the appropriate place in the Haggadah to mention this concept is here, near the conclusion of the Haggadah, then why mention it at all in the beginning?

of unconnected paragraphs in confusing disarray. The lack of coherence glares at us so blatantly that we become accustomed to the confusion, and after just a few hours of it each year we return the Haggadah to the shelves with faith that at least the person who put it together knew what he was talking about.

Of course, it is inconceivable that one of the most important books of Jewish observance would follow no meticulous order, or at least no order which the ordinary reader could not discern, follow, and learn from. What is the order behind the Haggadah of Pesach, and what did our Sages intend to teach with it?

Let us begin with the basics.

Step One. On the first night of Pesach, every Jew is required to perform five mitzvos. Two are required by the Torah: (1) To eat matzah (Shemos 12:18); (2) To recount the story of the Exodus from Egypt (Shemos 13:8). The other three are rabbinical ordinances: (1) To drink four cups of wine; (2) To eat maror; (3) To recite Hallel, the psalms of praise.

Because of their status as Torah commandments, the mitzvah to eat matzah and the mitzvah to recount the story of the Exodus stand out as the central motifs of the Pesach Seder. We fulfill the mitzvah to eat matzah, of course, by eating matzah. We drink wine, eat maror, and recite the passages of Hallel to fulfill the three rabbinical mitzvos of the evening. But how do we fulfill the mitzvah to recount the story of the Exodus?

For this mitzvah we have the Haggadah. Although we commonly refer to the entire book as the Haggadah, the term Haggadah technically refers to the middle part of the Hag-

gadah, or what we commonly call the *Maggid* section. Since this section is where we fulfill the mitzvah to recount the story of the Exodus, it is upon this section that our discussion is focused.

Step Two. The source for the obligation to recount the story of the Exodus is the verse (Exodus 13:8):

והגדת לבנך ביום ההוא לאמר בעבור זה עשה ה׳ לי בצאתי ממצרים

And you shall relate to your child on that day, saying: "It is because of this that Hashem acted for me when I came forth out of Egypt."

Although there are other verses in the Torah which command us to recount the story of the Exodus, this is the only verse which requires us to tell the story regardless of whether or not we are prompted by a child's question. The other verses command us to tell the story only if a child asks about the Exodus. Since the commandment of this verse, however, applies whether or not a child asks, it serves as the source for the mitzvah of Pesach night for every Jew to tell the story of the Exodus from Egypt.

Step Three. Since this verse is the source for the mitzvah to recount the Exodus and, therefore, the basis for the Haggadah, the compiler of the Haggadah composed its content and order to correspond to the phrases in the verse והגדת.

Step Four. This "Source Verse" has six parts:

1) והגדת לבנך — And you shall relate to your child
2) ביום ההוא — On that day
3) לאמר — Saying
4) בעבור זה — It is because of this
5) עשה ה׳ לי — Hashem acted for me

6) בצאתי ממצרים — When I came forth out of Egypt

The Haggadah, too, is divided into six sections, corresponding to these six phrases. Through the lens of this simple assumption we will begin to see the true colors and pattern of this marvelous masterpiece we call the Haggadah.

The First Section

והגדת לבנך — *And You Shall Relate To Your Child*

The first eight paragraphs, beginning with עבדים היינו and concluding with ושאינו יודע לשאול, were placed at the beginning of the Haggadah to correspond with והגדת לבנך, the first phrase of the Source Verse. Each paragraph contributes an essential element to describe the words והגדת לבנך, *And you shall relate to your child.*

When we read the paragraph of עבדים היינו, it sounds like the beginning of the story. Indeed, many commentators on the Haggadah maintain that the paragraph עבדים היינו is a narrative account, the first episode in the saga of our slavery in Egypt[5]. However, if we step back and view עבדים היינו in the broad perspective of the entirety of the Haggadah, we will see that it is, in fact, not part of the story of the Exodus.

This common misinterpretation arises from the innuendo of the first twelve words of עבדים היינו, which certainly do sound like a story:

עבדים היינו לפרעה במצרים ויוציאנו ה' אלקינו משם ביד חזקה

---

5. It is so widely accepted to be a narration that the custom has evolved to preface the recitation of עבדים היינו by saying, "The answer to the four questions of Mah Nishtana is as follows...".

ובזרוע נטויה — *We were slaves unto Pharaoh in Egypt, and Hashem our God took us out from there with a strong hand and an outstretched arm.*

Aside from these few words, however, nothing else in this paragraph, or in the following eight paragraphs, even slightly resembles a narrated story. We find no story until we come to the paragraph מתחלה עובדי עבודה זרה (nine paragraphs later!). But now we are left with a question. If עבדים היינו is not telling us part of the story, then what is it telling us? The answer has profound implications.

The sentence עבדים היינו לפרעה במצרים ויוציאנו ה' אלקינו משם ביד חזקה ובזרוע נטויה, *We were slaves unto Pharaoh in Egypt, and Hashem our God took us out from there with a strong hand and an outstretched arm* is not the beginning of the story of the Exodus, but is the declaration of the fundamental reason *why* we are all obligated to recount the Exodus story.

Because we were slaves unto Pharaoh in Egypt, we are obligated to tell the story of the Exodus and to express our enormous gratitude to our Redeemer, for had He not brought us forth from Egypt we would still be there. עבדים היינו is the reason *why* we have the mitzvah to tell the story; it is not the story itself.

Let us delve deeper by asking another basic question. Why must every Jew recount the Exodus, why must even the wisest sage tell the story, each and every year, which everyone already knows?

At first thought, we could say that the reason for this obligation is for everyone to recognize that our lives and our freedom come from God. Through remembering the Exodus,

we are reminded that it is God's omnipotently open hand which gives us everything we need. This renewed recognition inspires us to strengthen our love, awe, and service for God.

This is certainly an appropriate explanation for the obligation to recount the Exodus. But still — there seems to be something more to this mitzvah, for if its purpose was solely to enhance our devotion to God, then why are the wise, holy, righteous Jews, who are constantly cognizant of God's greatness, obligated to recount the Exodus? There must be some greater purpose behind this mitzvah. It is this purpose which will give us profound insight into the mitzvah of recounting the Exodus.

Indeed, recounting the events of the Exodus is not solely for our own spiritual benefit. But it is also for our children's. For when we recount the Exodus, we not only ensure that *we* do not forget what God did for us, but we also guarantee that our children and future generations will recall the Exodus and realize that their lives, too, were fundamentally affected by that awesome event, and they will, as a consequence, acknowledge their personal responsibility to praise and thank the Almighty. To ensure this perennial awareness of what God did for His people, every Jew is commanded to tell and elaborate upon the events of the Exodus, regardless of his wisdom and knowledge, for it is not only for his benefit, but for the benefit of the future generations of the Jewish people.

If particular individuals had been exempted from this obligation, it would have been conceivable for the Exodus to be forgotten. Any Jew acquainted with history would exempt himself by justifying that he already knows the historical events.

Exempt from telling the story of the Exodus, he would leave his children ignorant of the significance of their past, and unaware of their purpose for the present and their responsibilities for the future. By requiring every person to recount the Exodus, regardless of his knowledge, the Torah circumvents this problem. The continued consciousness of our collective history and the responsibilities and privileges that it bore is guaranteed.

We now understand the paragraph עבדים היינו. The sole but critical purpose of עבדים היינו is to inform us that the obligation to tell the story of the Exodus falls upon every Jew, even if he already knows it and has no need to retell it. For it is not only for his sake that he must tell it, but for the sake of all following generations. עבדים היינו therefore says:

> We were slaves to an oppressive king and to an oppressive nation. Only God, through His miraculous Divine providence, took us out from there. Had God not delivered us, we, our children, and our children's children would still have been subjugated to Pharaoh in Egypt. All subsequent generations would have been born into the oppression of Egypt. Therefore, since all later generations were also included in the redemption, they are also obligated to praise and thank God for the deliverance from slavery to freedom. In order to ensure that they will be aware of their privileged responsibility, we are all obligated to recount the Exodus *and even if we were all wise.* For that is the failsafe strategem to keep alive the events of the Exodus in the mind and heart of the Jewish people.

Our questions begin to disappear.

1) עבדים היינו has a distinct purpose and is not out of order

in the Haggadah. Since it is not meant to be part of the story but rather the impetus to tell the story, it is appropriately placed at the beginning of the Haggadah, before the telling of the story.

The statement ואלו לא הוציא הקדוש ברוך הוא...משעבדים היינו לפרעה במצרים *And if the Holy One, blessed be He, had not taken our fathers out of Egypt, then we, our children, and our children's children would still have been subjugated to Pharaoh in Egypt* is not repeating the idea that appears later in בכל דור ודור, *that we must view ourselves as if we were personally redeemed from Egypt*. Rather, it is declaring the purpose for our obligation to recount the Exodus — if not for ourselves, then for our children who were also affected by the event.

2) Once we understand that the purpose of recounting the Exodus is not only for ourselves, but for our children and future generations, we can understand why we must recount the Exodus even if we were all wise — ואפילו כלנו חכמים. The purpose of the recounting is not for us, but for our children. Requiring every individual to recount the Exodus, regardless of his level of knowledge, is the infallible method to ensure that our children will always be aware of it and its import.

3) We now understand why the word "and" was added to ואפילו כלנו חכמים, *and even if we were all wise... we would nevertheless be obligated to recount the story of the Exodus from Egypt*. ואפילו כלנו חכמים is not a self-contained statement, but the corollary of the preceding sentence, ...our children, and our children's children, would still have been subjugated to Pharaoh in Egypt. Once we know that the *raison d'être* of the obligation is for the sake of our children, to ensure that they will know that they were redeemed as well, it follows

logically that every one of us must recount it, *and even if we were all wise... we would nevertheless be obligated to recount the story of the Exodus from Egypt.*

The Torah itself subtly implied this reason for the obligation when it phrased the command, והגדת לבנך, *And you shall tell your child*..., using the verb "tell" and emphasizing telling *your child.* If the purpose was for us and not for our children, the command would be phrased, וזכרת, *And you shall remember....*

The Sages, following the Torah's lead that the purpose of telling the story of the Exodus is not only for us but for our children, introduced additional customs for the sake of the children, such as removing the Seder plate before the meal begins, and having the children snatch away the Afikoman. These customs were introduced to attract the attention and interest of the children and to encourage their questions, thereby assisting us to instill in them the awareness of the Exodus.

In conclusion, עבדים היינו is not the beginning of a story, but a pedagogical statement giving the reason why we are obligated to recount the Exodus even if we are all wise. The inclusion of עבדים היינו here is based on the words והגדת לבנך, the first words in the verse והגדת לבנך ביום ההוא לאמר בעבור זה עשה ה' לי בצאתי ממצרים. עבדים היינו encapsulates the essence of והגדת לבנך, *And you shall relate to your child*: the purpose for recounting the Exodus is for our children to be aware of what God did for us and for them.

The seven paragraphs that follow are also based on the words והגדת לבנך:

מעשה ברבי אליעזר is an example of telling the story *even if we were all wise.* Five of the greatest Tannaim, Rabbi Eliezer,

Rabbi Yehoshua, Rabbi Elazar ben Azarya, Rabbi Akiva, and Rabbi Tarfon, eminent sages whose minds were immersed in the depths of every realm of Torah, nevertheless elaborated upon the Exodus story throughout the night. They knew that the purpose of the obligation was not solely for the individual, but for ensuing generations — והגדת לבנך.

אמר רבי אלעזר בן עזריה is also an important addition to this part of the Haggadah. Although there is an obligation to mention the Exodus every night of the year, the obligation on Pesach night is different. Every other night one is required merely to mention the Exodus to himself, whereas on Pesach night he must tell the story to someone else, and even if there is no one else present, he must tell the story to himself in order to safeguard against it ever being forgotten.

The paragraphs dealing with the Four Sons follow, depicting the responses to the questions of the four types of children. These paragraphs appropriately appear in the section of the Haggadah which corresponds to והגדת לבנך, *And you shall relate to your child*. The response to the last son, the son who does not know how to ask, is the very verse which is the source for the obligation to tell the story of the Exodus, והגדת לבנך ביום ההוא לאמר בעבור זה עשה ה׳ לי בצאתי ממצרים — an appropriate ending to this section of the Haggadah.

The Second Section
ביום ההוא — *On That Day*

After the section which corresponds to the words והגדת לבנך and which describes the obligation to recount the Exodus, comes

the section which corresponds to the next words ביום ההוא, *on that day*, and which describes the proper time for this obligation.

The Haggadah derives from the words ביום ההוא that the obligation of והגדת לבנך — telling about the Exodus — must be fulfilled *on that day*, the day *when matzah and maror are in front of you* — that is, the Fifteenth of Nissan.

Therefore, following the order of words in the Source Verse, והגדת לבנך ביום ההוא, *And you shall relate to your child on that day*, this is certainly the fitting place for the paragraph יכול מראש חדש. This answers our sixth question.

The Third Section

לאמר — *Saying*

We now come to the third section of the Haggadah, which corresponds to the third phrase לאמר, *saying*, in the Source Verse. We have seen that the compiler of the Haggadah established the order of the Haggadah based upon the sequence of words in the Source Verse, והגדת (Shemos 13:8). We have seen that he placed the description of the obligation to recount the Exodus first, corresponding to the words והגדת לבנך. Next, he placed the details of when to fulfill this obligation, corresponding to the next words in the verse, ביום ההוא. Likewise, the third section corresponds to the third phrase, לאמר, *saying*, and contains the actual saying of the story of the Exodus.

Not only was the compiler of the Haggadah consistent with the order of words in the Source Verse, but he also achieved a logical progression by first introducing the obligation to recount the Exodus (והגדת לבנך), then instructing when to fulfill

this obligation (ביום ההוא), and then including the actual fulfillment of the obligation (לאמר).

This section of the Haggadah starts with the paragraph מתחלה עובדי עבודה זרה and continues with צא ולמד. Here, the Haggadah begins its analysis of the verses in Devarim 26:5-8 which describe the history of the Exodus. Each word of these verses depicts a particular component of the Exodus story so that together these four verses encapsulate the essence of our experience — the suffering of slavery, the relief of redemption, and the awesome miracles and wonders which God wrought for our sake. The Haggadah cites each verse and shows how the details of the Exodus are inherent in each word.

Following the elucidation of the verses comes the paragraphs כמה מעלות טובות and על אחת כמה וכמה. These paragraphs list the bountiful kindnesses God bestowed upon us when He brought us forth from Egypt, when He guided us through the wilderness, and when He escorted us into the Holy Land. They were placed at the conclusion of the recounting of the story of the Exodus because they include additional accounts of God's benevolence which were not mentioned in the verses which the Haggadah cited, such as God's enriching us with the wealth of Egypt, the splitting of the Sea, the provision of our needs in the wilderness, and additional acts of kindness which the Exodus led to, including the giving of the Sabbath, the receiving of the Torah, the entry into the land of Israel, and the building of the Holy Temple.

In conclusion, the compiler of the Haggadah placed this section — beginning with מתחלה עובדי עבודה זרה, ending with על אחת כמה וכמה, and containing the actual telling of the story of

the Exodus — as the third section of the Haggadah. It appropriately corresponds to the third phrase of the Source Verse upon which the Haggadah is based: the phrase לאמר in the verse והגדת לבנך ביום ההוא לאמר בעבור זה עשה ה׳ לי בצאתי ממצרים.

The Fourth Section

בעבור זה — *Because of This*

The fourth section corresponds to the fourth phrase, בעבור זה, *it is because of this*, in the Source Verse. With this simple assumption we can answer the seventh and eighth questions.

Rabban Gamliel's rule that one must explain the Pesach, matzah, and maror, corresponds to the phrase בעבור זה, which is why the compiler of the Haggadah placed the paragraph of Rabban Gamliel at this point in the Haggadah.

Rabban Gamliel's rule states that if one does not explain these three objects — Pesach (the Paschal offering), matzah, and maror, then one has not fulfilled the obligation to recount the Exodus. What is the source for this rule? His source is none other than the phrase to which this section of the Haggadah corresponds — בעבור זה.

How does Rabban Gamliel derive from these words the obligation to recite the explanation of the Pesach offering, matzah, and maror?

Rabban Gamliel reads the verse והגדת differently from the common reading. The common reading is,

> And you shall relate to your child on that day, saying: "It is because of this that Hashem acted for me when I came forth out of Egypt".

Rabban Gamliel, however, translates the verse as follows:

> And you shall relate to your child on that day, saying: "This is because of what Hashem acted for me when I came forth out of Egypt".

Rabban Gamliel translates בעבור זה as *this is because* or *the reason for this is*, which is indeed an accurate, simple translation of the words בעבור זה. The difference between the common way of reading the verse and Rabban Gamliel's way is whether the word זה, *this*, is the subject or the object of the subordinate clause. Rabban Gamliel learns that it is the subject ("this thing is because") and not the object ("because of this thing"). To illustrate, it is as if the phrase reads זה בעבור instead of בעבור זה, and as if the verse reads, והגדת לבנך ביום ההוא לאמר זה בעבור עשה ה׳ לי בצאתי ממצרים .

What does "this" refer to? "This" is the object on the table to which one can point and say, "*This* is because...", referring to the Pesach offering, the matzah, and the maror.

To summarize, Rabban Gamliel's rule is clearly written in the verse itself: *And you shall relate to your child on that day, saying: "This [the Pesach offering, matzah, and maror] is because of what Hashem acted for me when I came forth out of Egypt*". Consequently, in order to fulfill the obligation of relating the story of the Exodus to one's child, one must also relate the reason for the Pesach offering (*"Because the Holy One, blessed be He, passed over the houses of our fathers in Egypt*"), the reason for the matzah (*"Because the dough of our fathers did not have time to become leavened*"), and the reason for the maror (*"Because the Egyptians embittered the lives of*

our fathers in Egypt"). This obligation is part and parcel of the obligation to recount the Exodus, as is evident by its presence in the verse which commands us to recount the Exodus.

This also explains why we must say "This matzah" and "This maror", for "this" is the language of the verse, בעבור זה, *this is because.*[6]

The Fifth Section

עשה ה׳ לי —*Hashem Acted for Me*

After the section of the Haggadah based on the phrase בעבור זה, we come to the section based on the next words in the verse, עשה ה׳ לי. These words are the source for the obligation for each person to consider himself as if he personally had been redeemed from Egypt. Therefore, the compiler of the Haggadah placed the paragraph בכל דור ודור, which discusses this obligation, at this point in the Haggadah following the order of the verse. This answers our ninth question.

This paragraph states, *In every single generation one is obligated to look upon himself as if he personally had gone forth out of Egypt.* The paragraph continues to prove this obligation from the words עשה ה׳ לי, *Hashem acted for me*, in the Source Verse.

We asked that the idea of viewing oneself as having personally left Egypt already appeared at the beginning of the

---

6. We do not say "*This* Paschal lamb" because we no longer have the Pesach sacrifice to which we could point and say "This Paschal lamb". Since the destruction of the second Holy Temple, the text was changed from "This Paschal lamb which we eat" to "The Paschal lamb that our fathers used to eat at the time when the Holy Temple was still standing".

Haggadah in עבדים היינו, *We were slaves... And if the Holy One, Blessed be He, had not taken our fathers out of Egypt, then we, our children, and our children's children would still have been subjugated to Pharaoh in Egypt.* We already explained that the purpose of that statement is to explain why every individual is obligated to recount the Exodus *even if we were all wise.* It does not come to express the idea that one must view oneself as having personally left Egypt. For that comes the fifth section of the Haggadah, the paragraph בכל דור ודור, which corresponds to the phrase עשה ה' לי, *Hashem acted for me* — the fifth phrase in the Source Verse, והגדת.

The Sixth Section

בצאתי ממצרים — *When I came forth from Egypt*

The sixth section of the Haggadah begins with the paragraph לפיכך, *Therefore we are obliged to give thanks,* an introduction to the recital of Hallel, the psalms of praise to God for the miracles of the redemption from Egypt.

This paragraph states that we are obligated to thank God with abundant expressions of praise and exaltation for all the acts of kindness He bestowed and continually bestows upon us. This paragraph ends with the imperative, הללויה, *Praise God!,* an appropriate introduction to Hallel.

The recitation of Hallel was placed at the end of the Haggadah because it corresponds to the phrase בצאתי ממצרים, *when I came forth out of Egypt,* the sixth and final phrase of the Source Verse. The Hallel of the Seder commemorates the miracles of the redemption from Egypt and gratefully declares,

בצאת ישראל ממצרים, *When Israel went forth from Egypt,* echoing the words upon which its inclusion in the Haggadah is based, בצאתי ממצרים. This answers our eleventh question.

And our final question — why is this book called the Haggadah — has long since disappeared. Since the book's foundation from beginning to end is based on the words of the verse והגדת לבנך, it is obvious that the <u>most fitting title for</u> this book is the first word of that verse, הגדה.

In Conclusion

With a single, clear, simple answer, we have discovered an overwhelmingly logical and organized order in the Haggadah. The order of the Haggadah is the order of words in the verse which stands as the source for one of the Pesach Seder's, and, indeed, one of the entire year's, most important mitzvos:

והגדת לבנך	And you shall relate to your child;
ביום ההוא	On that day Saying
בעבור זה	It is because of this
עשה ה׳ לי	that Hashem acted for me
בצאתי ממצרים	When I came forth out of Egypt.

The Argument between Rav and Shmuel

The Mishnah in *Pesachim* (116a) teaches that our narration of the Exodus story on Pesach night must begin with the shameful parts of our history, to be followed by praises of God Who raised us from our shameful state.

The two Talmudic sages Rav and Shmuel disagree what

"shameful" refers to in the Mishnah. Rav explains that "shameful" refers to the paragraph מתחלה עובדי עבודה זרה, *At first our fathers were idol worshippers*, which discusses our shameful ancestry prior to Avraham. Shmuel, on the other hand, explains that "shameful" refers to the paragraph עבדים היינו, *We were slaves*, which discusses our shameful degradation in Egypt.

The Questions

1) The argument regarding the connotation of "shameful" is straightforward. What practical ramifications, however, does this argument bear on the text of the Haggadah? Does Shmuel maintain that we do not recite the paragraph מתחלה עובדי עבודה זרה at all, and does Rav maintain that we do not recite the paragraph עבדים היינו? If so, then according to each opinion, there would be no question regarding the chronological order of the two paragraphs (see our first question in the *Overview*), because there would only be *one* paragraph. However, according to the Halachic ruling that we read both paragraphs, the question remains, why do we read עבדים היינו before מתחלה עובדי עבודה זה; this order contradicts both the chronological sequence of events as well as the logical progression of the content of the paragraphs.

2) In practice, when we read the Haggadah we follow the view of Shmuel and commence with עבדים היינו. In Talmudic law, however, there is a rule that in any dispute between Rav and Shmuel concerning a non-monetary matter, we follow the opinion of Rav. Why, then, in the Haggadah, do we follow Shmuel's opinion?

One possibility is that we adopt Shmuel's ruling because

immediately following the account of the argument of Rav and Shmuel, the Talmud records an incident in which Rav Nachman started his recitation with עבדים היינו — just as Shmuel ruled. However, if we follow Shmuel's opinion because Rav Nachman did, then we are faced with another problem — why did Rav Nachman himself follow Shmuel's opinion?

Even if we suppose that Rav Nachman read *both* Shmuel's paragraph and Rav's paragraph, then the first question we asked returns: following the chronological and natural order of the content of the paragraphs, Rav Nachman should have read Rav's paragraph first.

Moreover, the actual ruling of the Halachic authorities itself is enigmatic. They rule that we follow both views by reading both paragraphs. How does this ruling follow *both* opinions, though, since the argument itself was which paragraph to start with; the ruling that we read both, beginning with עבדים היינו, effectively follows Shmuel's opinion, and not Rav's!

3) Both the opinion of Rav and the opinion of Shmuel pose problems. Does Rav, who states that we begin the Haggadah with מתחלה עובדי עבודה זרה, also hold that we omit all of the preceding paragraphs, or that we should insert them elsewhere in the Haggadah? It is difficult to conceive how Rav could omit so many essential paragraphs, considerably shortening the Haggadah. On the other hand, if Rav does not omit them from the Haggadah, where does he insert them?

Similarly, we can ask whether Shmuel, who states that we begin the Haggadah with עבדים היינו, holds that we omit מתחלה עובדי עבודה זרה, or whether we include it after עבדים היינו (like the text of our Haggadah). If the latter is

true, then the only point of dissent between Rav and Shmuel is *when*, and not *whether*, we read מתחלה עובדי עבודה זרה.

Once we know that the order of the Haggadah is based on the verse והגדת לבנך (see *Overview*), and we understand that every passage was purposefully placed in its particular place, we can understand the argument between Rav and Shmuel.

The Mishnah in *Pesachim* (116a) states that we must begin the Haggadah with the shameful part of Jewish history and conclude with the praises of God. The Mishnah does not say what the "shameful" part of Jewish history is; this is the subject of the dispute between Rav and Shmuel. Rav explains that "shameful" refers to our shameful ancestry of idol worshippers, described in the paragraph מתחלה עובדי עבודה זרה. Shmuel maintains that it refers to our shameful oppression in Egypt, descibed in the paragraph עבדים היינו.

If the order of the Haggadah is so precise, and every section in its exact place, then how do Rav and Shmuel disagree how the Haggadah starts? If the order of the Haggadah follows the verse, as we have shown, and the verse dictates that each section must be in its appropriate place, without any omissions or changes in the order, then how can Rav disrupt this clarity by starting the Haggadah with מתחלה עובדי עבודה זרה, the section based on the third, not the first, part of the verse? Is Rav not aware that the Haggadah has a basic order which cannot be altered?

Upon closer examination of the words of the Talmud, we will discover that Rav and Shmuel were not at all arguing about the order of passages in the Haggadah.

When the Mishnah states, "One begins with the shameful

part...", the Talmud does not ask, "With what part does one begin?". Instead, it asks, "What is the 'shameful' part?".

There was never any question how the Haggadah starts. Everyone agrees to the order of the Haggadah as based on the Biblical verse. Rav agrees that the Haggadah starts with עבדים היינו as the order of words in the "Source Verse" requires. Rather, they argue which part of the Haggadah was the Mishnah referring to when it said, "One begins with the shameful part". Does the Mishnah mean the beginning of the Haggadah, or does it mean the beginning of the section which tells the story of the Exodus?

This is the question which Rav and Shmuel come to answer. Rav answers that "shameful" refers to the beginning of the third section of the Haggadah, the most important section, for it contains the telling of the story of the Exodus (מתחלה עובדי עבודה זרה). The preceding sections are all introductory. Shmuel, however, learns the Mishnah literally, and answers that "shameful" refers to the very beginning of the Haggadah (עבדים היינו), and not the beginning of the third section.

Therefore, when Rav Nachman opened with עבדים היינו, he was not ruling like Shmuel, for even Rav agrees that the Haggadah opens with עבדים היינו.

The Origin of the Haggadah
Who wrote the Haggadah?

We usually allude to the author of the Haggadah in vague terms such as the *Ba'al HaHaggadah*. But who is this anony-

mous *Ba'al HaHaggadah?*

The commonly accepted assumption ascribes the compilation of the Haggadah to sometime during the Mishnaic or Talmudic periods (circa 3610/150 B.C.E. to 4210/450 C.E.). Of course, from the time of the Exodus (2448/1312 B.C.E.) the Jews have celebrated Pesach and have fulfilled the commandment of והגדת לבנך, *And you shall tell your child...*, as well as the other commandments of Pesach. However, the need for the formalization of the Haggadah for the benefit of ensuing generations arose only later in the history of the Jewish people. The actual compiler and the time of organization of the Haggadah is uncertain.

According to our assumption, however, we can deduce a precise time for the composition of the Haggadah as it appears before us, and we may even be able to suggest its author.

The latest Tanna (sage who lived during the period of the oral transmission of the law, the time of the Mishnah) mentioned in the Haggadah is Rabbi Yehudah, who is cited in the statement, *Rabbi Yehudah made a mnemonic [for the ten plagues]*. When the name of Rabbi Yehudah appears with no surname, it refers to Rabbi Yehudah bar (the son of) Rabbi Ela'ay (circa 160 B.C.E.), who was the teacher of Rabbeinu HaKadosh (Rabbeinu Yehudah HaNasi, commonly called *Rebbi*), the redactor of the Mishnah and the prestigious leader of Babylonian Jewry.

Therefore, the Haggadah could not have been written earlier than the time of Rabbeinu HaKadosh; otherwise, the writer could not have quoted Rabbi Yehudah, who would have lived later.

However, the *latest* time for the origin of the Haggadah remains unknown. According to most commentators on the Talmud, the Haggadah was still not in existence in the time of Rav and Shmuel. According to those commentators, when Rav and Shmuel argued the Mishnah's meaning of the word "shameful" (the Mishnah states that the recounting of the Exodus on Pesach night must begin with the "shameful" aspects of Jewish history), they were arguing which paragraph comes first in the Haggadah. If that is true, then even in the time of Rav and Shmuel (circa 230 C.E.), the Haggadah had not yet been formalized, or else they would not have argued how it should begin.

The Haggadah was, however, apparently organized by the time of Rav Nachman, for certain statements that he made imply that his Haggadah was identical to ours.

Who was Rav Nachman and when did he live? This is the subject of a dispute between *Rashi* and *Tosafos*. *Tosafos* (*Bava Basra 46b, s.v. Shalach*) states that when the name "Rav Nachman" appears unadorned, it refers to Rav Nachman bar Yaakov (circa 280 C.E.), who was a student of Rav and Shmuel. According to *Rashi*, the name "Rav Nachman" refers to Rav Nachman bar Yitzchak (circa 370 C.E.), who was a student of Rava. According to this opinion, the Haggadah was not written until the end of the period of the Talmudic sages.

According to our explanation of the order of the Haggadah, the Haggadah was written much earlier. We explained that Rav and Shmuel were not arguing which paragraph should begin the Haggadah. The Haggadah had already been formalized, and Rav and Shmuel each held in their hands the same text of

the Haggadah. Rather, they argued *where* in the existing Haggadah appears the "shameful" part of Jewish history mentioned in the Mishnah. Rav held that "shameful" refers to מתחלה עובדי עבודה זרה היו אבותינו. Although that is not the beginning of the Haggadah, it is the beginning of this specific section. This is how Rav interpreted the Mishnah, "We must begin with the shameful part."

Shmuel, on the other hand, held that the Mishnah was referring to the beginning of the entire Haggadah, the paragraph עבדים היינו. But they both agree to the actual text and order of the Haggadah.

We can, therefore, suggest that the Haggadah had been formalized no later than the time of Rav and Shmuel. Furthermore, Rav and Shmuel were students of Rabbeinu HaKadosh (Shmuel was also his physician). We mentioned above that the Haggadah could not have been written before the time of Rabbeinu HaKadosh because it cites his teacher, Rabbi Yehudah.

It follows that the time of the writing of the Haggadah concurred exactly with the time that Rabbeinu HaKadosh lived and the time that the Mishnah, the Oral Law, was committed to writing (circa 180 B.C.E.). In addition, the literary style of the Haggadah is very similar to the style of the Mishnah. Furthermore, no teachings of any Talmudic sages (who lived after the redaction of the Mishnah) are mentioned in the Haggadah, albeit there exist many teachings of the Talmudic sages relating to the verses cited in the Haggadah.

These factors suggest that the Haggadah was written during the time that the Mishnah was committed to writing. And if the

time of the writing of the Haggadah was precisely during the lifetime of Rabbeinu HaKadosh, then it is not unlikely that the compiler of the Haggadah was none other than the great leader of Jewry himself, the preserver of the Oral Law for all ensuing generations, the holy and renowned sage of the Mishnah, Rabbeinu HaKadosh.

Thanks to Rabbi Asher Balanson, Rabbi Yitzchok Lebovits, Rabbi Label Lopiansky, Rabbi Joseph Pearlman, Rabbi Daniel Taub, Rabbi Meir Tribits, Mrs. Corinne Fishman, Yechezkel Anis, Yechiel Greenbaum, Ian Jaeger, Daniel Taub, and to the many other individuals whose helpfulness contributed to the translation and research.

בְּדִיקַת חָמֵץ, בִּטוּלוֹ וּבְעוּרוֹ

Search for Chametz,
Annulling and
Destroying Chametz

On the evening of the 14th of Nissan (or, if this falls on Friday night, on the evening of the 13th), every corner of the house must be searched for chametz. Although some families have the custom of putting out ten (well-wrapped) pieces of bread to be found during the search, this is by no means a substitute for making a thorough search for all chametz present. The search is made by the light of a candle. However, in places where it is more convenient, a flashlight may be used.

Before starting the search, one is required to make the appropriate berachah. All those who will help in the search should be present and attentive when the berachah is recited by the head of the household or whoever is leading the search, having in mind that it is being said for them, too. Immediately after the recitation of the berachah, one may not speak or delay before beginning the search, and it is preferable not to speak at all until the search has been completed, except when necessary for the performance of the search. One should have the intention that this berachah is not only for the search but also for the annulling of the chametz immediately afterward, the burning of the chametz the next morning and the final annulling after that. The berachah is as follows:

בָּרוּךְ אַתָּה יהוה אֱלֹהֵינוּ מֶלֶךְ הָעוֹלָם אֲשֶׁר
קִדְּשָׁנוּ בְּמִצְוֹתָיו וְצִוָּנוּ עַל בְּעוּר חָמֵץ:

Blessed be You, Hashem our God, King of the universe, Who has sanctified us by His commandments and commanded us concerning the removal of chametz.

1

After the search, one should wrap the chametz which he intends to burn the following morning and store it in a place where it is safe from children and pests. Likewise, any chametz which he intends to eat until the permitted time expires should be similarly stored in a secure place.

At this point, all remaining chametz which is unknown to the head of the household is to be annulled. The following declaration is not a prayer but an act which, in order to be valid, must be understood. Therefore, it should be said in a language understood by the one reciting it.

כָּל חֲמִירָא וַחֲמִיעָא דְּאִכָּא בִרְשׁוּתִי. דְּלָא חֲמִיתֵּהּ וּדְלָא בַעַרְתֵּהּ וּדְלָא יְדַעְנָא לֵיהּ. לִבְטַל וְלֶהֱוֵי הֶפְקֵר כְּעַפְרָא דְאַרְעָא:

All leaven and leavened products in my possession, which I have neither seen nor removed nor know about shall be deemed of no value and ownerless like the dust of the earth.

On the morning of the 14th of Nissan (if it is not Shabbos) during the fifth hour of the day, all chametz previously put aside or left over from breakfast is to be burned. After it has been burned, a declaration annulling all remaining chametz must be said in a language understood by the one reciting it. If erev Pesach is on Shabbos, then the chametz from the search is burned on Friday morning, and the declaration is said on Shabbos morning, at the regular time, after disposing of any leftover chametz from the meal by flushing it down the drain. The declaration is as follows:

כָּל חֲמִירָא וַחֲמִיעָא דְּאִכָּא בִרְשׁוּתִי. דַּחֲזִתֵּהּ וּדְלָא חֲזִתֵּהּ דַּחֲמִתֵּהּ וּדְלָא חֲמִיתֵּהּ דְּבַעַרְתֵּהּ וּדְלָא בַעַרְתֵּהּ. לִבְטַל וְלֶהֱוֵי הֶפְקֵר כְּעַפְרָא דְאַרְעָא:

All leaven and leavened products in my possession, whether I have seen them or not, whether I removed them or not, shall be deemed of no value and ownerless like the dust of the earth.

2

סדר אמירת קרבן פסח

After the Minchah Service it is customary to recite the order of the Pesach Sacrificial Service as a substitute for the actual sacrifice which we are unable to perform:

רבונו של עולם, אתה צויתנו להקריב קרבן הפסח במועדו בארבעה עשר יום לחדש הראשון ולהיות כהנים בעבודתם ולוים בדוכנם וישראל במעמדם קוראים את־ההלל. ועתה בעונותינו חרב בית המקדש ובטל קרבן הפסח ואין לנו לא כהן בעבודתו ולא לוי בדוכנו ולא ישראל במעמדו, ואתה אמרת ונשלמה פרים שפתינו. לכן יהי רצון מלפניך יהוה אלהינו ואלהי אבותינו שיהא שיח שפתותינו חשוב לפניך כאילו הקרבנו את־הפסח במועדו ועמדנו על־מעמדנו ודברו הלוים בשיר והלל להודות ליהוה. ואתה תכונן מקדשך על־מכונו ונעלה ונקריב לפניך את־הפסח במועדו כמו שכתבת עלינו בתורתך על־ידי משה עבדך כאמור:

ויאמר יהוה אל־משה ואל־אהרן בארץ מצרים לאמר: החדש הזה לכם ראש חדשים ראשון הוא לכם לחדשי השנה: דברו אל־כל־עדת ישראל לאמר בעשר לחדש הזה ויקחו להם איש שה לבית־אבת שה לבית: ואם־ימעט הבית מהיות משה ולקח הוא ושכנו הקרב אל־ביתו במכסת נפשת איש לפי אכלו תכסו על־השה: שה תמים זכר בן־שנה יהיה לכם מן־הכבשים

3

The Order of the Pesach Sacrificial Service

After the Minchah Service it is customary to recite the order of the Pesach Sacrificial Service as a substitute for the actual sacrifice which we are unable to perform:

Master of the universe, You have commanded us to offer the Pesach Sacrifice in its appointed time, on the fourteenth day of the first month that the Kohanim perform their service, that the Levites be on their dais, and that the Israelites occupy their positions reciting the Hallel. But, now, because of our iniquities, our Holy Temple is destroyed and the Pesach Sacrifice is in abeyance; and we have no Kohen at his service, no Levite on his dais, and no Israelite standing in his position. You, however, have said: "...and we shall render for bullocks the offering of our lips" (*Hoshea* 14:3). Therefore, may it be Your will, Hashem, our God and God of our fathers, that the utterance of our lips be regarded before you as if we had offered the Paschal lamb in its appointed time and stood in our positions, and the Levites had spoken in song and praise to Hashem. And may You establish Your Holy Temple on its site, and then we shall ascend and offer the Pesach Sacrifice before You in its appointed time, as You have commanded us in Your Torah, by the hand of Moshe Your servant, as it says:

"And Hashem spoke unto Moshe and unto Aharon in the land of Egypt, saying: 'This renewal of the moon shall be unto you the beginning of new moons; it shall be the first month of the year to you. Speak unto the whole of the congregation of Yisrael saying: "On the tenth day of this month they shall take unto them every man a lamb, according to their fathers' houses, a lamb for each household. And if the household be too small for a lamb, then shall he and his neighbor who is near to his house take one according to the counting up of souls; according to every man's eating you shall make your count for the lamb. Your lamb shall be complete, without blemish, a male of the first year; you may

ומן־העזים תקחו: והיה לכם למשמרת עד ארבעה עשר יום
לחדש הזה ושחטו אתו כל קהל עדת־ישראל בין הערבים: ולקחו
מן־הדם ונתנו על־שתי המזוזת ועל־המשקוף על הבתים אשר־
יאכלו אתו בהם: ואכלו את־הבשר בלילה הזה צלי־אש ומצות
על־מררים יאכלהו: אל־תאכלו ממנו נא ובשל מבשל במים כי
אם־צלי־אש ראשו על־כרעיו ועל־קרבו: ולא־תותירו ממנו עד־
בקר והנתר ממנו עד־בקר באש תשרפו: וככה תאכלו אתו
מתניכם חגרים נעליכם ברגליכם ומקלכם בידכם ואכלתם אתו
בחפזון פסח הוא ליהוה:

ובכן כך היתה עבודת קרבן פסח בבית אלהינו ביום ארבעה עשר בניסן.

אין שוחטין אותו אלא אחר תמיד של בין־הערבים. ערב פסח בין בחול בין
בשבת היה התמיד נשחט בשבע ומחצה וקרב בשמונה ומחצה, ואם חל ע״פ
להיות בערב שבת היו שוחטין אותו בשש ומחצה וקרב בשבע ומחצה, והפסח
אחריו.

כל אדם מישראל, אחד האיש ואחד האשה, הגדולים והטהורים ונמולים
(וכשם שמילתו מעכבת מלעשות הפסח ומלאכול בו, כך מילת בניו הקטנים

ומילת עבדיו בין גדולים ובין קטנים וטבילת אמהותיו מעכבת) כל שיכול להגיע
לירושלים בשעת שחיטת הפסח חייב בקרבן־פסח.

מביאו מן הכבשים או מן העזים זכר תמים בן־שנה, ואינו טעון סמיכה,
ושוחטו בכל מקום בעזרה אחר גמר עבודת תמיד הערב ואחר הטבת הנרות. ואין
שוחטין הפסח ולא זורקין הדם ולא מקטירין החלב על החמץ (אפילו היה כזית
חמץ ברשותו של אחד מבני החבורה, בעת אחת מהעבודות של קרבן פסח, הוא
לוקה והפסח כשר).

take it from the sheep or from the goats. And it shall be to you for a safekeeping until the fourteenth day of the same month; then the whole assembly of the congregation of Yisrael shall slaughter it between the two evenings. And they shall take of the blood and put it on the two door posts and on the lintel, upon the houses wherein they shall eat it. And they shall eat the flesh, that night, roasted with fire; with unleavened bread and bitter herbs shall they eat it. Eat not of it half-cooked nor cooked in water as usual, in no other way but roasted with fire; its head with its legs and with its innards. And you shall let nothing remain of it until morning; and that which does remain of it when morning comes you shall burn with fire. And thus shall you eat it; with your loins girded, your shoes on your feet, and your staff in your hand; and you shall eat it in haste — it is a Pesach directed to Hashem" ' " (*Shemos* 12:1-11).

Thus was the service of the Pesach Sacrifice in the House of our God on the fourteenth of Nissan:

The Pesach Sacrifice is only slaughtered after the Daily Afternoon Sacrifice. On the day before Pesach, whether this was a weekday or a Shabbos, the Daily Sacrifice is slaughtered half an hour after the seventh hour and its offering is completed at half an hour after the eighth hour. If the day before Pesach falls on a Friday, however, the Daily Sacrifice is slaughtered half an hour after the sixth hour, its offering is completed one hour later, and the Pesach Sacrifice takes place immediately afterwards.

Every adult Jew, male or female, who is ritually pure, circumcised (just as an uncircumcised Jew may not offer or eat a Paschal lamb, so too, if his minor sons or adult or minor slaves have not undergone circumcision, or if his bondwomen have not undergone ritual immersion, he may not offer or eat the Paschal lamb), and able to reach Yerushalayim in time for the slaughtering is obliged to offer a Paschal lamb.

The Pesach Sacrifice is to consist of a male, unblemished sheep or goat in its first year. No Laying on of Hands is required. It may be slaughtered anywhere in the Temple court, after the completion of the Afternoon Sacrifice and the Setting in Order of the Lamps. It may not be slaughtered, its blood poured, or its fats burned together with the possession of chametz. (Even if there is an amount of chametz as small as an olive in the possession of any member of the group at the time any of the rituals involved in the Pesach

שחט השוחט (אפילו זר) וקבל דמו הכהן שבראש השורה ונתן לחברו, וחברו
לחברו, כהן הקרוב אצל המזבח זורקו זריקה אחת כנגד היסוד, וחוזר הכלי ריקם
לחברו, מקבל המלא ואח"כ מחזיר את הריקן. והיו הכהנים עומדים שורות
שורות, ובידיהם בזיכים שכולם כסף או כולם זהב, ולא היו מעורבים, ולא היו
לבזיכים שולים, שלא יניחום ויקרש הדם.

אח"כ תולין את הפסח באונקליות (או במקלות דקים, מניח על כתפו ועל
כתף חברו, ותולה), ומפשיט אותו כולו (ובשבת עד החזה, ומשם ולמטה בברזי),
וקורעין בטנו ומוציאין אימורים, החלב שעל הכרס, ויותרת הכבד, ושתי הכליות,
וחלב שעליהן, והאליה – אם היה ממין הכבשים – ולעומת העצה. נותן בכלי־
שרת ומולחן ומקטירין הכהן על המערכה, חלבי כל זבח וזבח לבדו, בחול ביום,
ולא בלילה שהוא יום־טוב, אבל אם חל ע"פ בשבת מקטירין והולכין כל הלילה,
ומוציא קרביו וממחה אותן עד שמסיר מהם הפרש (כדי שיהיו נקיים כשצולהו
עמם).

שחיטתו וזריקת דמו ומיחוי קרביו והקטר חלביו דוחין את השבת, שאר
ענייניו אין דוחין.

בשלש כתות הפסח נשחט, ואין כת פחותה משלשים אנשים, נכנסה כת
אחת נתמלאה העזרה נועלין אותה, ובעוד שהן שוחטין ומקריבין וכהנים תוקעין
החליל מכה לפני המזבח והלויים קוראין את ההלל, אם גמרו קודם שיקריבו את

כולם שנו, אם שנו שלשו, על כל קריאה תקעו והריעו ותקעו. גמרה כת אחת
להקריב פותחין העזרה, יצאה כת ראשונה נכנסה כת שניה, נעלו דלתות העזרה,
גמרה, יצאה שניה נכנסה שלישית, כמעשה הראשונה כך מעשה השניה
והשלישית.

Offering are performed, the guilty person incurs the penalty of lashes. The sacrifice nevertheless remains valid.)

Anyone (even a non-Kohen) may perform the slaughtering. The Kohen at the head of the column receives the blood and hands it to the Kohen next to him and that Kohen to the one next to him. The Kohen nearest to the altar pours the blood in a single action against the base and returns the empty basin to the Kohen next to him. First he receives the full basin, and then he returns the empty one. In any line there are gold or silver basins but never both. The bottoms of the basins are rounded to prevent their being set down and the blood from congealing.

The carcass is then suspended from hooks (or else from thin sticks held by the owner on his shoulder and that of his neighbor), and it is skinned in one piece. (On Shabbos, it is skinned down to the chest in one piece and thereafter in strips.) Its belly is then split open and the parts to be sacrificed extracted — that is, the fat on the innards, the diaphragm of the liver, the two kidneys, and the fat on them, and, in the case of a sheep, the fat tail is severed at the backbone. These parts are placed in utensils of service and salted. The Kohen burns the fats of each sacrifice separately on the pyre. On weekdays they burn during the day, but not at night, for by then it is yom tov. If the day before Pesach falls on Shabbos, however, the members will be burnt all night long. The innards are removed and cleansed of all dung (so that later the lamb may be roasted with them).

Slaughtering, pouring the blood, cleansing the innards and burning the fats override Shabbos. The other processes do not.

Three groups, one at a time, slaughter the Paschal lamb, no group consisting of less than thirty persons. The first group enter. When the Temple court is filled, it is locked. While the sacrifices are being slaughtered and offered up, the Kohanim blow the shofar, the flute is played before the altar, and the Levites read the Hallel. If they finish the Hallel before all has been offered, it is repeated; if the Hallel is read a second time and the sacrifices are not yet completed, they recite it a third time. For every reading, a tekiah, teruah, tekiah is sounded. When the first group are finished, the court gates are opened, the second group enter, and the doors are locked again. When the second group are finished, they depart and the third enter. The order of service is the same for all three groups.

After all have left, the court is washed of refuse from the blood, even on

אחר שיצאו כולן ורחצין העזרה מלכלוכי הדם, ואפילו בשבת, אמת־המים היתה עוברת בעזרה שכשרוצין להדיח הרצפה סותמין מקום יציאת המים והיא מתמלאת על כל גדותיה, עד שהמים עולין וצפין ומקבצין אליהם כל דם ולכלוך שבעזרה, אח"כ פותחין הסתימה ויוצאין המים עם הלכלוך, נמצאת הרצפה מנוקה, זהו כבוד הבית.

יצאו כל אחד עם פסחו (ועור שלו) וצלו אותם. כיצד צולין אותו, מביאין שפוד של רמון, תוחבו מתוך פיו עד בית נקובתו, ותולהו לתוך התנור והאש למטה, ותולה כרעיו ובני־מעיו חוצה לו, ואין מנקרין את הפסח כשאר בשר.

בשבת אין מוליכין את הפסח לביתם, אלא כת הראשונה יוצאין בפסחיהן ויושבין בהר־הבית, השניה יוצאין עם פסחיהן ויושבין בחיל, והשלישית במקומה עומדת. חשכה, יצאו וצלו את פסחיהן.

כשמקריבין את הפסח מקריבין עמו ביום ארבעה־עשר זבח שלמים, מן הבקר או מן הצאן, גדולים או קטנים, זכרים או נקבות, והיא נקראת חגיגת ארבעה־עשר, על זה נאמר בתורה וזבחת פסח ליי אלהיך צאן ובקר, ולא קבעה הכתוב חובה אלא רשות בלבד, מכל־מקום היא כחובה מדברי־סופרים, כדי שיהא הפסח נאכל על השובע.

אימתי מביאין עמו חגיגה, בזמן שהוא בא בחול, בטהרה, ובמועט, ונאכלת לשני־ימים ולילה אחד. ודינה ככל תורת זבחי שלמים, טעונה סמיכה ונסכים ומתן דמים שתים שהן ארבע ושפיכת שירים ליסוד.

זהו סדר עבודת קרבן פסח וחגיגה שעמו בבית אלהינו שיבנה במהרה בימינו אמן. אשרי העם שככה לו אשרי העם שיי אלהיו.

9

Shabbos. How is this done? A channel of water passes through the court. To wash the floor, the opening through which the water flows out is closed, making the water overflow the sides, rise, and collect all the blood and refuse in the court. Then the stopper is opened, and the water with all its refuse flows out, leaving the floor clean. This lends dignity to the court.

Each person departs with his Paschal lamb (and its hide) and roasts it. How is it roasted? A spit of pomegranate wood is brought and inserted from the animal's mouth to its buttocks. Then the animal is suspended in an oven — the fire burning underneath — with its legs and innards hanging down outside the carcass. The Paschal lamb is not gouged like other meat.

The Paschal lamb is not taken home on Shabbos. Instead the first group leave with their Paschal lambs and remain on the Temple Mount. The second depart with theirs and stay within the rampart. The third remain where they ate. When it becomes dark, they all go and roast their lambs.

When the Pesach Sacrifice is offered, a Peace Offering is offered with it on the fourteenth day of the month, either from the bullocks or the sheep, large or small, male or female. This is called the "Chagigah of the Fourteenth." Of it, the Torah states: "And you shall bring the Pesach as an offering of a meal to Hashem, your God; from flock and the herd..." (*Devarim* 16:2). Scripture did not make this mandatory, but optional. Nevertheless, the Sages made the Chagigah obligatory to ensure that the Pesach Sacrifice be eaten when one is no longer very hungry.

When is the Chagigah brought together with the Pesach Sacrifice? They are offered together only in a state of ritual purity on weekdays when the Paschal lamb is too small for all those eating. It may be eaten for two days and one night. It is governed by the same regulations as all Peace Offerings: it requires Laying on of Hands, Drink Offerings, two Applications of Blood which add up to four, and the Pouring of the Remainder of the Blood against the base of the altar.

This is the order of the Pesach Sacrifice and its accompanying Peace Offering in the House of our God, may it be rebuilt speedily, in our days, Amen. To salvation strides that nation with whom it is so. To salvation that nation whose God is Hashem.

אלהינו ואלהי אבותינו מלך רחמן רחם עלינו טוב ומטיב
הדרש לנו שובה אלינו בהמון רחמיך בגלל אבות שעשו רצונך
בנה ביתך כבתחלה וכונן בית מקדשך על מכונו והראנו בבנינו
ושמחנו בתקונו והשב שכינתך לתוכו והשב כהנים לעבודתם
ולוים לשירם ולזמרם והשב ישראל לנויהם ושם נעלה ונראה
ונשתחוה לפניך בשלש פעמי רגלינו ונאכל שם מן הזבחים ומן
הפסחים אשר יגיע דמם על קיר מזבך לרצון. יהיו לרצון אמרי פי
והגיון לבי לפני יהוה צורי וגאלי.

Our God and God of our fathers, compassionate King, have compassion upon us, cause us to find You a good and beneficent Being. Return to us in the fullness of Your compassion, for the sake of the fathers who did Your will; build Your House as at the beginning and establish Your Sanctuary upon its site. And let us behold its rebuilding and gladden us by its restoration, return Your Presence within it, and restore the Priests to their service, and the Levites to their songs and praises. Lead Yisrael back to their dwelling places, and there we shall ascend and appear and cast ourselves down before You at the three seasons of our pilgrimage, and we shall eat there from the sacrifices and from the Pesach Offerings whose blood will be sprinkled on the sides of Your altar for gracious acceptance. May the words of my mouth and the meditation of my heart be pleasing before Your countenance, o' Hashem, my Rock and my Redeemer.

עֵרוּב תַּבְשִׁילִין

If the first day of Pesach falls on a Thursday, those who live in chutz la'aretz must prepare an eruv tavshilin on erev yom tov so that one may make preparations on Yom tov for Shabbos. A matzah is taken with some of the food which was cooked on erev yom tov (usually an egg, meat or fish) and the following berachah is said:

בָּרוּךְ אַתָּה יהוה אֱלֹהֵינוּ מֶלֶךְ הָעוֹלָם אֲשֶׁר קִדְּשָׁנוּ בְּמִצְוֹתָיו וְצִוָּנוּ עַל־מִצְוַת עֵרוּב:

Blessed be You, Hashem our God, King of the universe, Who has sanctifies us by His commandments and commanded us concerning the commandment of the eruv.

בְּדֵן עֵרוּבָא יְהֵא שָׁרֵא לָנָא לְמֵיפֵא וּלְבַשָּׁלָא וּלְאַטְמָנָא וּלְאַדְלָקָא שְׁרָגָא וּלְמֶעְבַּד כָּל צָרְכָּנָא מִיּוֹמָא טָבָא לְשַׁבַּתָּא לָנוּ וּלְכָל הַדָּרִים בָּעִיר הַזֹּאת.

By means of this eruv may we be permitted to bake, cook, keep food warm, kindle lights and prepare on yom tov all that we require for the Shabbos, we and all the inhabitants of this city.

Requirements for the Seder

"In every single generation, one is obligated to look upon himself as if he personally had gone forth out of Egypt" (*Haggadah text*).

In order to fulfill this obligation properly at the Seder, one must experience both the bondage and the servitude of the slaves and the freedom of the redeemed. The ritual is arranged into a definite pattern designed to help one achieve this experience. This is one of the reasons why the Seder is called the Seder, meaning order. Throughout the evening there are various requirements and customs, some symbolizing the state of bondage and some the state of freedom, some both and some either.

The leader of the Seder personifies the epitome of freedom, a king, and, consequently, ought to act and be treated accordingly. In many communities, he conducts the Seder clothed in a white kittel. Interestingly, among the reasons given for this custom, one says that it is to liken him to Heavenly angels, and, in contrast, another says that it is to remind him of the shroud of the dead, lest in the expression of so much honor and freedom he forget that he is still a servant of Hashem.

Twice during the Seder the leader washes his hands, and both times the washbasin and towel are brought to his seat. In some homes, another person even pours the water over his hands. His cup is always filled by someone else, just as a king is always served by others (in many homes the custom is that everyone's cup is filled by someone else).

At the start of the Seder, the Seder plate is brought and

placed before the leader. With certain exceptions, he and the other participants in the Seder eat and drink in a reclining position (leaning to the left). In many homes, a cushion or pillow is placed at the left to recline upon.

MATZAH: The matzah represents both the bondage and the redemption (*Shelah*). It is a "poor man's bread," being unleavened and without eggs or additives, and it was the staple that the slaves in Egypt existed upon, since it was neither expensive nor time-consuming to prepare. Therefore, it is broken at the start of the Seder, when we begin to experience the feeling of slavery and poverty, and it is introduced as the "bread of affliction."

For the Jewish people, however, the matzah has a unique additional significance. Towards the end of the narration of maggid, the leader of the Seder again shows the matzah to all the participants, but this time he describes it as the bread of freedom. Our redemption came so quickly that we "had been driven out of Egypt and could not tarry," and so, we ate unleavened bread, matzah, instead of leavened bread. Therefore we recline when we eat the matzah as a sign of our independence.

The matzah of the Seder has a special meaning and must be shemurah, "guarded" for this specific purpose from any wetness or anything else which could cause it to become chametz from the time the wheat was cut until the matzah is finally baked. Some are particular that it be produced by hand, and some insist that it be round.

MAROR: The word means "bitterness" and the aim of the maror is to help us recall the bitterness we were forced to

suffer in Egypt. For this reason, many use horseradish, whose sharp taste serves as an excellent reminder. However, because it is so very sharp, it is difficult to eat the minimum required amounts and to fulfill one's obligation on Pesach night. Therefore, romaine lettuce is commonly used, even though it does not taste bitter, since if left in the ground long enough it will develop a bitter taste. One must keep in mind that it is extremely difficult to clean its leaves, as they are usually heavily infested with tiny insects. The recommended solution is to cut away and discard the green leaves altogether and to use only the white center, which can (and must) be easily cleaned and inspected. Some use endives as another suitable alternative, since they have very little leafy green around a white center. Some even use iceberg lettuce. The required amounts differ, depending upon what is used, as will be explained below.

During the Seder, maror is eaten twice: once alone and again with matzah in korech. On some Seder plates (which will be described below), there is one place for maror and another for chazeres, the bitter herbs combined with the matzah and eaten together in korech. Some use the same type twice, some use one type the first time and another type the second time, and some mix types.

ZEROA AND BEYTZAH: At the time of the Beis Hamikdash, the roasted Pesach Sacrifice was the focal point of the Seder. A second sacrifice, known as the Chagigah, was also offered, on erev Pesach, to be eaten together with the Pesach. Unfortunately, due to our many sins, our Holy Temple no longer stands in Yerushalayim and the altar is no more, and we are forbidden to offer sacrifices anywhere else. Therefore,

we prepare the zeroa as a remembrance of the Korban Pesach and the beytzah to commemorate the Chagigah.

The zeroa is any roasted bone with some meat on it, usually the shank bone of a lamb. However, it is important to keep in mind that today it is forbidden to designate anything to serve as a sacrifice or even to appear to do so. Therefore, some do not roast the zeroa at all but rather cook it, and some even prefer to use a part of a chicken. For this reason, too, one should be careful not to refer to the zeroa as the Pesach, and we do not lift it up or point to it when we describe, in the narration of the maggid, the Pesach that our fathers used to eat...when the Holy Temple was still standing.

The beytzah, in remembrance of the Chagigah, is a hard-boiled egg. In some homes, the egg is also roasted a bit.

CHAROSES: This is a mixture of apples, (figs and pomegranates) walnuts, almonds, cinnamon sticks (and ginger), grated together to form a thick texture. The charoses symbolizes the mortar we were forced to mix and build with in Egypt. Some red wine, symbolizing the blood, is then added to make it slightly liquidy. The maror and the korech are dipped into it. This serves to neutralize the sharp taste of the maror and protect us from any harmful effects it might have. However, in order not to lose the taste of the maror completely, it must not remain in the charoses too long, and one must shake off any excess charoses which may stick to it. (Those who wish to eat this delicious mixture may do so at the meal.)

KARPAS: Towards the beginning of the Seder, a small piece of the karpas is dipped into salt water or vinegar and eaten. Karpas must be a vegetable whose berachah is borei pri

ha'adama but not any one of the aforementioned bitter herbs which may be used for maror. The karpas must be served in a manner in which most people would normally eat it, whether that be raw or cooked. Usually, parsley, celery or radishes are used (but they must first be thoroughly cleaned and inspected for insects). Some have a family custom to use potatoes, since in certain parts of Europe, no other vegetable was available (or affordable) at Pesach time.

There is an indication in the Hebrew letters of the word "karpas" that 60 (the letter "samech") times 10,000 *toiled* (the word *perech* formed from the remaining three letters) in bondage in Egypt. On the other hand, dipping an appetizer before a meal is a sign of luxury. Therefore, there are differing customs whether or not to recline while eating the karpas.

SALT WATER: A mixture of salt and water or a portion of vinegar should be prepared in a bowl in order to dip the karpas. In accordance with the first explanation given for the karpas, the salt water is to symbolize the bitterness of the bondage or the tears of the slaves.

WINE: During the course of the Seder, everyone will be required to drink four cups of wine (the required measurements and amounts are discussed below). Wine is a free man's beverage and, therefore, the four cups must be drunk while reclining. Red wine is preferable, but children, women or one who finds it difficult to drink wine may use as a substitute pure grape juice or a mixture of both. (According to the opinion of Hagaon Harav Moshe Feinstein zt"l, unless one will become bedridden or will not be able to complete the Seder, he should force himself to use intoxicating wine, even though he will

suffer extreme discomfort as a result.) Enough wine should be prepared for everyone attending the Seder, and all bottles should be opened before yom tov.

CUPS: Unlike the kiddush of Shabbos and other yom tov days, everyone must have his or her own cup from which to drink the required four cups of wine. The cups should be elegant (within one's means) and whole. An extra cup for Eliyahu Hanavi should be prepared as well.

TABLE SPREAD: The table should be covered with an elegant clean tablecloth and decorated with the finest dishes and silverware one possesses. Even utensils not usually used, owing to their value, should be used or at least displayed on Pesach Eve as a sign of our freedom and dignity. During the year, we refrain from putting out all of our finery as a remembrance of the destruction of the Beis Hamikdash. On the Seder night, however, it is a mitzvah to do so.

AFIKOMAN HOLDER: One should prepare a clean pillow-case or some other sort of cloth in which to wrap the afikoman which he will hide until after the meal.

SEDER PLATE: A large plate upon which will be placed samplings of the items to be used at the Seder should be prepared. The arrangement of these items on the plate is described below. However, one should note that some commercial "seder plates" sold in stores do not conform with any of the customs, and one should avoid using them.

TREATS: It is of utmost importance that the children remain awake throughout the Seder, so that the father can fulfill his obligation to relate to them the story of the Exodus from Egypt. A child who has the ability to understand should not be put

19

to sleep after he has successfully "asked" or, rather, recited the four questions. On the contrary, he should remain at the Seder until after his father has answered his questions by reading "We were slaves...". Preferably, he should remain at least until after the matzah, maror and korech have been eaten.

For this reason, one should endeavor to keep his child awake in spite of the late hour. There are several ways to accomplish this: 1) the child should take a nap in the afternoon before the Seder; 2) one should have everything prepared and the Seder table completely set before yom tov, so that one can begin the Seder immediately upon arriving home from shul, taking care to make kiddush after nightfall; 3) the order of the Seder, by its requiring that we do many things differently from the whole year, is designed to arouse the child's curiosity and hold his interest; 4) one should let the child "steal" the afikoman and hold it for a "ransom" at the end of the meal; 5) one should distribute nuts and candies and fruits to the children during the Seder.

CANDLES: The candles for the Seder should be big enough to burn until after the yom tov meal.

HAGGADOS: Enough haggados should be prepared for everyone attending the Seder (children will want one, too). Haggados should be stored all year round in a place free of chametz.

Women, as well as men, share in all of the required mitzvos of the Seder, including the recitation of the Haggadah and the Hallel. The only exception is the mitzvah of reclining, about which they are not commanded, but they may do so if they wish to. If the wife or a helper must spend some time in the

kitchen preparing the meal, she should not leave until after she drinks the first cup after the kiddush is said, and she should be called back before reading "Rabban Gamliel used to say...", whereupon she should remain until the maggid is completed with the drinking of the second cup. If possible, she should also be present when the ten plagues are read and explained.

Required Measurements (Shiurim) and Amounts

These measurements and amounts are based upon the decisions of Hagaon Harav Moshe Feinstein, zt"l in *Sefer Kol Dodi* (second edition) by Rabbi Dovid Feinstein, shlitah. Other opinions do exist.

All of these required measurements and amounts apply to women as well as to men. Regarding children, there are more lenient laws, depending upon their ages.

CUPS: The cup of every man and woman attending the Seder must hold at least a revi'is, which is 2.9 fluid ounces. If, however, it is Friday night then the first cup over which the kiddush is recited must hold 4.42 fl. ozs. However, the cups of those who are hearing kiddush from the leader of the Seder need only hold 2.9 fluid ounces as usual.

WINE: One should preferably drink the entire contents of each of the four cups. However, if this is difficult, then one should drink more than half the wine in the cup.

MATZAH: One kezayis of matzah is the equivalent of enough thin matzah to cover an area of 7" x 4". When eating two kezaysim, however, the equivalent of enough thin matzah

21

to cover an area of 7" x 6 1/4" is sufficient.

One who is old or, because of health reasons, cannot chew matzah may use shemurah matzah meal. For motzi-matzah he should consume an amount of meal that can be packed into a 1.5 fl. oz. cup. For korech he need only eat an amount of meal that can be packed into a 1.1 fl. oz. cup.

For motzi-matzah, one kezayis total of *both* the upper and middle matzos is required. However, it is preferable to eat two kezaysim. Some are of the opinion that if the other participants in the Seder cannot obtain a full kezayis from *each* of the two matzos of the leader of the Seder, then they are not required to eat more than one kezayis. For korech, the requirement is for one kezayis of matzah to be combined with one kezayis of maror. For afikoman, only one kezayis of matzah is required but two are preferable.

MAROR: One kezayis of maror is required after reciting the berachah on maror, and another kezayis is needed for korech. The measurement of the kezayis depends upon what is being used for maror:

If using romaine lettuce stalks or endives: enough to cover an area of 3" x 5".

If using romaine or iceberg lettuce leaves: enough to cover an area of 8" x 10".

If using pure grated horseradish: for maror — 1.1 fl. ozs (if this is difficult, one may use only .7 fl. ozs.); for korech — .7 fl. ozs.

PLEASE NOTE: In order to be able to measure the matzah and the maror during the Seder, one should prepare a sheet of paper which has been marked off according to the proper

dimensions. Likewise, if he uses grated horseradish or matzah meal, he should prepare a jigger of the required volume.

REQUIRED TIME PERIOD FOR EATING AND DRINKING: One has fulfilled his obligation only when he consumes the proper amount of matzah, maror and wine within the required period of time. There are many conflicting views concerning how long this time period actually is. Regarding a kezayis, opinions range from the most stringent of two minutes to the most lenient of nine. Therefore, since the eating of the matzah the first time is a Torah commandment, one should attempt to satisfy the stricter opinion. At other times when eating the matzah or the maror or both, one may rely on the more lenient opinions. Since the time for eating a kezayis does not begin until one has actually begun to *swallow*, one should attempt to chew the food as much as possible before swallowing so as to speed up the process of consumption.

If one is drinking the entire cup, he should preferably finish it in two quick swallows. If he only drinks most of the cup, it should preferably be done in one quick swallow. However, there are many authorities who allow the wine to be consumed within the time span of two to nine minutes.

IMPORTANT NOTE: Anyone who, for health reasons, is not able to comply with these amounts and measurements, should consult a competent rabbi.

Preparations before the Seder

As mentioned before, all preparations for the Seder should be finished early so that the Seder may begin immediately upon

returning from shul. (However, contrary to other Shabbos and yom tov evenings, kiddush on Pesach Seder nights may not be said before dark, since all the mitzvos of this evening must be performed when it is night.)

Another reason to prepare early is to avoid the possibility of violating one or more of the yom tov laws relevant to these preparations. These include bereirah (selecting), techina (grinding), shechittah (drowning the bugs and worms) and ibud (tanning). Early preparation is even more important if Pesach begins on a Friday night.

One should prepare in advance enough matzos, maror, wine, Haggados and all other items necessary for all of his guests. This will save him precious time later and enable him to truly enjoy his Seder.

Arrangement of the Matzos and the Seder Plate

Three shemurah matzos are placed on the table, one above the other, in front of the leader of the Seder (according to the custom of the Gaon of Vilna, only two matzos are used). They are separated by napkins or the like. Some place the Seder plate over the matzos, while some put the matzos on the Seder plate.

A sampling of the items which will be used during the Seder should be arranged on the Seder plate.

In most homes, it is common to arrange the Seder plate according to the custom of the Arizal, Rabbi Yitzchak Luria. Some follow the custom of the Gaon of Vilna, while others

follow the instructions of the Rama.

As mentioned previously, these are only samplings. The proper amount of matzah, maror, etc. for all assembled at the Seder must be prepared separately.

THE SEDER PLATE
ACCORDING TO:

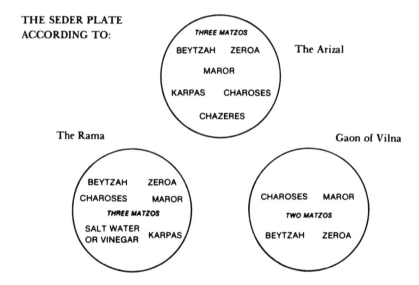

The Arizal

The Rama

Gaon of Vilna

הַדְלָקַת הַנֵּרוֹת

Kindling of the Candles

The lady of the house kindles the yom tov lights. She then extends her hands, placing them between her eyes and the lights, and recites the following berachah:

בָּרוּךְ אַתָּה יהוה אֱלֹהֵינוּ מֶלֶךְ הָעוֹלָם אֲשֶׁר קִדְּשָׁנוּ בְּמִצְוֹתָיו וְצִוָּנוּ לְהַדְלִיק נֵר שֶׁל (שַׁבָּת וְשֶׁל) יוֹם טוֹב:

Blessed be You, Hashem our God, King of the universe, Who has sanctified us by His commandments and commanded us to kindle the (Shabbos and) yom tov light.

In many communities the women also say:

בָּרוּךְ אַתָּה יהוה אֱלֹהֵינוּ מֶלֶךְ הָעוֹלָם שֶׁהֶחֱיָנוּ וְקִיְּמָנוּ וְהִגִּיעָנוּ לַזְּמַן הַזֶּה:

Blessed be You, Hashem our God, King of the universe, Who has kept us alive and preserved us, and enabled us to attain this season.

26

The Traditional Order of the Seder

This order is attributed to Rashi. Many announce each new step at its appropriate time throughout the Seder (but Motzi-Matzah must be announced before washing the hands since afterwards one should not speak unnecessarily).

Kaddesh   קדש
Kiddush, the sanctification of the Festival

Urechatz   ורחץ
Washing the hands in preparation for karpas

Karpas   כרפס
Eating a bit of vegetable dipped in salt water or vinegar

Yachatz   יחץ
Dividing the middle matzah and hiding the larger part

Maggid   מגיד
Reciting the Haggadah, the story of our Exodus and liberation

Rochtzah   רחצה
Washing the hands before the meal

Motzi   מוציא

Blessing over the matzah

Matzah   מצה
  *Special blessing before performing the mitzvah of eating
  matzah at the Seder, and eating it*

Maror   מרור
  *Special blessing before performing the mitzvah of eating
  the bitter herbs, and eating them*

Korech   כורך
  *Combining the maror with matzah and eating them
  together*

Shulchan Orech   שלחן עורך
  Eating the yom tov meal

Tzafun   צפון
  *Eating the afikoman, that part of the matzah
  which was hidden*

Barech   ברך
  Birkas hamazon, grace after meals

Hallel   הלל
  Chanting psalms of praise and affirmation of faith in God

Nirtzah   נרצה
  *Concluding the Seder with the hope and prayer that it was
  properly observed and was acceptable to God*

קַדֵּשׁ

The matzos are covered and the first cup of wine is poured. Everyone should have in mind that, with this cup, it is his intention to fulfill the requirement of reciting kiddush on (Shabbos and on) yom tov over wine and also of drinking the first of the four cups of wine.

בלחש: וַיְהִי־עֶרֶב וַיְהִי־בֹקֶר

יוֹם הַשִּׁשִּׁי: וַיְכֻלּוּ הַשָּׁמַיִם וְהָאָרֶץ וְכָל צְבָאָם: וַיְכַל אֱלֹהִים בַּיּוֹם הַשְּׁבִיעִי מְלַאכְתּוֹ אֲשֶׁר עָשָׂה וַיִּשְׁבֹּת בַּיּוֹם הַשְּׁבִיעִי מִכָּל מְלַאכְתּוֹ אֲשֶׁר עָשָׂה: וַיְבָרֶךְ אֱלֹהִים אֶת יוֹם הַשְּׁבִיעִי וַיְקַדֵּשׁ אֹתוֹ כִּי בוֹ שָׁבַת מִכָּל מְלַאכְתּוֹ אֲשֶׁר בָּרָא אֱלֹהִים לַעֲשׂוֹת:

סַבְרִי מָרָנָן וְרַבָּנָן וְרַבּוֹתַי:

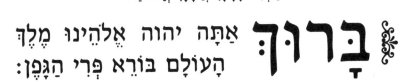

בָּרוּךְ אַתָּה יהוה אֱלֹהֵינוּ מֶלֶךְ הָעוֹלָם בּוֹרֵא פְּרִי הַגָּפֶן:

בָּרוּךְ אַתָּה יהוה אֱלֹהֵינוּ מֶלֶךְ הָעוֹלָם אֲשֶׁר בָּחַר בָּנוּ מִכָּל־עָם וְרוֹמְמָנוּ מִכָּל־לָשׁוֹן וְקִדְּשָׁנוּ בְּמִצְוֹתָיו. וַתִּתֶּן לָנוּ יהוה אֱלֹהֵינוּ בְּאַהֲבָה (שַׁבָּתוֹת לִמְנוּחָה וּ)מוֹעֲדִים לְשִׂמְחָה חַגִּים וּזְמַנִּים לְשָׂשׂוֹן אֶת יוֹם

Kaddesh

The matzos are covered and the first cup of wine is poured. Everyone should have in mind that, with this cup, it is his intention to fulfill the requirement of reciting kiddush on (Shabbos and on) yom tov over wine and also of drinking the first of the four cups of wine.

Quietly:
And it was evening and it was morning,

The sixth day: Thus the heaven and the earth and their whole host were brought to their destined completion. Then God completed with the seventh day His work that He had made, and with the seventh day He ceased from all of His work that He had made. And God blessed the seventh day and made it holy, for with it He had ceased from all of His work which He, God, had created in order to continue shaping it.

By your leave, my masters and teachers:

BLESSED be You, Hashem our God, King of the universe, Who creates the fruit of the vine.

Blessed be You, Hashem our God, King of the universe, Who has chosen us from among all peoples, exalted us above all tongues, and has sanctified us by His commandments. And You have given us, Hashem our God, in love, (Sabbaths for rest and) festivals of assembly for rejoicing, feasts of rallying and seasons for delight, (this Shabbos day and) the day of this

(הַשַּׁבָּת הַזֶּה וְאֶת־יוֹם) חַג הַמַּצּוֹת הַזֶּה זְמַן חֵרוּתֵנוּ (בְּאַהֲבָה) מִקְרָא קֹדֶשׁ זֵכֶר לִיצִיאַת מִצְרָיִם. כִּי בָנוּ בָחַרְתָּ וְאוֹתָנוּ קִדַּשְׁתָּ מִכָּל־הָעַמִּים (וְשַׁבָּת) וּמוֹעֲדֵי קָדְשֶׁךָ (בְּאַהֲבָה וּבְרָצוֹן) בְּשִׂמְחָה וּבְשָׂשׂוֹן הִנְחַלְתָּנוּ. בָּרוּךְ אַתָּה יהוה מְקַדֵּשׁ (הַשַּׁבָּת וְ)יִשְׂרָאֵל וְהַזְּמַנִּים:

At the close of Shabbos add the following two berachos:

בָּרוּךְ אַתָּה יהוה אֱלֹהֵינוּ מֶלֶךְ הָעוֹלָם בּוֹרֵא מְאוֹרֵי הָאֵשׁ:

בָּרוּךְ אַתָּה יהוה אֱלֹהֵינוּ מֶלֶךְ הָעוֹלָם הַמַּבְדִּיל בֵּין קֹדֶשׁ לְחוֹל בֵּין אוֹר לְחשֶׁךְ בֵּין יִשְׂרָאֵל לָעַמִּים בֵּין יוֹם הַשְּׁבִיעִי לְשֵׁשֶׁת יְמֵי הַמַּעֲשֶׂה. בֵּין קְדֻשַּׁת שַׁבָּת לִקְדֻשַּׁת יוֹם טוֹב הִבְדַּלְתָּ וְאֶת יוֹם הַשְּׁבִיעִי מִשֵּׁשֶׁת יְמֵי הַמַּעֲשֶׂה קִדַּשְׁתָּ. הִבְדַּלְתָּ וְקִדַּשְׁתָּ אֶת עַמְּךָ יִשְׂרָאֵל בִּקְדֻשָּׁתֶךָ. בָּרוּךְ אַתָּה יהוה הַמַּבְדִּיל בֵּין קֹדֶשׁ לְקֹדֶשׁ:

One should have in mind that the following berachah pertains to the yom tov as well as all the mitzvos of the evening.

בָּרוּךְ אַתָּה יהוה אֱלֹהֵינוּ מֶלֶךְ הָעוֹלָם שֶׁהֶחֱיָנוּ וְקִיְּמָנוּ וְהִגִּיעָנוּ לַזְּמַן הַזֶּה:

The required amount of the first cup should be drunk (see Required Measurements and Amounts, page 21), within the required period of time, while reclining to the left.

31

Festival of Unleavened Bread, the season of our freedom, (in love), a convocation to the Sanctuary, a remembrance of the departure from Egypt. For You have chosen us and You have sanctified us from among all peoples; and (Shabbos and) Your holy festivals of assembly (in love and in favor) in joy and delight have You given us as an inheritance. Blessed be You, Hashem, Who sanctifies (Shabbos,) Yisrael and the festive seasons.

At the close of Shabbos add the following two berachos:

Blessed be You, Hashem our God, King of the universe, Who creates the flames of the fire.

Blessed be You, Hashem our God, King of the universe, Who has made a distinction between holy and profane, between light and darkness, between Yisrael and the nations, between the seventh day and the six days of toil. You have made a distinction between the sanctity of Shabbos and the sanctity of the festival, and You have sanctified the seventh day above the six working days. You have set apart Your people Yisrael and sanctified them by Your holiness. Blessed be You, Hashem, Who has made a distinction between holy and holy.

One should have in mind that the following berachah pertains to the yom tov as well as all the mitzvos of the evening.

Blessed be You, Hashem our God, King of the universe, Who has kept us alive and preserved us, and enabled us to attain this season.

The required amount of the first cup should be drunk (see Required Measurements and Amounts, page 21), within the required period of time, while reclining to the left.

Urechatz

*A washbasin is brought to the leader of the Seder who
proceeds to wash his hands without reciting a
berachah. In some communities, the one who brings
the water also pours it over the leader's hands, and in
many homes, all the participants of the Seder wash
their hands, too.*

Karpas

*The leader of the Seder takes a piece of karpas (less
than a kezayis so as not to incur the obligation of
saying a berachah acharonah), dips it in vinegar or
salt water, and distributes similar pieces to all
assembled at the Seder. Then the following berachah is
recited with the intention that it refers also to the
maror which will be eaten later on:*

בָּרוּךְ אַתָּה יהוה אֱלֹהֵינוּ מֶלֶךְ
הָעוֹלָם בּוֹרֵא פְּרִי הָאֲדָמָה:

BLESSED be You, Hashem
our God, King of
the universe, Who creates the fruit of the earth.

*In some communities, the custom is to eat the karpas
while reclining, while in some communities they do
not recline.*

Yachatz

*The leader of the Seder then takes the middle matzah
and breaks it in two. The larger portion is hidden
away for the afikoman, while the smaller portion is to
be replaced between the two whole matzos.*

Maggid

*Before the beginning of the narrative part of the
Haggadah, everyone should have in mind that it is his
intention to fulfill his obligation to recount the Exodus
from Egypt. The narrative should be read or explained
in a language that is understood by all those
assembled at the Seder, including the women and the
children.*

*Upon beginning the narrative, the leader of the Seder
displays the broken piece of matzah to those assembled
and recites the following (many lift the entire Seder
plate in order to display the uncovered matzos thereon
and some first remove the zeroa and the egg):*

הָא לַחְמָא עַנְיָא דִּי אֲכָלוּ אַבְהָתָנָא בְּאַרְעָא דְמִצְרָיִם. כָּל דִּכְפִין יֵיתֵי וְיֵכֻל. כָּל דִּצְרִיךְ יֵיתֵי וְיִפְסַח. הָשַׁתָּא הָכָא לַשָׁנָה הַבָּאָה בְּאַרְעָא דְיִשְׂרָאֵל. הָשַׁתָּא עַבְדֵי לַשָׁנָה הַבָּאָה בְּנֵי חוֹרִין:

הא לחמא — This is the bread of affliction

The Questions

1 Why does the Haggadah begin with this paragraph?

2 Why is this paragraph written in Aramaic, while the rest of the Haggadah is in Hebrew?

3 Why are certain phrases repeated?

The phrase *Whoever is hungry, let him come and eat* is repeated as, *whoever is in need, let him come and celebrate the Pesach.*

In addition, the idea expressed in *This year we are here; next year may we be in the Land of Israel* is repeated in *This year we are in bondage; next year may we be free men.*

4 Why do we invite the needy to come and eat when the festival has already entered, we have closed our doors, we have sat down at our tables and have begun the Seder, and there is no poor person present to hear our invitation?

5 How can we invite the needy, on Pesach night, to come and take

35

❧THIS is the bread of affliction which our fathers ate in the land of

Egypt. Whoever is hungry, let him come and eat; whoever is in need, let him come and celebrate the Pesach. This year we are here; next year may we be in the Land of Yisrael. This year we are in bondage; next year may we be free men.

part in the Pesach sacrifice? According to Halacha, only those who were expressly included in the sacrifice before it was slaughtered the day before Pesach may participate in its consumption Pesach night.[1]

הא לחמא *This is the bread of affliction.* This paragraph was instituted during the Babylonian exile, in the vernacular Aramaic so that the masses would understand it (at that time Hebrew had fallen into disuse as the common language).

For the sake of the poor, a public invitation was announced on the day before Pesach, proclaiming, *Whoever is hungry, let him come and eat! This year we are here, next year may we be in the Land of Israel!* However, in order to protect the poor from embarrassment, the announcement was introduced with, *This is the bread of affliction which our fathers ate in the land of Egypt*, where they made the Pesach sacrifice and they ate matzah, activities which sub-

---

1. *Pesachim 61a; Zevachim 5:8; Hilchos Korban Pesach 2:1.*

sequently became commandments for all generations to come, as it says, *You shall celebrate this day as a festival to God throughout your generations, you shall celebrate it as an everlasting ordinance* (Shemos 12:14).

When our invitation to the poor is accompanied by an announcement about the mitzvah to eat matzah, we give the impression that we are inviting them to come not because of their poverty and their lack of food, but because of their obligation to fulfill the mitzvah of eating matzah. We thus avoid embarrassing them, for then it appears that they are coming in order to fulfill the mitzvah, and not because they are hungry.

When the Babylonian exile came to an end and the people returned to the land of Israel, rebuilt the Holy Temple, and reinstituted the Pesach sacrifice, their invitation to the poor changed. They now announced every year on the day before Pesach, *Whoever is in need* of partaking of the Pesach sacrifice, *let him come and celebrate the Pesach*, let him come and be included among the participants in the Pesach sacrifice. They continued to announce *Whoever is hungry, let him come and eat*, because the Pesach sacrifice may be eaten only after a satisfying meal.[2]

Another change which was made when the people returned to the land of Israel was the addition of the declaration, *This year we are in bondage* under the dominion of the Persian and Greek empires; *next year may we be free men.* The former declaration, *This year we are here; next year may we be in the*

---

2. *Mishnah Torah, Hilchos Korban Pesach 8:3.*

37

Land of Israel was no longer relevant once they returned to Israel.

Our text of the Haggadah incorporates both variations to commemorate those times when they used to announce the invitation to people in need. We recite it at the beginning of the Haggadah just as they used to announce it prior to the service of the Pesach sacrifice and Seder.

Another explanation of הא לחמא takes into account the important practice of Pesach night of encouraging the children to ask questions. During the Seder we remove the Seder plate from the table in order to arouse the curiousity of the children.[3] It is possible, however, that in practice the children will be away playing somewhere in the home and will not notice the odd occurrence that the Seder plate has been removed before the meal has even begun. The Sages, therefore, instituted this paragraph in the language the children and all the members of the household would understand, which was, at the time, Aramaic. When the head of the Seder would declare, *This is the bread of affliction which our fathers ate in the land of Egypt,* the children would hasten to gather around the table and take note of the matzah. They would see the table all ready for the meal, and when the Seder plate would be removed from the table before the meal their curiousity would be aroused.

The leader would also call to the other members of the houehold, *Whoever is hungry, let him come and eat.* When the people returned from the exile to the land of Israel, the Sages added the declaration, *Whoever is in need,* that is, whoever in

---

3. *Pesachim 115b; Shulchan Aruch 473:6.*

38

*The second cup is then poured. Some have the custom
to cover the matzos, some move the Seder plate to the
other end of the table, and some remove it from the
table completely, while others do none of these. And
now the youngest child (or, if there are no children
present, the wife or some other adult present) asks the
Four Questions:*

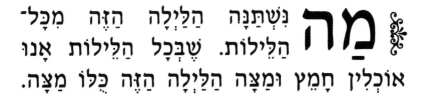

מַה נִּשְׁתַּנָּה הַלַּיְלָה הַזֶּה מִכָּל־
הַלֵּילוֹת. שֶׁבְּכָל הַלֵּילוֹת אָנוּ
אוֹכְלִין חָמֵץ וּמַצָּה הַלַּיְלָה הַזֶּה כֻּלּוֹ מַצָּה.

the family needs to eat from the Pesach sacrifice who, before
it was slaughtered, had been specifically included to partake
in it, let him come and celebrate the Pesach.

To further inspire the children to question, the leader
would say at the beginning of the Seder, *This year we are here;
next year may we be in the Land of Israel.* This hopeful prayer
was usually pronounced after every meal (we still recite it after
the Seder meal), and when the leader would recite it *before*
the meal, the children would ask about the strange order.
When the people returned to the land of Israel, they replaced
their former prayer with another: *This year we are in bondage;
next year may we be free men.*

The second cup is then poured. Some have the custom to cover the matzos, some move the Seder plate to the other end of the table, and some remove it from the table completely, while others do none of these. And now the youngest child (or, if there are no children present, the wife or some other adult present) asks the Four Questions:

✿**WHY** is this night different from all other nights? On all other nights, we may eat leavened or unleavened bread; tonight we must eat only matzah.

מה נשתנה — **Why is this night different**

The Questions

1 How does removing the Seder plate from the table encourage the children to ask the Four Questions?

At this point in the Seder, we are instructed to remove the Seder plate from the table in order to arouse the children's curiosity[4] so that they will ask the Four Questions. When the children see us removing the Seder plate before the meal has started, they will surely ask about this strange custom. But what relevance does this have to the Four Questions? How will removing the Seder plate cause the children to ask four questions which have nothing to do with the Seder plate?

---

4. *Pesachim 115b; Shulchan Aruch 473:6.*

שֶׁבְּכָל הַלֵּילוֹת אָנוּ אוֹכְלִין שְׁאָר יְרָקוֹת
הַלַּיְלָה הַזֶּה מָרוֹר. שֶׁבְּכָל הַלֵּילוֹת אֵין אָנוּ
מַטְבִּילִין אֲפִילוּ פַּעַם אֶחָת הַלַּיְלָה הַזֶּה שְׁתֵּי
פְעָמִים. שֶׁבְּכָל הַלֵּילוֹת אָנוּ אוֹכְלִין בֵּין יוֹשְׁבִין
וּבֵין מְסֻבִּין הַלַּיְלָה הַזֶּה כֻּלָּנוּ מְסֻבִּין:

*In some communities, the leader of the Seder repeats
the Four Questions.*

Furthermore, how can we expect all the children, children of
diverse experiences, knowledge, and intellectual abilities, to ask
the same four questions?

2 Why are we obligated to recite the Four Questions to ourselves if
there is no one else to ask?

The Halacha states that if one is alone on Seder night, one is
nevertheless required to ask oneself the Four Questions[5]. What is
the purpose of this obligation?

3 Why is the Pesach sacrifice not included in the differences
between this night and all other nights?

The Four Questions present four basic differences between the
night of Pesach and all other nights, but the most obvious
difference — the Pesach sacrifice — is not mentioned.

4 Why is the obligation to drink the four cups of wine not included
in the differences between this night and all other nights?

Although the requirement to drink four cups of wine is as unique
to this night as matzah, maror, dipping twice, and reclining, this

---

5. *Pesachim 116a; Shulchan Aruch 473:7.*

41

On all other nights, we may eat all kinds of vegetables; tonight we must eat bitter herbs. On all other nights, we are not required to dip even once; tonight we are required to dip twice. On all other nights, we may eat either sitting or reclining; tonight we must all recline.

In some communities, the leader of the Seder repeats the Four Questions.

feature of Pesach night is not mentioned in the Four Questions. Some commentators answer that the children who ask these questions do not yet know that we will be drinking four cups of wine; at this point in the Seder we have only drunk one cup of wine, the wine from Kiddush. However, neither do the children know that we will be dipping twice, but they nevertheless ask why we dip twice. Furthermore, even the adults who are aware that there will be four cups of wine are obligated to ask the Four Questions, and yet the obligation to drink four cups of wine is not included in these questions. Why not?

מה נשתנה *Why is this night different?* The Talmud teaches, "Why do we remove the table?[6] The school of Rabbi Yannai said, 'In order that the children should notice [the unusual occurrence] and be inspired to ask questions.'" (*Pesachim 115b*)

---

6. In the time of the Talmud, each person had his own small, individual table upon which his meal would be served. Before reciting מה נשתנה, the leader's table was removed from the room. Nowadays, since we generally eat together on one large table, the custom is to remove the Seder plate instead of the table. (*Rashbam, Pesachim 115b*)

The questions referred to in this Talmudic passage are not the Four Questions, the מה נשתנה. They are whatever questions the children are inspired to ask, according to each child's own level of understanding and knowledge. We encourage the children to ask questions on this night by altering the usual procedure of events, in the hope that their questions will offer us the opportunity to open a discussion with them about the events we commemorate and re-experience on Pesach night.

This procedure — of encouraging the children's curiousity and inquisitiveness in order to open a discussion with them — is depicted clearly later in the Haggadah in the paragraph which instructs us how to speak to the son who does not know how to ask: את פתח לו, *You must open the conversation with him.* The word פתח means *open,* from which comes the word פתח, *doorway.* Thus, "make for him a doorway through which he will enter into a discussion with you."

The text of מה נשתנה, however, was not intended to be asked spontaneously. If the child is not yet knowledgeable enough to ask the Four Questions on his own, then the father teaches them to him. If there are no children, then the adults have an obligation to ask the Four Questions to each other.

The Sages ruled that we must recite this paragraph, the Four Questions, immediately before we recount the Exodus story. Why did the Sages institute the obligation to recite מה נשתנה specifically at this point in the Seder? The reason has profound significance.

The four differences between Pesach night and all other nights mentioned in מה נשתנה comprise two contrasting categories. The first two questions, regarding matzah and maror,

represent the concept of slavery and oppression, hardship and bitterness. The last two questions, regarding dipping food and reclining, on the other hand, correspond to the concept of emancipation and liberty, redemption and freedom.

Through the sudden and startling contrast of these two antithetical states of being represented by the very items and actions which are part and parcel of the evening's activity, we create within ourselves a sincere and heartfelt appreciation for the kindness God has done for us, and we enhance our desire to thank and praise God. When we face the facts that at one moment we were eating matzah and maror, living painful and frustrated lives as slaves to a persecuting Pharaoh, and at the next moment our lives were turned around and we were dipping our food and reclining during our meals like noble aristocrats, our natural reaction is to feel full of gratitude to God for His magnificent magnanimity.

With this awareness and feeling which comes from reciting מה נשתנה, the elements of which symbolically remind us of the progression of events from our subjugation to our liberty, we can immediately proceed to recount the Exodus story with fervor and excitement. Without מה נשתנה, the arousal of our feelings of joy and gratefulness to God would take time and would come only *after* recounting the Exodus story, *after* recounting the events which show the contrast between our state of enslavement and our state of freedom, and consequently our praise of God on this important evening would be diminished.

Therefore, since the contrast of our condition from the painful beginning of the Exodus experience to its joyous

culmination is highlighted by the elements we mention in מה נשתנה, we can easily understand why one who is alone on Seder night must ask himself these four questions. Their purpose is to generate a spiritual and intellectual awakening via the recognition of the sudden and massive change which took place at the Exodus, in order for the individual to proceed to the next section of the Haggadah — the recounting of the Exodus story — with a genuine feeling of love and gratitude towards God and a desire to praise and give glory to Him.

By increasing our awareness of the affliction, suffering, and bitterness that preceded the redemption from Egypt, the more our hearts and minds will appreciate the necessity to express genuine thanksgiving to our Redeemer. The recital of the Exodus story will then be an emotionally and intellectually uplifting experience, and not merely an onerous, mechanical fulfillment of an obligation.

Now that we understand the purpose of מה נשתנה, we can understand why its author selected these four specific features as the subjects of the Four Questions. Since the questions of מה נשתנה help us engender emotional enthusiasm and intellectual awareness in order to thank God, the author of the Haggadah chose the most effective way of activating emotional response — to highlight those points that relate directly to slavery and those that relate directly to liberation.

1) אכילת מצה *Matzah.* The matzah, called the "bread of affliction" (Devarim 16:3), is the food of slaves. The matzah reminds us of the slavery and subjugation we suffered.

2) אכילת מרור *Maror.* The maror, the bitter herbs, reminds us of the bitterness and affliction we endured.

3) טבול המרור בחרוסת *Dipping the Maror in Charoses.* The dipping of the bitter maror in the sweet charoses to dilute its bitterness symbolizes freedom from enslavement. In addition, the act of dipping itself is a sign of freedom, because it is generally done with fine delicacies, the food of the free.[7]

4) הסיבה *Reclining.* Reclining at one's leasure is a sign of freedom. In the time of the Talmud it was the manner of the wealthy to eat while reclining on couches.

These four unique features of Pesach night remind us of our slavery, and then of our freedom. They influence our thoughts and emotions and awaken us to become ever more cognizant of the dramatic change which God introduced into the life of our nation.

On the other hand, the four cups of wine do not commemorate any tangible manifestation of being enslaved or being freed. The four cups were instituted merely as an allusion to the four expressions of redemption God used when He assured the downtrodden Jewish people that He would redeem them (Shemos 6:6-7): *I will bring you out, I will free you, I will redeem you, I will take you*[8]. Mentioning the four cups of

---

7. According to Rabbi Eliezer bar Rabbi Tzadok (*Pesachim 114a, 116a*) the charoses is also a reminder of the bitterness of slavery, because it resembles the clay with which we were forced to make bricks and mortar.

8. Our Sages teach that the four cups of wine of the Seder also correspond to the four times the word "cup" is mentioned in Bereishis 40:9-13, in the account of the butler's dream and Yosef's interpretation of it. The four cups also correspond to the four cups of poison that the destroyers of the Temple will be forced to drink, and the four cups of comfort which the Jewish people will drink. (See *Bereishis Rabbah 88:5; Yerushalmi Pesachim 10:1*)

According to none of these explanations do the four cups symbolize actual physical slavery or freedom like the other four unique features of the Seder do.

*If the matzos were covered or removed, they are now
returned and/or uncovered and are to remain so
throughout the narration of the Haggadah, except
when the cups of wine are lifted.*

*The narration of the Haggadah is not said reclining,
but rather in a spirit of awe and fear of the Almighty.*

עֲבָדִים הָיִינוּ לְפַרְעֹה בְּמִצְרָיִם. וַיּוֹצִיאֵנוּ יהוה אֱלֹהֵינוּ מִשָּׁם בְּיָד חֲזָקָה וּבִזְרוֹעַ נְטוּיָה. וְאִלּוּ לֹא

wine in מה נשתנה would not achieve the emotional impact necessary to increase our thankfulness to God. They were, therefore, not included in the Four Questions.

Our analysis of מה נשתנה, which indicates that the criterion for inclusion in מה נשתנה is that the elements included must symbolize or commemorate actual slavery or redemption, does not explain why the Pesach sacrifice is not included. After all, the Pesach sacrifice commemorates God's "passing over" the Jewish homes when He killed the Egyptian firstborn, which was one of the most significant stages in the redemption. Mentioning the Pesach sacrifice should certainly enliven our desire to give thanks to God!

Indeed, the original text of the מה נשתנה includes the Pesach sacrifice as one of the Four Questions[9]. However, since

---

9. *Pesachim 10:4.*

*If the matzos were covered or removed, they are now
returned and/or uncovered and are to remain so
throughout the narration of the Haggadah, except
when the cups of wine are lifted.*

*The narration of the Haggadah is not said reclining,
but rather in a spirit of awe and fear of the Almighty.*

WE were slaves unto Pharaoh in Egypt, and Hashem our God took us out from there with a strong hand and an outstretched arm. And if the Holy One, Blessed be He, had not

nowadays we cannot offer the sacrifices, the question was replaced with the observation that on Seder night we recline while we eat. This question was not included in the original text, for in the time of the Mishnah it was common to recline while eating, and therefore reclining was not a distinctive feature of Seder night. Nowadays, however, we *only* recline on Seder night, and therefore reclining *is* a distinctive feature of Seder night.

עבדים היינו — We were slaves

The Questions

1 Why are several phrases in this paragraph repeated in different words?

We were slaves to Pharaoh in Egypt. The phrase *in Egypt* is redundant; where else could we have been slaves to Pharaoh?

הוֹצִיא הַקָּדוֹשׁ בָּרוּךְ הוּא אֶת אֲבוֹתֵינוּ מִמִּצְרָיִם. הֲרֵי אָנוּ וּבָנֵינוּ וּבְנֵי בָנֵינוּ. מְשֻׁעְבָּדִים הָיִינוּ לְפַרְעֹה בְּמִצְרָיִם. וַאֲפִילוּ כֻּלָּנוּ חֲכָמִים. כֻּלָּנוּ נְבוֹנִים. כֻּלָּנוּ זְקֵנִים. כֻּלָּנוּ יוֹדְעִים אֶת הַתּוֹרָה. מִצְוָה עָלֵינוּ לְסַפֵּר בִּיצִיאַת מִצְרָיִם. וְכָל הַמַּרְבֶּה לְסַפֵּר בִּיצִיאַת מִצְרַיִם הֲרֵי זֶה מְשֻׁבָּח:

The phrases *with a strong hand* and *with an outstretched arm* are seemingly synonymous. One would have sufficed.

What is the difference between *wise, understanding,* and *versed in the Torah*? Why are all three adjectives necessary?

2 *We were slaves unto Pharaoh in Egypt, and Hashem our God took us out from there.*

Why do we say "from there"? It would have sufficed to say, *We were slaves to Pharaoh in Egypt, and Hashem our God took us out.* Once we have said *where* we were slaves (i.e. in Egypt), it is obvious that God took us out *from there!*

3 *And if the Holy One, Blessed be He, had not taken our fathers out of Egypt.*

Why do we repeat the name of God here? Since we just said, *and Hashem our God took us out from there,* it would have sufficed to say, *And if **He** had not taken our fathers out of Egypt...!*

4 *We were slaves to Pharaoh.... And if the Holy One, Blessed be He, had not taken our fathers out of Egypt.*

Why does the Haggadah switch from the first-person plural subject to the third-person plural subject? The subject of the

49

taken our fathers out of Egypt, then we, our children, and our children's children would still have been subjugated to Pharaoh in Egypt. Therefore, even if we were all wise, all understanding, all experienced, and all versed in the Torah, we would nevertheless be obligated to recount the story of the departure from Egypt; and he who elaborates upon the story of the departure from Egypt is worthy of praise.

previous sentence was *we*, and the subject of this sentence is *our fathers*. The Haggadah should have said, *And if the Holy One, Blessed be He, had not taken **us** out of Egypt...!*

5 *...then we, our children, and our children's children would still have been subjugated to Pharaoh in Egypt. Therefore, even if we were all wise... we would nevertheless be obligated to recount the story of the departure from Egypt.*

Why should the assertion that we and our descendants would still be subjugated to Pharaoh in Egypt logically imply ("therefore") that *even if we were all wise... we would nevertheless be obligated to recount the story of the departure from Egypt*?

6 *Therefore, even if we were all wise... we would nevertheless be obligated to recount the story of the departure from Egypt.*

Why should those who already know the story be obligated to recount it?

7 *We were slaves to Pharaoh... we would still have been subjugated to Pharaoh.*

Why does the Haggadah first refer to our status in Egypt as slaves, and then refer to our status as *subjugated?* It would have

sufficed to say, we would still have been **slaves** to Pharaoh.

8 *...we would nevertheless be obligated to recount the story of the departure from Egypt; and he who elaborates upon the story of the departure from Egypt is worthy of praise.*

Why does the Haggadah first call our duty to recount the Exodus story an *obligation,* and then call it an act which is *worthy of praise?* Why is the fulfillment of this particular obligation especially worthy of praise?

עבדים היינו We were slaves. At first glance, עבדים היינו appears to be a narrative paragraph, the beginning of the story of our Exodus. However, the Exodus story does not begin until later in this section of the Haggadah, with the paragraph מתחלה עובדי עבודה זרה, *At first our fathers were idol worshippers,* which narrates our history from the time of Avraham's father until the Exodus and describes in detail the conditions of our enslavement and liberation.

עבדים היינו is not a narrative paragraph, but an instructive one. עבדים היינו comes to teach us of our obligation to recount the Exodus story "even if we were all wise, all understanding, and all versed in the Torah," and to explain to us the reason for that seemingly odd obligation. עבדים היינו tells us that our obligation to recount the Exodus story is a logical consequence of what occurred at the Exodus.

We were slaves, hopelessly bound in the shackles of merciless masters. To gain our freedom was not humanly possible. The Egyptian grip that bound us was so strong that nothing but a miracle could save us. And nothing but a miracle did.

Had the natural course of history been allowed to continue, the Jewish people would never have become the Jewish

people; we would have remained a class of slaves to the North African country of Egypt *forever*. But God intervened and gave our future a new direction. All subsequent generations, ours included, are direct beneficiaries of that intervention. Therefore, it is logical that we should be obligated to recall it every year, to remember God's kindness, and to see to it that the miracle of the Exodus never be forgotten from the heart and mind of the Jewish people. That is what עבדים היינו tells us. (See *Overview* for a discussion of this idea.)

With that understanding we can proceed to explain the paragraph of עבדים היינו.

עבדים היינו לפרעה *We were slaves to Pharaoh*, a tyrannical ruler, במצרים *in Egypt*, a tyrannical regime. The despotic disposition of that nation is indicated by its very name, מצרים, *Mitzrayim*, which comes from the root מצר, *to oppress*. *Mitzrayim*, in the plural, implies a nation of oppressors and persecutors.

ויוציאנו ה׳ אלקינו *And Hashem our God took us out* against the will of Pharaoh, the most powerful person in the world, משם, *from there* — and, moreover, against the will of Egypt, the mightiest nation in the world. Only God, with His almighty and unlimited power, could have succeeded in carrying out such a mission. ביד חזקה *with a strong hand* God smote the Egyptians, compelling them to free us against their will, ובזרוע נטויה *and an outstretched arm*, revealing Himself so that there should exist no doubt that it was God's intervention, His outstretched arm, that freed us, and not the forces of nature.

עבדים היינו *And if [He] had not taken us out....* If עבדים היינו had been a narrative paragraph, the story would have contin-

ued, *If [He] had not taken us out...*, without the word "and"; this would have been an independent statement with no connection to the previous statement. However, since עבדים היינו is not narrative, but didactic, the word "and" was added so that this sentence would be a continuation of the previous sentence, forming a chain of logical reasoning for the obligation to recount the story *even if we were all wise.* That is, (1) we were slaves, (2) God freed us, (3) had He not freed us, we would still be slaves, (4) therefore we are obligated to remember what He did for us.

ואלו לא הוציא הקדוש ברוך הוא *And if the Holy One, Blessed be He, had not taken us out....* The Haggadah here refers to God as *the Holy One, Blessed be He* to emphasize that only through the power of the Holy One, and through no other force, were we freed. And had the Holy One, Blessed be He, not wrought miracles to liberate us, הרי אנו ובנינו ובני בנינו, *then we, our children, and our children's children* for all subsequent generations, משעבדים היינו *would still have been subjugated* to the same tyrannical monarch, לפרעה *to Pharaoh*, and to the same tyrannical nation, במצרים *in Egypt*.

In the syntax of this sentence we find special emphasis on two important concepts of עבדים היינו.

First, the Haggadah uses the word "subjugated" rather than "slaves" to emphasize the depravity which would have resulted had we not been redeemed. A slave is required to work; his master's control over him is limited to labor. To be subjugated, however, means to be under the complete domination of the master who is free to do anything he pleases with his subject. Our situation in Egypt would have degenerated from that of

slaves to that of being completely subjugated if not for God's miraculous intercedence.

Second, the Haggadah repeats the phrase "to Pharaoh in Egypt" to stress the despondency and hopelessness of aspiring for freedom. It was far beyond the imagination to conceive of being liberated from the superpower of the ancient world. But it is just that hopelessness which makes us truly appreciate what God did for us, and therefore, ואפילו כלנו חכמים *even if we were all wise*, even if we were familiar with the Torah's account of the Exodus, logic would still require us to recount it in gratitude; even if כלנו נבונים, *we were all understanding*, able to infer the implicit meaning from the literal text; even if כלנו זקנים, *we were all experienced* and remembered the miracles which the Jews saw with their own eyes; even if כלנו יודעים את התורה, *we were all versed in the Torah*, that is, the Torah in its entirety, a level of knowledge superior to that of the "wise" man.

In each of these progressively advanced levels of wisdom, the phrase "*[even if] we were all...*" is repeated. The purpose of this repetition is to convey that even if there was not a single member of our nation who was not wise, understanding, experienced, and erudite in the knowledge of the Torah, so that not a single soul needed to be educated about the Exodus, מצוה עלינו, *we would nevertheless be obligated* to perform this absolute duty, לספר ביציאת מצרים, *to recount the story of the Exodus from Egypt*.

The rationale for this obligation follows from the previous statements in this paragraph: *And if the Holy One, Blessed be He, had not taken our fathers out of Egypt, then we, our children, and our children's children would still have been*

מַעֲשֶׂה בְּרַבִּי אֱלִיעֶזֶר וְרַבִּי יְהוֹשֻׁעַ וְרַבִּי
אֶלְעָזָר בֶּן־עֲזַרְיָה וְרַבִּי עֲקִיבָא וְרַבִּי טַרְפוֹן שֶׁהָיוּ
מְסֻבִּין בִּבְנֵי־בְרַק וְהָיוּ מְסַפְּרִים בִּיצִיאַת מִצְרַיִם
כָּל־אוֹתוֹ הַלַּיְלָה עַד שֶׁבָּאוּ תַלְמִידֵיהֶם וְאָמְרוּ לָהֶם.
רַבּוֹתֵינוּ הִגִּיעַ זְמַן קְרִיאַת שְׁמַע שֶׁל שַׁחֲרִית:

subjugated to Pharaoh in Egypt. The awareness of this historical fact of our liberation from bondage obliges us and inspires in us intense feelings of gratitude, as well as the obligation to ensure that this awareness — and consequent sense of gratitude — will be equally experienced by all subsequent generations. Therefore, we do not necessarily recount the Exodus story because we need to hear it. Rather, *even if we were all wise, all understanding, all experienced, and all versed in the Torah,* we would still be duty-bound to recount the story each year *for the sake of our children and their children,* to ensure that *they* never lose touch with *their* debt of gratitude to God.

The purpose of this obligation is expressed by the verse in the Torah which commands us to recite the Exodus story:

And you shall relate to your child on that day, saying: "It is because of this that Hashem acted for me when I came forth out of Egypt" (Shemos 13:8).

"And you shall relate to your child" tells us that the essence of the obligation is the education of the next generation.

It happened that Rabbi Eliezer, Rabbi Yehoshua, Rabbi Elazar ben Azaryah, Rabbi Akiva and Rabbi Tarfon were reclining [at the Seder table] in Bnei Berak, and were recounting the story of the departure from Egypt. They continued the entire night until their pupils came and said to them: "Our teachers! The time for the recital of the morning Shema has arrived."

Accordingly, the extent of one's knowledge about the Exodus is irrelevant; one is still required to recount the Exodus story for the sake of one's children. (See *Overview.*)

מצוה עלינו לספר. To fulfill the mitzvah, the bare minimal obligation, all we would need to do is mention a cursory remark about God taking us out of Egypt. However, there is no limit to the fulfillment of this obligation, and as such, כל המרבה לספר, he who elaborates upon the story of the departure from Egypt — even though he is not Halachically required to, but nevertheless raises himself above and beyond the bare minimal duty — הרי זה משבח, is worthy of praise.

מעשה ברבי אליעזר — It happened that Rabbi Eliezer

The previous paragraph taught us two fundamental ideas:
1) Even if we were all wise...we would nevertheless be

אָמַר רַבִּי אֶלְעָזָר בֶּן־עֲזַרְיָה. הֲרֵי אֲנִי כְּבֶן שִׁבְעִים שָׁנָה. וְלֹא זָכִיתִי שֶׁתֵּאָמֵר יְצִיאַת מִצְרַיִם בַּלֵּילוֹת. עַד שֶׁדְּרָשָׁהּ בֶּן זוֹמָא. שֶׁנֶּאֱמַר לְמַעַן תִּזְכֹּר אֶת יוֹם צֵאתְךָ מֵאֶרֶץ מִצְרַיִם כֹּל יְמֵי חַיֶּיךָ. יְמֵי חַיֶּיךָ הַיָּמִים. כֹּל יְמֵי חַיֶּיךָ הַלֵּילוֹת. וַחֲכָמִים אוֹמְרִים. יְמֵי חַיֶּיךָ הָעוֹלָם הַזֶּה. כֹּל יְמֵי חַיֶּיךָ לְהָבִיא לִימוֹת הַמָּשִׁיחַ:

obligated to recount the story of the departure from Egypt.

2) He who elaborates upon the story of the departure from Egypt is worthy of praise.

The paragraph of מעשה ברבי אליעזר illustrates each of these ideas.

1) *It happened that Rabbi Eliezer, Rabbi Yehoshua, Rabbi Elazar ben Azaryah, Rabbi Akiva and Rabbi Tarfon....* These five individuals were the greatest and wisest sages of their time. They were experts in every area of Torah, and their knowledge certainly encompassed every detail of the story of the Exodus. Since they were fully aware of everything that occurred during the departure from Egypt, they had no need to learn about it or to remind themselves of it, but, nonetheless, they *were recounting the story of the departure from Egypt.*

Said Rabbi Elazar ben Azaryah: "Behold! I am like a man of seventy years old, and I did not succeed in proving that the Departure must be mentioned at night, until Ben Zoma explained that the Torah states...'so that you may remember the day when you came forth out of the land of Egypt *all* the days of your life' (*Devarim* 16:3). 'The days of your life' — includes nighttime as well. But the Sages say 'the days of your life' indicates your life in the present; '*all* the days of your life' refers to the time of the Mashiach as well."

2) ...*the entire night.* They continued to recount the story the entire night and were so deeply involved in it that they failed to notice that dawn had arrived *until their pupils came and said to them: "Our teachers! The time for the recital of the morning Shema has arrived."*

אמר רבי אלעזר בן עזריה — Said Rabbi Elazar ben Azaryah

The Questions

1 If, until now, Rabbi Elazar ben Azaryah never knew Ben Zoma's explanation of the verse "...all the days of your life" (Devarim 16:3), then what was his source for the mitzvah of mentioning the departure from Egypt at night?

2 ולא זכיתי *I did not succeed.* Rabbi Elazar ben Azaryah said, "I am *like* a man of seventy years old." Had he indeed been an elderly man, his statement would have expressed the difficulty in proving that there is an obligation to recite the Shema at night. However, since he was not actually an old man and thus had not spent many years attempting to establish this view, the fact that he did not succeed in proving the obligation does not indicate how difficult it was to prove. Why, then, did he say, *I did not succeed in proving*, implying extensive effort?

3 What is the argument between Ben Zoma and the Sages? Why does Ben Zoma understand the verse to mean one thing, and the Sages understand it to mean something entirely different?

4 Both Ben Zoma and the Sages derive from this verse a specific Halacha regarding the recounting of the departure from Egypt in the daily recital of the Shema. Ben Zoma maintains that the departure from Egypt must be included in the recital of the nighttime Shema as well as the daytime Shema. The Sages argue and maintain that it need not be mentioned in the nighttime Shema. They instead learn from this verse that the Exodus story must be mentioned in the daytime Shema in the time of the Mashiach as well as in the present time. Both Ben Zoma and the Sages learn a specific Halacha about the Shema from this verse.

The problem is that this verse contains absolutely no mention of the Shema.

If we examine the verse in context, we will notice that this verse's command to recount the departure from Egypt is not a daily obligation, but an annual one. The verse discusses remembering the Exodus by means of the Pesach sacrifice and the matzah, but not by reciting the Shema[10].

---

10. *In the place that God will choose to dedicate to His name, you shall sacrifice the Pesach offering to Hashem your God, sheep and cattle. Do not eat any leaven with it. For seven days you shall eat bread of poverty, because in haste you left Egypt, so that you may remember the day when you came forth out of the land of Egypt all the days of your life* (Devarim 16:2-3).

If the verse discusses remembering the Exodus during Pesach, then how did Ben Zoma and the Sages derive the Halacha that the Exodus must be mentioned in the Shema?

אמר רבי אלעזר בן עזריה *Said Rabbi Elazar ben Azaryah.* Since Rabbi Elazar ben Azaryah was one of the sages who were reclining and retelling the story of the departure from Egypt as depicted in the previous paragraph, the Haggadah continues here with his statement concerning the mentioning of the Exodus and the teaching of Ben Zoma, expounded on the day that Rabbi Elazar ben Azaryah was appointed as *Nasi*, the head of the Sanhedrin, the supreme judicial and legislative authority.

הרי אני כבן שבעים שנה *Said Rabbi Elazar ben Azaryah, "Behold! I am like a man of seventy years old"* — but not actually seventy years old. Rabbi Elazar ben Azaryah was appointed head of the Sanhedrin at the unusually young age of eighteen. Although he was fully qualified for the position, and his selection was based on his scholarship and leadership abilities, the appointment of such a young leader was bound to cause dissent among some of the people. His physical demeanor, therefore, was miraculously altered to appear as though he were an older man and deserving of the prestigious position he had just received[11]. That is why he said, "I am like a man of seventy years old": Even though I am like a man of seventy years — that is, even though my wisdom earned me the position as leader, I have still been unsuccessful in having the Halacha (of when to mention the

---

11. *Berachos 28a.*

Exodus) decided in accordance with my opinion.[12]

שתאמר יציאת מצרים בלילות *that the departure must be mentioned at night*. In which part of the nightly liturgy was Rabbi Elazar ben Azaryah attempting to prove that we must mention the Exodus? In the third paragraph of the nighttime Shema: *I am Hashem your God who brought you out of Egypt to be your God, I am Hashem your God* (Bamidbar 15:41). The established Halacha at the time was that the third paragraph of the Shema need not be recited at night.[13]

עד שדרשה בן זומא *until Ben Zoma explained that the Torah states... 'so that you may remember the day when you came forth out of the land of Egypt **all** the days of your life'* (Devarim

---

12. Some read Rabbi Elazar ben Azaryah's statement as simply, "I am a man of like seventy years old", that is: I am an elderly man, approximately seventy years old. It was at this time, over fifty years after Rabbi Elazar ben Azaryah was appointed as the leader, that Ben Zoma explained his interpretation of the verse. According to this, the phrase "and I did not succeed in proving" is very relevant: Even though I am an aged man of many years, I still did not succeed in proving my view of the Halacha. (*Sefer Hayuchasin; Yerushalmi Berachos 1:6*)

13. Originally, the third paragraph of the Shema was not recited at nighttime, because that paragraph deals primarily with the Mitzvah of *Tzitzis* which does not apply at night. However, there was another reason to include the third paragraph. The Talmud introduces a requirement, based on verses in the Torah, that the *Geula*, the redemption from Egypt, must be mentioned immediately before *Tefillah*, the Shemoneh Esreh — לסמוך גאולה לתפילה (*Berachos 4b*). Everyone agrees that this requirement applies during the morning prayers. They argue, however, whether or not it applies during the nighttime prayers.

The dispute revolves around another argument.

When did the redemption from Egypt occur? Everyone agrees that the Jews left Egypt during the daytime, the morning of the fifteenth of Nissan. However, Rabbi Yochanan maintains that since Pharaoh had told the Jews to leave the night before, the nighttime is also considered to be the time of redemption.

16:3). Although this verse discusses remembering the departure from Egypt by eating the Pesach sacrifice and matzah, as we see from its context, there are three extra words from which we deduce the obligation to mention the Exodus every day: כל ימי חייך *all the days of your life.*

If the sole purpose of the verse was to instruct us to remember the Exodus through eating the Pesach sacrifice and matzah, then it would have sufficed to say, "so that you may remember the day when you came forth out of the land of Egypt", without the extra words, "all the days of your life".[14]

Why did the Torah add the words "all the days of your

Rabbi Elazar ben Azaryah agrees with the reasoning of Rabbi Yochanan that the nighttime is also the time of redemption. Therefore, he holds that the departure from Egypt should also be mentioned in the nighttime Shema. (*Berachos 1:5*)

Rabbi Elazar ben Azaryah's opinion in this Halacha is consistent with his position in another disagreement. The Talmud discusses the proper time for eating the Pesach sacrifice (*Berachos 9a*). Rabbi Elazar ben Azaryah holds that it may be eaten until midnight. Rabbi Akiva argues and holds that it may be eaten past midnight, until daybreak. The Talmud concludes that this dispute is based on the interpretation of the verse, "and you shall eat it [the Pesach sacrifice] in haste" (Shemos 12:11). Rabbi Elazar ben Azaryah learns that this "haste" is the speed with which the Egyptians urged the Jews to leave Egypt, which occurred at night. Rabbi Akiva learns that this "haste" is the alacrity with which the Jews actually left Egypt, which occurred during the day.

Therefore, Rabbi Elazar ben Azaryah, in accordance with his view that the departure from Egypt occurred at night as well as during the day, maintains that the Exodus must be mentioned in the nighttime Shema. The Sages who argue maintain that the redemption only occurred during the day, and therefore we mention the Exodus only during the morning Shema. The Halacha followed their opinion, until Ben Zoma's teaching.

14. One might argue that the words "all the days of your life" are necessary in order to establish that the obligation of remembering the Exodus by eating

life"? It must be that this phrase comes to include an additional continual obligation — to remember the departure from Egypt *all the days of your life*[15]; not merely once a year through eating the Pesach sacrifice and matzah, but every single day and night of the year as well in the recitation of the Shema.

This is how Ben Zoma understands the seemingly super-fluous words at the end of this verse. Had the verse not included "all the days of your life", then there would be no obligation to remember the departure from Egypt every day. Had the verse written, "so that you may remember the day when you came forth out of the land of Egypt the days of your life" without the word "all", we would have understood the Torah's intention to include only the days in this new obliga-tion, and not the nights. " 'The days of your life' refers to the daytime," says Ben Zoma. But now that the Torah writes "*all* the days of your life", the additional word "all" teaches us to include the nights in this new obligation as well. " '*All* the days

---

the Pesach sacrifice and matzah applies each year, and, therefore, the words "all the days of your life" are not superfluous.

This cannot be so, because the verse already instructs, "Keep the month of the springtime and observe the Pesach" (Devarim 16:1), and continues, "...so that you may remember the day when you came forth out of the land of Egypt all the days of your life" (ibid. 16:3). Therefore, we know already from verse one that the command to remember the Exodus by eating the Pesach sacrifice and matzah applies every year, and thus the words "all the days of your life" *are* superfluous.

15. The words "so that you may remember" serve a dual purpose. First, they are the continuation of Devarim 13:1, "Keep the month of springtime and observe the Peasch," referring to the Pesach sacrifice and matzah. Second, they relate to the end of Devarim 13:3, "all the days of your life," teaching us that there is another *daily* obligation to remember the Exodus — that is, in the Shema.

of your life' includes nighttime as well."

וחכמים אומרים ימי חייך העולם הזה *But the Sages say 'the days of your life' indicates your life in the present.* The Sages interpret the extra words of this verse differently than Ben Zoma. They understand "the days of your life" to refer not to each day of the year, but to one's lifetime, including all the days and all the nights. Whereas Ben Zoma places the emphasis of the verse upon *"the days* of your life", the Sages place the emphasis upon "the days of *your life"*. The Sages do not learn that without the word "all", the word "days" would have excluded the nighttime from this obligation. Rather, they learn that the words "your life", that is, your present mode of living, would have excluded the different type of life that will exist in the time of the Mashiach. The word "all" comes to include even that time of life, the time of the Mashiach, in the obligation to remember the departure from Egypt. " '*All* the days of your life' refers to the time of the Mashiach," the Sages say.

Following the exposition of Ben Zoma, the practical Halacha is that we mention the departure from Egypt at nighttime as well as during the day. There are several reasons for this Halachic ruling. First, once Rabbi Elazar ben Azaryah cited proof to his opinion that the Exodus must also be mentioned at nighttime, his view was endorsed by the majority. Second, Ben Zoma's interpretation of the extra words "all the days of your life" is more straightforward than the Sages' way of understanding those words. Third, the word חייך, "your life," is conjugated in the singular, implying an obligation on the individual; according to the Sages who maintain that "your life"

בָּרוּךְ הַמָּקוֹם. בָּרוּךְ הוּא. בָּרוּךְ שֶׁנָּתַן תּוֹרָה לְעַמּוֹ יִשְׂרָאֵל. בָּרוּךְ הוּא.

כְּנֶגֶד אַרְבָּעָה בָנִים דִּבְּרָה תוֹרָה. אֶחָד חָכָם. וְאֶחָד רָשָׁע. וְאֶחָד תָּם. וְאֶחָד שֶׁאֵינוֹ יוֹדֵעַ לִשְׁאוֹל:

refers to the pre-Messianic era, the verse is addressing the Jewish people as a whole, and thus the grammatical form is less accurate.

ברוך המקום — Blessed is the Omnipresent

Until now the Haggadah has elucidated the obligation to recount the Exodus story, explaining the necessity of such an obligation solely upon the basis of logic and common sense. That is, if God had not liberated our fathers from Egypt, we and all of our descendants would still have been subjugated to Egypt, and, therefore, we are obligated to retell the story of the redemption in order to ensure that our children remain aware of God's great beneficence. Now the Haggadah turns to the Torah-source of the obligation to recount the story of the departure from Egypt.

BLESSED be the Omnipresent, Blessed be He! Blessed be He Who has given the Torah to His people Yisrael, Blessed be He.

The Torah spoke about four sons: one wise, one wicked, one simple, and one who does not know how to ask.

We find four instances in the Torah where we we are instructed to tell our children about the departure from Egypt. In three of these four our words to the children are preceded and prompted by specific questions from the children themselves. However, the obligation to recount the Exodus story is binding even when no questions are asked. Therefore, none of these three places can be the source for this obligation.

The fourth command with which the Torah instructs us to tell the Exodus story is not prompted by any questioning on behalf of the child. Therefore, this verse must be the Torah-source for this obligation:

And you shall relate to your child on that day, saying: "It is because of this that Hashem acted for me when I came forth out of Egypt" (Shemos 13:8).

The four verses which command us to tell our children about the bondage in Egypt and God's miraculous intervention

represent four different ways of teaching them, corresponding to the four different types of children: wise, wicked, simple, and the one who does not know how to ask. The exact nature and character of each child represented by each verse is evident from the complexity and tone of the question which the child asks, or does not ask. For example, when the Torah commands, "When your son will ask you in time to come, saying, 'What are the testimonies, the statutes, and the social ordinances which Hashem our God has commanded you?'" (Devarim 6:20) we know that this verse is telling us what to respond to the wise child. When the Torah states, "And you shall relate to your child..." (Shemos 13:8) with no question from the child, we know that this verse is referring to the child who does not know how to ask.

Since the Haggadah's purpose here is to cite the verse which serves as the Torah-source for the all-inclusive obligation to retell the story of the Exodus, it would have sufficed to mention only the verse which addresses the son who does not know how to ask. Nevertheless, the Haggadah also brings the other three verses to complete the discussion and to inform us how to fulfill our obligation under diverse circumstances. The Haggadah brings these verses in a progressive order, and not necessarily in the order in which they appear in the Torah, leading up to its goal — the verse, *And you shall relate to your child on that day, saying...* (Shemos 13:8).

Since the Haggadah now turns to the Torah, it preludes with words of praise and thanksgiving to God for having given the Torah to the Jewish people.

ברוך המקום *Blessed be the Omnipresent.* God is often called

67

HaMakom — "the Omnipresent", or literally, "the Place". Referring to God in such a way reminds us that God is not limited by the confines of space; He is not located anywhere in the world. Rather, the world is located somewhere in Him.[16]

ברוך הוא *Blessed be He!* The compiler of the Haggadah arranged this section of praise in the form of a responsive refrain. The leader first declares, "Blessed be the Omnipresent!" to which the others respond, "Blessed be He!" The leader then declares, "Blessed be He Who has given the Torah to His people Israel!" to which the others again respond, "Blessed be He!" in affirmation.

כנגד ארבעה בנים דברה תורה *The Torah spoke about four sons.* Following the introductory declarations of praise to God for His Torah, the Haggadah now turns to the Torah itself, to the four separate verses with which the Torah commands us to teach our four different types of children about the Exodus, and they are...

אחד חכם ואחד רשע ואחד תם ואחד שאינו יודע לשאול *one wise, one wicked, one simple, and one who does not know how to ask.* The Haggadah lists these types of children in a different order than that in which they appear in the Torah. The Torah presents the four sons in the following order: the wicked son (Shemos 12:26), the son who does not know how to ask (Shemos 13:8), the simple son (Shemos 13:14), and the wise son (Devarim 6:20).

The Haggadah, though, places the wise son first, a position befitting the honor which his righteousness earns for him. Next, the Haggadah mentions the wicked son, the antagonist

---

16. *Bereishis Rabbah 68:9.*

חָכָם מַה הוּא אוֹמֵר. מָה הָעֵדֹת וְהַחֻקִּים
וְהַמִּשְׁפָּטִים אֲשֶׁר צִוָּה יהוה אֱלֹהֵינוּ אֶתְכֶם. וְאַף
אַתָּה אֱמָר־לוֹ כְּהִלְכוֹת הַפֶּסַח. אֵין מַפְטִירִין אַחַר
הַפֶּסַח אֲפִיקוֹמָן:

of the wise son, to show the contrast between the two sons.
In addition, the Haggadah chooses to mention the wicked son
second because in the Torah he is mentioned before the other
two sons. The Haggadah then mentions the simple son and
the son who does not know how to ask; they follow the wicked
son in the order of their ability. In addition, the son who does
not know how to ask is mentioned last so that this section of
the Haggadah will conclude with its raison d'etre, the Torah-
source for the positive commandment to recount the story of
the departure from Egypt on Seder night.

The wise son — חכם מה הוא אומר — what does he say?

The Questions

1 *And you should even instruct him regarding the laws of the Pesach:
"After the Pesach offering, no dessert is to be eaten!"*
This is the answer which the Haggadah instructs us to give to
the wise son. However, the Torah explicitly specifies, at length, a
different response to the wise son:

69

The wise son — what does he say? "What are the testimonies, the statutes, and the social ordinances which Hashem our God has commanded you?" (see *Devarim* 6:20). You should even instruct him regarding the laws of the Pesach: "After the Pesach offering, no dessert is to be eaten!"

And you shall say to your son, "We were slaves to Pharaoh in Egypt, but God brought us forth from Egypt with a mighty hand. God brought signs and wonders, great and terrifying, upon Egypt, upon Pharaoh, and upon all his household before our eyes. And He brought us forth from there, in order to bring us and to give us the land which He swore to our fathers. God commanded us to keep all of these statutes, to fear Hashem our God, for our good all the days, so that He will keep us alive like today. It will be righteousness for us if we observe to do all of this law before Hashem our God, as He commanded us" (Devarim 6:21-25).

Why does the Haggadah abandon the Torah's answer and compose a completely different one?

2 ואף אתה אמר לו *And you should even instruct him regarding....*

What purpose does the word אף, "even", serve? It would have sufficed to say, "And you should instruct him regarding..." and not, "And you should even instruct him regarding...".

3 כהלכות הפסח *And you should even instruct him regarding the laws of the Pesach....*

Why do we say כהלכות הפסח, literally, "...instruct him regarding *like* the laws of the Pesach"?

4 *...instruct him regarding the laws of the Pesach: "After the Pesach offering, no dessert is to be eaten!"*

Why is "laws" in the plural, when the response concludes with only one law? The Haggadah should have said, "...instruct him regarding a *law* of Pesach...".

5 *"After the Pesach offering, no dessert is to be eaten!"*

Why was this law, of all the laws of Pesach, chosen as the response to the child's question? Furthermore, how does this law answer the question, *What are the testimonies, the statutes, and the social ordinances which Hashem our God has commanded you?*

חכם מה הוא אומר *The wise son — what does he say?* Perhaps a more accurate translation of חכם מה הוא אומר would be, *The wise son — what does it [the verse in the Torah] say [about him],* and not, *what does he say.*[17]

This understanding of מה הוא אומר makes sense, because the previous sentence stated, *The Torah spoke about four sons;* now the Haggadah logically asks what the Torah said about those four sons.

The wise son — what does the Torah say about him? The Haggadah answers with the verses of the Torah which discuss the wise son. Although the Haggadah cites only the son's question, *What are the testimonies, the statutes, and the social ordinances which Hashem our God has commanded you?* (Devarim 6:20), it is clear from these verses that the Torah is talking about a wise and righteous son.

First, the Torah introduces this son's question with the words, "When your son will ask you in time to come, saying...". In contrast, when the Torah introduces the question of the wicked son, it says, "...when your children will say to you...".

---

17. We find the phrase מה הוא אומר used this way later in the Haggadah, in the paragraph of Rabbi Yose the Galilean p. 153.

The difference in diction is obvious; in one place the Torah says the child will *ask you*, and in the other it says the child will *say to you*. What does this difference mean?

When the child *asks you*, "What are these testimonies...", he is questioning sincerely. He earnestly desires the knowledge he lacks and is making an honest attempt to obtain it. His mind is open and he is fully prepared to give ear to the answer, to listen, to understand, to accept and to fulfill all that we tell him. This is the righteous son.

When the child *says to you*, "What is this service to you?", even though his words are in question form, he is not questioning, but making a statement. He is saying outright that these laws mean nothing to him. This is the wicked son.

Second, "When your son will ask you *in time to come*" implies that the son will ask in the future, because he himself did not experience the Exodus and did not witness the miracles God wrought. His motive for questioning is to fill the gaps in his knowledge concerning the events in history which he was not present to behold. "In time to come" tells us that he is not asking out of malice or resentment.

This differs from the wording the Torah uses in regards to the wicked son's question. There, the Torah does not say "in time to come". This indicates that the son is asking even though he witnessed the departure from Egypt and is not lacking knowledge of it; rather, he is questioning out of his spirit of rebelliousness.

Third, the son, in his question, distinguishes between three types of commandments:

מה העדות What are the testimonies. These are the com-

mandments which testify to the miracles and wonders that God performed for us.

והחקים *and the statutes.* These are the commandments whose reasons are beyond human comprehension.

והמשפטים *and the social ordinances.* These are the commandments which regulate the relationships between man and his fellow (such as providing charity and respecting the property of others), for which our common sense would oblige us even without the Torah's command.

This distinction between the various types of commandments displays a keen awareness of the Torah, expresses an ardent desire to understand its many facets, and is additional evidence that the enquirer is indeed wise. This is in stark contrast to the wicked son's question. The wicked son includes all of the commandments in one general term — "service", making no differentiation between the varied forms of service. This shows a feeling of apathy at best, and derision at worst, for what the Torah has to offer.

Fourth, the son says, "...*which Hashem our God has commanded...*". Not only does he include mention of the Almighty in his question, but he also says "*our* God", thus including himself as one who faithfully trusts in and serves God. The wicked son, on the other hand, makes no mention of God in his question.

אשר צוה ה׳ אלקינו אתכם ...*which Hashem our God has commanded you.* When the wise son says "commanded *you*", and not "commanded *us*", he does not intend to exlude himself from the commandments, as the Haggadah indeed deduces from the wicked son's use of the same phrase — "to *you*, but

not to *him*". What is the difference?

We have already seen that the wise son's question arises from his lack of knowledge, which itself is merely a consequence of not personally witnessing the Exodus. Just as he did not experience the Exodus, he was also not physically present for the Revelation at Sinai, when the entire nation heard God speak to them. Therefore, he asks, "What are the testimonies... which God has commanded *you*," which God spoke unto *you*; I am certainly included in the commandments, but God did not speak directly to me as he did to you.

The wicked son, however, says, "What is this service to *you*"; even though he may have experienced the Revelation and heard God speak to him, he still says "to *you*" to stress his self-imposed exclusion from the community.

This difference between the "*you*" of the wise son and the "*you*" of the wicked son is evident in the two Hebrew forms of what seems to be the same pronoun. The wise son says אתכם, which literally means "with you". He is not implying that God's words were directed *to you* and not to him; he is merely asking what God said when he spoke *with you*. He understands that God's words are directed to every Jewish person without exception, but that God only actually spoke with those who lived at the time of the Revelation. The wicked son says לכם, which literally means "to you". He believes that even though he may have heard God speak, God's words were directed not to him, but to you.

The Haggadah began this section with a question, *The wise son — what does the Torah say about him?*, and proceeded to guide us to the section of the Torah which addresses the

רָשָׁע מַה הוּא אוֹמֵר. מַה הָעֲבוֹדָה הַזֹּאת
לָכֶם. לָכֶם וְלֹא לוֹ. וּלְפִי שֶׁהוֹצִיא אֶת־עַצְמוֹ מִן
הַכְּלָל כָּפַר בְּעִקָּר. וְאַף אַתָּה הַקְהֵה אֶת־שִׁנָּיו וֶאֱמָר
לוֹ בַּעֲבוּר זֶה עָשָׂה יהוה לִי בְּצֵאתִי מִמִּצְרָיִם. לִי
וְלֹא לוֹ. אִלּוּ הָיָה שָׁם לֹא הָיָה נִגְאָל:

question of the wise son. Once it has informed us where in
the Torah the wise son's question is discussed, the Haggadah
has no need to tell us what to answer him. The answer is
already there, in the Torah, and we now know where to find
it. It is quite obvious that we answer the wise son with the
reply that the Torah teaches us to answer. Nevertheless, the
Haggadah wishes to emphasize that we must answer the wise
son by teaching him all of the laws of the Pesach offering, from
the beginning of the service until the end.

ואף אתה אמר לו *And you should even instruct him.* In
addition to what the Torah commands you to answer him, you
should even tell him...

כהלכות הפסח *...like the laws of the Pesach....* Just as you
teach him all of the laws of the Pesach sacrifice — which is
what he asked for — from the beginning of the service until
the end, you should also teach him all of the laws which apply

The wicked son — what does he say? "What is this service to you?" (see *Shemos* 12:26) To *you* — but not to *him*! Since he has excluded himself from the community, he has denied the essentials of our faith. Therefore, you should even blunt his teeth, and say to him: "It is because of this [service] that Hashem acted for me when I came forth out of Egypt" (see *Shemos* 13:8). For *me* — but not for *him*! Had he been there, he would not have been redeemed.

after the consumption of the Paschal lamb, such as... אין מפטירין אחר הפסח אפיקומן *"After the Pesach offering, no dessert is to be eaten!"*

רשע מה הוא אומר — The wicked son — what does he say?

The Questions

1 *"What is this service to you?" To you — but not to him! Since he has excluded himself from the community, he has denied the essentials of our faith.*

Why is this question different from that of the wise son, who also said, "What are the testimonies... which Hashem our God has commanded you"?

2 *Therefore, you should even blunt his teeth, and say to him: "It is because of this [service] that Hashem acted for me when I came forth out of Egypt" (Shemos 13:8).*

This is the answer which the Haggadah instructs us to give to the wicked son. However, the Torah explicitly specifies a different response to the wicked son:

You shall say, "It is a meal of a salvation performed through a pass-over, dedicated to God Who passed over the homes of the Children of Israel in Egypt when He mortally smote the Egyptians, and our homes He saved..." (Shemos 12:27).

Why does the Haggadah ignore the reply the Torah instructs for the wicked son, and, instead, cite a different response — the response to the son who does not know how to ask: *It is because of this that Hashem acted for me when I came forth out of Egypt* (Shemos 13:8)?

3 ואף אתה הקהה את שניו *Therefore, you should even blunt his teeth, and say....*

What purpose does the word אף, "even", serve? It would have sufficed to say, "Therefore, you should blunt his teeth and say...", and not, "Therefore, you should *even* blunt his teeth, and say...".

4 *...blunt his teeth...*

Why must we "blunt his teeth"? What is the significance of this expression?

רשע מה הוא אומר *The wicked son — what does he say?* As we noted above in the section pertaining to the wise son, perhaps a more accurate translation of רשע מה הוא אומר would be, *The wicked son — what does it [the verse in the Torah] say [about him],* and not, *what does he say.*

The wicked son — what does the Torah say about him? The Haggadah answers with the verses of the Torah which discuss the wicked son. Although the Haggadah cites only the son's question, *What is this service to you?* (Shemos 12:26), it is clear from these verses that the Torah is talking about a wicked son.

First, the Torah introduces this son's question with the

77

words, "When your children will *say* to you...", and not, "When your son will *ask* you...", as it says regarding the wise son and the simple son. The fact that he is *saying* this to you implies an unequivocal conviction to the "question" he is posing; when he asks, "What is this service to you?", he is really saying, "This service means nothing to me." He does not care for an answer. His position is final. This is the wicked son.

Second, the Torah here states, "When your children will say to you...", whereas regarding the wise son the Torah states, "When your son will ask you *in time to come*...". This omission suggests that this son poses his question not "in time to come", but now — in the generation that experienced the Exodus and witnessed the Revelation at Sinai. He asks not to fill the gaps in his knowledge, but to mock and to criticize.[18]

---

18. This understanding of the wicked son's question may seem problematic in light of the preceding verse which states, "When you come to the land that God will give you as He promised, you shall observe this service" (Shemos 12:25). This implies that the wicked son will ask you only *after* the people of Israel have entered the land of Israel. Since they entered the land forty years after the Exodus, this son must have been born some time after the departure from Egypt at Revelation at Sinai. And if so, his question may indeed be merely a request for knowledge, and we have no indication that he is asking mockingly.

In truth, however, this verse poses no problem. This section of the Torah, in Shemos, chapter twelve, takes place immediately prior to the departure from Egypt. Upon God's command, Moshe and Aharon instruct the people to take the necessary actions in anticipation of the events to occur beginning at midnight that fateful night. Moshe adds, after instructing the people to prepare the Pesach sacrifice, that in time to come their children may ask them about this service, and he tells them what they are to reply. At this point in time, prior to the actual Exodus and prior to the sin of the spies, the providential itinerary called for entering the land of Israel immediately after departing from Egypt, with no lengthy delay in between. This plan was altered, however,

Third, this son makes no mention of God's name in his question, suggesting that he does not believe that this service was divinely ordained.

Fourth, since this son says, "What is this עבודה, *service*, to you," without mentioning "service of *God*", he is clearly using the word service to denote burdensome labor.

Fifth, he uses the phrase "to you" which implies *to you —* *but not to him;* he excludes himself from the service of God.

Sixth, when the Torah gives us the response to this son's question, it states ואמרתם זבח פסח, *You shall say, "It is a meal* *of a salvation...".* The Torah does not say, "You shall say *to* *him*", as it says when it addresses the other three sons.[19]

By not instructing us to say *to him,* the Torah is telling us that we are *not to respond* to his derisive question. He has made up his mind; nothing will change it. Instead, we are to address *ourselves;* we are to speak to ourselves to assure that his mocking words have no adverse effect upon our own faith.

From these six points it is clear that this is the section of the Torah which discusses the wicked son. Thus, the Haggadah has answered its question, *The wicked son — what does the* *Torah say about him?*

ולפי שהוציא את עצמו מן הכלל *Since he has excluded himself*

---

upon the sin of the spies (Bamidbar 13, 14:1-25); only then did God decree that the people of Israel would wander in the wilderness for forty years (Bamidbar 14:32-34).

Therefore, when Moshe said, "When you come to the land that God will give you" (verse 25) that arrival to the land was imminent, and thus "your children" (verse 26) who will ask you about the Pesach service would have indeed experienced the Exodus themselves.

19. See Shemos 13:8; 13:14; Devarim 6:21.

from the community by emphasizing, "What is this service *to you*", כפר בעקר *he has denied the essentials of our faith* by denying the Divine origin and the validity of the commandments.

ואף אתה הקהה את שניו *Therefore, you should even blunt his teeth*. The purpose of the apparently superfluous word "even" is the same purpose which we described to explain the extra word "even" in the paragraph of the wise son.

The Haggadah began this section with a question, *The wicked son — what does the Torah say about him?*, and proceeded to guide us to the section of the Torah which addresses the question of the wicked son. Once it has informed us where in the Torah the wicked son's question is discussed, the Haggadah has no need to tell us what to answer him. The answer is already there, in the Torah, and we now know where to find it. It is quite obvious that we respond to the wicked son's sneering gesture with the statement that the Torah instructs. Nevertheless, the Haggadah wishes to emphasize an additional element in our response to the wicked son's ridicule. Not only "you shall say" what the Torah commands you to say, but "you should *even* blunt his teeth."

We now understand the reason for the extra word, "even". But why should we blunt his teeth?

The often painful and damaging act of blunting or gnashing one's teeth is usually executed unintentionally by the victim himself, while chewing his food. In other words, it is a self-inflicted injury.

Similarly, when we respond to the wicked son's question, we are to use his own style of expression against him, to show him that he, in effect, has damaged himself. He said "to you" and

תָּם מַה הוּא אוֹמֵר. מַה זֹּאת. וְאָמַרְתָּ אֵלָיו
בְּחֹזֶק יָד הוֹצִיאָנוּ יהוה מִמִּצְרַיִם מִבֵּית־עֲבָדִים.

excluded himself from the community, and we are to reply,
ליולא לו...בעבור זה עשה ה׳ לי *"It is because of this that Hashem acted for me when I came forth out of Egypt." For **me** — but not for **him**.* He said "to you" and excluded himself, so we say "for me" and exclude him as well.

אלו היה שם לא היה נגאל *Had he been there, he would not have been redeemed.* We learned that our response to the wicked son's question should be directed not to him, for nothing will change his mind, but to ourselves, to strengthen our own beliefs against the onslaught of his heresy. The Haggadah utilizes this approach and says, "...but not for *him*," in the third person. Since we are not to talk directly to the wicked son, the Haggadah does not say, "but not to *you*."

תם מה הוא אומר — The simple son — what does he say?

The Questions

1. *"What is this? And you shall say to him: By strength of Hand did Hashem bring us out from Egypt, from the house of bondage" (Shemos 13:14).*

   Why, for the question of the simple son, does the Haggadah cite the response which is given in the Torah, whereas for the questions of the wise son and the wicked son, the Haggadah does not?

The simple son — what does he say? "What is this?" (see *Shemos* 13:14). And you shall say to him: "By strength of Hand did Hashem bring us out from Egypt, from the house of bondage" (*ibid.*).

2 ואמרת אליו And you shall say to him.
Why does the Haggadah not say, "And you shall *even* say to him," with the extra word "even", as it says in regards to the wise son and the wicked son?

תם מה הוא אומר *The simple son — what does he say?* As we explained, a more appropriate translation would be, *The simple son — what does the Torah say about him.* To this the Haggadah answers,

מה זאת *What is this?* (Shemos 13:14). This is the verse in the Torah which deals with the simple son. How do we know that this verse refers to the simple son?

First, the Torah introduces this son's question with the words, "And it will be when your child *asks* you..."; the word "asks" indicates a sincere desire to know (see p. 72). This indicates to us that the enquirer here is not the wicked son who "says" and does not "ask".

Second, the simple phrasing of the question, "What is this?", with no analysis or breakdown of the different types of components of the service, indicates that the enquirer is not the wise son. If this child is not wicked, nor wise, then he must be the simple one.

Since the Haggadah had nothing to add to the reply written

in the Torah, it did not use the word "even", which indicates something additional, as we have seen in the paragraphs regarding the wise son and the wicked son, where the Haggadah does indeed add something to the Torah's response.

However, we still must answer our first question: why does the Haggadah cite the response given in the Torah to the question of the simple son, and does not cite the responses to the questions of the wise and the wicked sons?

The answer is simple. The Haggadah does not need to cite *any* of the replies given in the Torah, for, as we have explained, once we know which section of the Torah discusses which son, we can open our *chumashim* and read the responses ourselves. Why, then, does the Haggadah cite the Torah's response to the simple son?

Since the Torah's response to the simple son immediately follows the son's question in the same verse, the Haggadah simply preferred to cite the entire verse, from the son's question until the end.[20] The questions of the wise son and the wicked son, on the other hand, each complete their verses in the Torah. Therefore, there was no reason to include the Torah's responses to their questions.

---

20. (Eds.) This is based on a Talmudic principle, כל פסוקא דלא פסקיה משה אנן לא פסקינן ליה, *any verse which Moshe did not divide, we are not permitted to divide* (*Megillah 22a*). This is generally understood to mean that any time a verse is quoted, it must be quoted in its entirety.

The Commentary uses this principle five times throughout the Haggadah in the following paragraphs to explain why parts of verses are cited which have no relation to the topic at hand:

1) *The simple son — what does he say*: Shemos 13:14.

2) *Few in number*: Devarim 10:22.

3) *And numerous*: Yechezkel 16:7.

83

4) *And the Egyptians ill-treated us*: Shemos 1:10.

5) *And our labor*: Shemos 1:22.

However, upon examining all the verses cited in the Haggadah, we find several verses which are not quoted in their entirety, apparently violating the rule that *any verse which Moshe did not divide, we are not permitted to divide*:

1) *Said Rabbi Elazar ben Azaryah*: Devarim 6:3 is not quoted in full.

2) *The wise son —what does he say*: Devarim 6:20 is not quoted in full.

3) *The wicked son — what does he say*: Shemos 12:26 is not quoted in full.

4) *And our labor*: Shemos 1:22 is not quoted in full. This instance is especially problematic. While the Commentary explains that the end of this verse ("and every daughter you shall let live") is cited because of the principle that a verse must be cited in its entirety, the opening words of the verse ("And Pharaoh commanded all his people saying") are omitted!

5) *And our oppression*: Shemos 3:9 is not quoted in full.

6) *And with an outstretched arm*: Divrei Hayamim I, 21:16 is not quoted in full. This instance could be resolved by speculating that the principle of quoting a verse in its entirety applies only to verses in the Pentateuch and not to verses in the Prophets and Scriptures (such as Divrei Hayamim) (see *Magen Avraham, Orech Chaim 422:8*). However, the Commentary applies this principle to a verse in Yechezkel, obviously of the view that this principle applies even to verses that are not in the Pentateuch.

The solution seems to be that the principle *any verse which Moshe did not divide, we are not permitted to divide* does not require verses to be quoted in their *entirety*. Rather, it requires that from whatever point the quotation starts, it must continue until the end of the verse. The first words of the verse may be omitted. It is the end of the verse, from the point at which the quotation begins, which one may not omit. (See Rav Reuven Margolios, *Nefesh Chayah*, Tel Aviv, 5714/1938, appendix pp. 3-4, who brings proof to this suggestion from *Bikkurim 3:6* and *Berachos* 28b, and justifies with it the recitation of incomplete verses in the texts of Kiddush of Friday night and Shabbos morning.)

This understanding of the principle is embodied within the phrasing of the principle itself. The words כל פסוקא דלא פסקיה משה אנן לא פסקינן ליה literally mean *any stop which Moshe did not stop, we are not permitted to stop*. The emphasis of the rule is on *stopping* the verse at a point at which Moshe did not stop the verse; we may, however, *begin* the verse from wherever we want.

Examining all of the cases of incomplete quotations of verses in the Haggadah, we find that in each and every case it is only the opening words which have been omitted; the verses are always quoted until the end.

84

וְשֶׁאֵינוֹ יוֹדֵעַ לִשְׁאוֹל אַתְּ פְּתַח לוֹ. שֶׁנֶּאֱמַר
וְהִגַּדְתָּ לְבִנְךָ בַּיּוֹם הַהוּא לֵאמֹר בַּעֲבוּר זֶה עָשָׂה
יהוה לִי בְּצֵאתִי מִמִּצְרָיִם:

ושאינו יודע לשאול — As for the son who does not know how to ask

The Questions

1 *As for the son who does not know how to ask — you must begin the conversation with him.*

According to the traditional way of translating the phrase מה הוא אומר, *what does he say*, we understand why this paragraph does not follow the pattern of the previous three paragraphs and say, *The son who does not know how to ask — what does he say*. By definition this son does not say anything.

According to our explanation, however, that מה הוא אומר means, *what does the Torah say about him*, we are faced with a question — why does the Haggadah omit this phrase in this paragraph? According to our explanation, the Haggadah should read, ושאינו יודע לשאול מה הוא אומר, *As for the son who does not know how to ask — what does the Torah say about him?*

2 את פתח לו *you must begin the conversation with him.*

את פתח לו literally means *you should open for him*. Why did the Haggadah not use the conventional, "You should say to him"?

85

As for the son who does not know how to ask — you must begin the conversation with him, as it is stated in the Torah: "And you shall relate to your child on that day, saying: 'It is because of this that Hashem acted for me when I came forth out of Egypt' " (*Shemos* 13:8).

ושאינו יודע לשאול *As for the son who does not know how to ask.* We know that in four verses the Torah commands the father to tell his child about the departure from Egypt. We also know that each of the four verses represents one of four different types of children. The only part we are missing is which of the four sections in the Torah refer to which of the four children. This is what the Haggadah informs us.

Until now, the Haggadah has identified three of the four sections of the Torah and to which sons they refer. We have learned about the wise son, the wicked son, and the simple son. The only one left is the son who does not know how to ask. However, there is no need to tell us which section of the Torah discusses this son; by the process of elimination we can assume that the only section which the Haggadah has not explained to refer to any particular type of son is the section which refers to the son who does not know how to ask.

Therefore, this paragraph does not say, *what does the Torah say about him,* because we know by elimination what the Torah says about him.

את פתח לו *you must begin the conversation,* or literally, *you*

must open for him. Although he is incapable of asking on his own initiative, we are not instructed merely to tell him what he does not know how to ask for. Rather, we are instructed to "open for him"; we are to stimulate and encourage him to ask his own question, whatever it may be, which we will use as an introduction for teaching him about the departure from Egypt. We are not to carry him into the room of knowledge; we are merely to *open for him* the door so that he can walk into it himself.

This invaluable instrument of education — not to merely teach, but to inspire questions and to encourage a desire to learn and to know — is subtly elucidated in the words of the Torah, in the very verse which discusses the son who does not know how to ask:

שנאמר והגדת לבנך ביום ההוא לאמר as it is stated in the Torah: "And you shall relate to your child on that day, saying..." (Shemos 13:8). The word "saying" seems superfluous. But in truth, the Torah is teaching an indispensable lesson in education. This is how we are to understand the verse: And you shall relate to your child on that day (והגדת לבנך ביום ההוא), telling him something which will inspire him to question, so that you will need *to respond* (לאמר) to him, *"It is because of this that Hashem acted for me when I came forth out of Egypt."*

For this reason we customarily remove the Seder plate prior to the start of the meal. The young children innocently notice something strange — the grown-ups are taking away the food before we've started eating! They will pose their inquisitive question to the perpetrators of this pretense, thus giving us the opportunity to answer them with the story of the departure from Egypt.

With the conclusion of the paragraph of the son who does not know how to ask, the Haggadah has accomplished its objective — to show the Torah-source of the obligation to recount the story of the Exodus on Seder night. The source is the verse *And you shall relate to your child...* (Shemos 13:8), because this is the sole source in the Torah for telling one's child about the Exodus independent of any question or statement from the child.[21]

---

21. This concludes the section of the Haggadah which corresponds to the phrase והגדת לבנך in Shemos 13:8. (See *Overview.*)

יָכוֹל מֵרֹאשׁ חֹדֶשׁ. תַּלְמוּד לוֹמַר בַּיּוֹם הַהוּא. אִי בַּיּוֹם הַהוּא יָכוֹל מִבְּעוֹד יוֹם. תַּלְמוּד לוֹמַר בַּעֲבוּר זֶה. בַּעֲבוּר זֶה לֹא אָמַרְתִּי אֶלָּא בְּשָׁעָה שֶׁיֵּשׁ מַצָּה וּמָרוֹר מֻנָּחִים לְפָנֶיךָ:

One might think — יכול מראש חדש

The Questions

1 *One might think that the obligation to recount the story of the departure from Egypt begins from the first day of the month of Nissan.*

Why would one think this? The departure from Egypt occurred on the fifteenth of Nissan; why would one think that the obligation to discuss it falls two weeks earlier?

2 *However, the Torah states: "on that day." "On that day" might be understood to mean while it is still day. Therefore, the text specifies "it is because of this." I can say "it is because of this" only at such a time when the matzah and the maror are in front of you.*

If the obligation applies only *at such a time when the matzah and the maror are in front of you*, that is, at nighttime, then what is the purpose of the words *on that day*, which imply daytime?[22]

---

22. Even if we assume *on that day* refers not to daytime but to the the day of the fifteenth of Nissan, including the night, the phrase is still unnecessary, because the verse already informs us that the obligation applies *when the matzah and the maror are in front of you*, i.e. the fifteenth of Nissan.

One might think that the obligation to recount the story of the departure from Egypt begins from the first day of the month of Nissan. However, the Torah states: "on that day." "On that *day*" might be understood to mean *while it is still day*. Therefore, the text specifies "it is because of *this*." I can say "it is because of this" only at such time when the matzah and the maror are in front of you.

יכול מראש חדש *One might think that the obligation to recount the story of the departure from Egypt begins from the first day of the month of Nissan.* Why would one think this?

The command to tell one's child the Exodus story appears in the following context:

*(5) When God will bring you to the land of the Canaanites... you shall perform this service **during this month**. (6) For seven days you shall eat matzahs, and the seventh day shall be a festival to God. (7) ...no leaven may be found in your possession. (8) And you shall relate to your child on that day, saying.... (Shemos 13:5-8).*

Without the words *on that day*, we could have feasibly understood this verse to be referring back to verse five. That is, when verse eight exhorts us to relate the Exodus story to our children, we would have wondered when this ordinance takes place. We would have looked back at verse five and seen *during this month*, the only hint of when this ordinance should

take place. Notwithstanding any other specification, we would have construed *during this month* to mean the first day of the month, and, consequently, *one might think that the obligation to recount the story of the departure from Egypt begins from the first day of the month of Nissan.*

תלמוד לומר ביום ההוא *However the Torah states: "on that day"* — not on the first day of the month, but *on that day*, on the first day of Pesach, the fifteenth of Nissan.

אי ביום ההוא יכול מבעוד יום *"On that **day**" might be understood to mean while it is still day.* Without the words בעבור זה, *it is because of this*, we might have thought that the command to tell our children about the departure from Egypt applies during the day. During what day? Since the Pesach sacrifice was prepared during the afternoon before the first night of Pesach (Vayikra 23:5), we might have learned that the recounting of the Exodus story should also take place *on that day, while it is still day.*

תלמוד לומר בעבור זה *Therefore, the text specifies "it is because of this."* The word *this* designates something that is present, in front of the person speaking.

בעבור זה לא אמרתי אלא בשעה שיש מצה ומרור מנחים לפניך *I can say "it is because of this" only at such a time when the matzah and maror are in front of you.* The Torah obliges the father to say *"it is because of this"* only on Pesach night, for only then can he point to the matzah and maror in front of him and say *"this".*

However, if the obligation to recount the Exodus story applies only at Seder night, why does the verse state *on that day*, which apparently implies during the daytime?

When the Torah uses the word "day", it connotes both daytime and nighttime.[23] Without the phrase *it is because of this*, we would have explained the word "day" here in its simplest meaning — daytime; we would have concluded that the specified time for the recounting of the Exodus story is the daytime, the afternoon of Pesach eve.

However, once the verse states *it is because of this*, we know that we must recount the story of the Exodus at such a time when we can point to *this*, the matzah and maror — that is, at nighttime.

But once we know when to recount the Exodus, what use are the words *on that day?* After all, the words *it is because of this* already tell us exactly when to recount the Exodus story!

We can answer this question similarly to the way we answered the first question. The verses state,

For seven days you shall eat matzahs, and the seventh day shall be a festival to God. Since matzahs must be eaten these seven days... no leaven may be found in your possession. And you shall relate to your child on that day, saying.... (Shemos 13:6-8)

Without the phrase *on that day*, we might reasonably have inferred that the obligation to recount the Exodus story is binding on *all* seven days of Pesach, just as the commandments to eat matzah and not to own leaven apply all seven days. We would have understood *it is because of this* to refer to the matzah which is in front of us all seven days.

The verse, therefore, had no choice but to add *on that day* in order to limit the obligation to just one day, and not seven

23. For example, *And it was evening and it was morning, one day* (Bereishis 1:5).

92

מִתְּחִלָּה עוֹבְדֵי עֲבוֹדָה זָרָה הָיוּ אֲבוֹתֵינוּ.
וְעַכְשָׁו קֵרְבָנוּ הַמָּקוֹם לַעֲבוֹדָתוֹ. שֶׁנֶּאֱמַר וַיֹּאמֶר
יְהוֹשֻׁעַ אֶל־כָּל־הָעָם כֹּה־אָמַר יהוה אֱלֹהֵי יִשְׂרָאֵל
בְּעֵבֶר הַנָּהָר יָשְׁבוּ אֲבוֹתֵיכֶם מֵעוֹלָם תֶּרַח אֲבִי
אַבְרָהָם וַאֲבִי נָחוֹר וַיַּעַבְדוּ אֱלֹהִים אֲחֵרִים: וָאֶקַּח
אֶת־אֲבִיכֶם אֶת־אַבְרָהָם מֵעֵבֶר הַנָּהָר וָאוֹלֵךְ אוֹתוֹ
בְּכָל־אֶרֶץ כְּנָעַן וָאַרְבֶּה אֶת זַרְעוֹ וָאֶתֶּן לוֹ אֶת־
יִצְחָק: וָאֶתֵּן לְיִצְחָק אֶת־יַעֲקֹב וְאֶת עֵשָׂו וָאֶתֵּן
לְעֵשָׂו אֶת־הַר שֵׂעִיר לָרֶשֶׁת אוֹתוֹ וְיַעֲקֹב וּבָנָיו יָרְדוּ
מִצְרָיִם:

days. Once the obligation is limited to one day, then the phrase
it is because of this comes to identify *that day* as the night when
the matzah and maror are in front of us, Seder night. Thus,
both phrases are necessary.[24]

---

24. Following the order of words in the verse והגדת לבנך, this section of the
Haggadah corresponds to the phrase, ביום ההוא, *on that day*. (See *Overview.*)

At first our fathers were idol worshippers, but now the Omnipresent has brought us near to His service, as it is said: "And Yehoshua said to all the people: 'Thus said Hashem, the God of Iisrael: "On the other side of the river, your fathers dwelt of old, Terach, father of Avraham and father of Nachor, and they served other gods. And I took your father Avraham from the other side of the river and led him through the whole land of Canaan, and I multiplied his descendants and gave him Yitzchak. And to Yitzchak I gave Yaakov and Esav; to Esav I gave Mount Seir for an inheritance, and Yaakov and his children went down to Egypt" ' " (*Yehoshua* 24:2-4).

מתחלה — **At first**

מתחלה *At first.* From here begins the central feature of Seder night — the story of the departure from Egypt.[25]

The compiler of the Haggadah chose to start the story from the early annals of Jewish history, going back as far as the era before our forefathers, before the monotheistic truth was propounded by Avraham. This historical account encompasses

---

25. Following the order of words in the verse והגדת לבנך, this part of the Haggadah corresponds to the word לאמר, *saying*, which refers to the actual saying of the Exodus story. (See *Overview*.)

the redemption from Egypt and the giving of the Torah on Sinai, and continues through the next four hundred years until the building of the First Temple.

Why does the Haggadah depict such a broad span of historical detail, when all we really need is the story of the departure from Egypt?

The purpose of chronicling so much history in the Haggadah is in order to achieve the most astounding contrast between the moments of the lowest spiritual degredation of our ancestors and the moments of the most exalted spiritual zenith of our nation. That distinction is starkest when we consider the state of our ancestors who worshipped idols compared to the state of our nation when we received the Torah at Sinai and, later, when we built the Holy Temple.

And what is the purpose of this contrast?

Only when we are shown the most ignoble depths to which we sank by the side of the most noble heights which we attained can we begin to sincerely appreciate the great kindness God has done for us by raising us from the wretched abyss of idolatry to the eternal blessing of being His chosen people. To open our minds to God's greatness, to inspire our hearts to praise Him on this Pesach night — that is the purpose of this historical account.

The narration begins with this contrast encapsulated in one sentence: *At first our fathers were idol worshippers, but now the Omnipresent has brought us near to His service.* After mentioning the two extremes of our collective condition, the Haggadah proceeds to a more detailed account.

Of course, to discuss in detail Jewish history from the time

of Terach until the Revelation at Sinai, contained in the books of Bereishis and Shemos, would be impractical, tedious, even boring and, thus, self-defeating in purpose. Needless to say, it would take considerably more time than that available on Seder night.

To resolve this dilemma without curtailing crucial elements of history, the Sages wisely chose a series of verses from the Book of Yehoshua (24:2-4) and from the Book of Devarim (26:5-8) which together concisely outline and summarize Jewish history from before Avraham until the redemption from Egypt. The verses from Yehoshua record the idolatry of our ancestors, Avraham's departure from his homeland, Ur Kasdim, to the land of Canaan, and the births and geneology of the forefathers until Yaakov's descent to Egypt.

The verses from Devarim, which comprise the text which one recites upon bringing the annual first fruits to the Temple, continue this compendium of Jewish history with the slavery in Egypt and the details of the miracles of our liberation.

Let us look more closely at these verses which the Haggadah cites.

ויאמר יהושע אל כל העם כה אמר ה׳ אלקי ישראל בעבר הנהר ישבו אבותיכם מעולם תרח אבי אברהם ואבי נחור ויעבדו אלהים אחרים *As it is said: "And Yehoshua said to all the people: 'Thus said Hashem, the God of Israel: "On the other side of the river, your fathers dwelt of old, Terach, father of Avraham and father of Nachor, and they served other gods...." ' "*

Why does the verse mention "on the other side of the river"? Why is Terach called "father of Avraham and father of Nachor," when "father of Avraham" would have been sufficient?

It was their dwelling *on the other side of the river* that brought about their idolatrous beliefs and practices, because *the other side of the river* lacks the positive spiritual influence which permeates the land of Israel.

The verse describes Terach as both "father of Avraham and father of Nachor" in order to demonstrate that Avraham's momentous recognition of the Creator was solely his own merit. Avraham was not instructed in such teachings by his father, for if he was, both sons would have been educated equally, and thus both Avraham and Nachor would have moved from Ur Kasdim. Yet we know that Nachor remained in Ur Kasdim immersed in idolatry. Therefore, it must have been Avraham's own greatness which led him to realize the existence of God.

"*And I took your father Avraham from the other side of the river.*" This verse in Yehoshua refers to God's command to Avraham, *Go away from your land and from your birthplace and from your father's home, to the land which I will show you* (Bereishis 12:1).

Why does the verse again describe Avraham as "your father", when it already called him "your father" in the same verse?

The verse repeats the phrase "your father" to teach us that only Avraham is considered our father; our spiritual history began with him, and not with Terach or any other previous generation. Only from Avraham onwards is the term "father" appropriate.[26]

---

26. Why is the Hebrew article את used twice — את אביכם את אברהם, when, grammatically, only the first את is necessary?

"*...and led him through the whole land of Canaan*", as we read, *Rise, walk the land, through its length and breadth, because to you shall I give it.* (Bereishis 13:17).

"*...and I multiplied his descendants*" — the sons of Yishmael, Avraham's older son, and the sons of Ketura, Avraham's wife after the death of Sarah (see Bereishis 25:1-4, 12-16).

"*...and gave him Yitzchak.*" Not only did I multiply his descendants, but I gave him Yitzchak as well. Yitzchak is not included in "his descendants", because he is the primary descendant, the heir to the spiritual dynasty established by Avraham.[27]

"*And to Yitzchak I gave Yaakov and Esav*". Of the children of Yitzchak, the primary descendant was Yaakov, for only through Yaakov and his descendants were the promises and prophecies of God to Avraham concerning his descendants fulfilled. What were those promises?

First, *to Esav I gave Mount Seir*, and I did not give him the land of Canaan which I had promised to give to the descendants of Avraham and Yitzchak.

Second, the gift of Mount Seir was *for an inheritance*, a permanent possession. Esav and his descendants will live peacefully, and will not suffer the oppressive ordeals which God prophecized for the descendants of Avraham, *Your seed shall be a stranger in a land that is not theirs* (Bereishis 15:13).

The word את is used twice to hint that Terach, Avraham's father, also left Ur Kasdim with Avraham to travel to Canaan (although Terach never reached Canaan; he died in Haran on the way). See Bereishis 11:31.

27. This is alluded to in the verse, *It is through Yitzchak that offspring will be considered yours* (Bereishis 21:12).

בָּרוּךְ שׁוֹמֵר הַבְטָחָתוֹ לְיִשְׂרָאֵל. בָּרוּךְ הוּא.
שֶׁהַקָּדוֹשׁ בָּרוּךְ הוּא חִשַּׁב אֶת הַקֵּץ לַעֲשׂוֹת כְּמָה
שֶׁאָמַר לְאַבְרָהָם אָבִינוּ בִּבְרִית בֵּין הַבְּתָרִים.
שֶׁנֶּאֱמַר וַיֹּאמֶר לְאַבְרָם יָדֹעַ תֵּדַע כִּי־גֵר יִהְיֶה זַרְעֲךָ
בְּאֶרֶץ לֹא לָהֶם וַעֲבָדוּם וְעִנּוּ אֹתָם אַרְבַּע מֵאוֹת
שָׁנָה: וְגַם אֶת־הַגּוֹי אֲשֶׁר יַעֲבֹדוּ דָן אָנֹכִי וְאַחֲרֵי כֵן
יֵצְאוּ בִּרְכֻשׁ גָּדוֹל:

Rather, only *Yaakov and his children went down to Egypt*; this is proof that they are Avraham's sole heirs.

These few verses briefly encompass several generations of our history as described in the Book of Bereishis.

ברוך שומר הבטחתו — **Blessed be He who keeps His promise**

Although the verses quoted from Yehoshua summarize the essential points on the timeline of Jewish history from the time of Terach until the descent into Egypt, they omit one event crucial to the Egyptian exile and, indeed, to all of Jewish history — the ברית בין הבתרים, *Covenant between the Portions*. In this covenant, God told Avraham, *Your seed shall be a stranger in*

Blessed be He Who keeps His promise to Yisrael. Blessed be He. For the Holy One, Blessed be He, calculated the end [of their exile], to do as He had said to our father Avraham at the Covenant between the Portions, as it is written: "He said to Avram: 'Know for sure that your seed shall be a stranger in a land that is not theirs, and they will enslave them and afflict them four hundred years. But also that nation whom they shall serve, do I judge, and afterwards they shall go forth with great possessions.' " (*Bereishis* 15:13-14).

a land that is not theirs, and promised, *But also that nation whom they shall serve, do I judge, and afterwards they shall go forth with great possessions* (Bereishis 15:13-14).

Since this fundamental pact is not mentioned in the verses quoted from Yehoshua and Devarim, it was inserted before the detailed discussion of our experiences in Egypt. We prelude the account of God's promise to redeem us from Egypt with expressions of praise and gratitude. The leader of the Seder proclaims, *Blessed be He Who keeps His promise to Israel*, and everyone responds, *Blessed be He*. We then proceed to explain how He kept His promise.

For the Holy One, Blessed be He, calculated the end of the four hundred years of prophecized exile (see Bereishis 15:13), *to do as He had said to our father Avraham at the Covenant*

between the Portions. We continue to describe exactly how God "calculated the end" of the Egyptian exile.

...as it is written: "He said to Avram: 'Know for sure that your seed shall be a stranger in a land that is not theirs.....'" *Your seed* refers to Yitzchak. God considered the beginning of the four hundred year exile to be the birth of Yitzchak, because at that moment *your seed* had already become *a stranger in a land that is not theirs*, for Canaan was under gentile dominion. The four hundred years of exile which God swore to bring upon the descendants of Avraham began with the birth of Yitzchak (see *Rashi* to Bereishis 15:13).

"*...and they will enslave them and afflict them four hundred years.*" This verse actually contains three different periods of time.

1) *...your seed shall be a stranger in a land that is not theirs.* This is Yitzchak, the immediate "seed" of Avraham, who was a stranger in Canaan under gentile dominion.

2) *...and they will enslave them.* This is the period of enslavement to Egypt.

3) *...and afflict them.* This refers to the period of increased affliction, the harsh and brutal subjugation which Israel suffered during the last eighty-six years of their enslavement in Egypt.[28]

The sum of these periods constitute the four hundred years of exile.

This answers a basic question: Why are we praising God

---

28. From the birth of Miriam (2362) until the Exodus (2448). See *Medrash Tanchuma* [Buber] *Parshas Bo*, ch. 7, which cites the *Seder Olam*, ch. 3. However, in the *Seder Olam* itself (ch. 3), the number is eighty-seven. (Eds.)

so profusely for fulfilling His promise? It is basic, moral protocol — nothing that deserves any extra praise — for any decent person to keep his word, let alone the Almighty.

In truth, however, we are praising God for much more than just keeping His word. We are praising God for fulfilling his promise in such a manner that He alleviated as much suffering as He could which might result from the exile. God's promise called for four hundred years of exile. God had deemed it necessary that the Jewish people undergo exile, and His Divine plan required that part of that exile include insufferable degrees of torment. This agony could have lasted four hundred years. But God, in His great mercy, minimized the suffering as much as He could while nevertheless fulfilling His purpose and His words to Avraham. He considered the exile to begin with the birth of Yitzchak and, consequently, substantially reduced the amount of time that the Jewish people would have to suffer in Egypt generations later.

"But also that nation whom they shall serve, do I judge, and afterwards they shall go forth with great possessions". But also refers back to the words *know for sure.* God assured Avraham that *the nation whom they shall serve, do I judge, and afterwards they shall go forth with great possessions.* And the Holy One, Blessed be He, indeed fulfilled all of His promises.

Cover the matzos and raise the cup of wine:

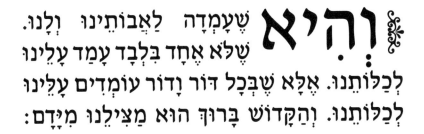

וְהִיא שֶׁעָמְדָה לַאֲבוֹתֵינוּ וְלָנוּ. שֶׁלֹּא אֶחָד בִּלְבָד עָמַד עָלֵינוּ לְכַלּוֹתֵנוּ. אֶלָּא שֶׁבְּכָל דּוֹר וָדוֹר עוֹמְדִים עָלֵינוּ לְכַלּוֹתֵנוּ. וְהַקָּדוֹשׁ בָּרוּךְ הוּא מַצִּילֵנוּ מִיָּדָם:

והיא שעמדה — **And it is this which stood by our fathers**

והיא שעמדה *And it is this which stood by our fathers and by us.* The generally accepted understanding of this phrase is that *this* refers to the promise God made to Avraham, cited in the previous paragraph. It was this promise *which stood by our fathers* in their moments of suffering, giving them the courage to endure their fate, and it was the actualization of this promise that eventually redeemed them from their troubles. It is also this promise which stands *by us*; in difficult times we, too, rely on this everlasting promise God made to Avraham to save his descendants from the persecuting hands of their enemies.

However, the promise made to Avraham at the *Covenant between the Portions* was specifically stated regarding the exile in Egypt. *This* promise that stands by us, therefore, cannot be the promise which was made to Avraham at that time, for that

103

Cover the matzos and raise the cup of wine:

🎗️AND it is this [promise] which stood by our fathers and by us, for not just one has risen up against us to destroy us, but in every single generation they rise up against us to destroy us, and the Holy One, Blessed be He, delivers us from their hand.

promise did not apply to any other hardship.

An alternative approach understands that *this* refers back to the first phrase of the previous paragraph, *Blessed be He Who keeps His promise to Israel* — this is the promise which has stood by us in every generation. And which promise is it? *This* is the all-encompassing, immutable guarantee in Vayikra (26:44), *And yet for all that, even when they are in the land of their enemies, I will not grow so disgusted with them nor abhor them that I would destroy them.*[29]

The paragraph of והיא שעמדה introduces the following description of the persecution of Yaakov at the hands of Lavan and our subsequent descent to Egypt. Throughout history, God saved His people from every threatening situation, just as He promised.

---

29. The Commentary cites this explanation in the name of HaRav Dov Ber Bampi, zt'l. (Eds.)

Put down the cup and uncover the matzos:

צֵא וּלְמַד. מַה בִּקֵּשׁ לָבָן הָאֲרַמִּי לַעֲשׂוֹת לְיַעֲקֹב אָבִינוּ. שֶׁפַּרְעֹה לֹא גָזַר אֶלָּא עַל הַזְּכָרִים וְלָבָן בִּקֵּשׁ לַעֲקוֹר אֶת הַכֹּל. שֶׁנֶּאֱמַר: אֲרַמִּי אֹבֵד אָבִי וַיֵּרֶד מִצְרַיְמָה וַיָּגָר שָׁם בִּמְתֵי מְעָט וַיְהִי שָׁם לְגוֹי גָּדוֹל עָצוּם וָרָב:

צא ולמד — Go and learn

צא ולמד. Following the summary of Jewish history from the father of Avraham until the descent into Egypt, the Haggadah continues with its summary by citing verses from the Book of Devarim (26:5-8). These four verses, commonly called *Parshas Bikkurim* since one reads them when bringing the annual first fruits (*Bikkurim*) to the Temple, portray, in condensed form, Jewish history from where the verses in Yehoshua left off; from the descent into Egypt until the miracles of the redemption.

From here on is the most important chapter of our history so far, for the following pages present the unfolding of events that led to the departure from Egypt. The discussion of these events serve as the fulfillment of the chief mitzvah of Seder night, the obligation to retell the story of the Exodus.

105

Put down the cup and uncover the matzos:

GO out and learn what Lavan the Aramean planned to do to our father Yaakov. For while Pharaoh's decree applied only to the male children, Lavan sought to uproot all, for it says: **"...an Aramean sought to destroy my father, and he went down to Egypt and sojourned there as a stranger, few in number; and there he became a nation, great, strong and numerous"** (*Devarim* 26:5).

Furthermore, in order to enable us to fulfill the dictum, *he who elaborates upon the story of the departure from Egypt is worthy of praise*, every relevant detail is recorded in these verses and expressed by the Haggadah.[30]

---

30. These four verses, therefore, concisely include all of the fundamental details of the Exodus. In order to incorporate so many details into so little space, not all are written in the verses explicitly; rather, some are tacitly alluded to. Our Sages used four methods to find the details contained within these verses:

1) Some are expressed explicitly.

2) Some are derived from the language and structure of the sentences.

3) Some are derived from the particular positioning of one phrase next to another.

4) Some are derived from the specific word that is used, as opposed to any other, seemingly synonymous word.

For every point that the four verses from Devarim express, the Haggadah cites additional verses from the Book of Shemos and other books of Tanach which also express that point. The second verse is not cited as proof to the

The Questions

1 צא ולמד *Go out and learn.*

Why are we told to *go out* and learn? Where should we go out to?

2 צא ולמד *Go out and learn.*

The words *and learn* imply that the following idea is not written explicitly but must be deduced from the text. However, the verse clearly states, *an Aramean sought to destroy my father.*

3 *For while Pharaoh's decree applied only to the male children, Lavan sought to uproot all.*

This night is the divinely appointed time to express the wickedness of Pharaoh. Why, then, does the Haggadah mention that he spared the female children?

4 Furthermore, why does the Haggadah mention Pharaoh at all? It would have sufficed to say *Lavan sought to uproot all* without any mention of Pharaoh.

5 ארמי אבד אבי *An Aramean sought to destroy my father.*

This is how we understand the phrase, ארמי אבד אבי — *an Aramean [Lavan] sought to destroy my father [Yaakov].* However, the grammatical structure of the words suggests that the simplest

---

point deduced from Devarim (why should a second verse expressing the same detail be more convincing than the first?), but merely to show that the four verses the Sages chose to include in the Haggadah concisely contain the many details of the Exodus recorded in other parts of the Torah.

This explains why the phrase כמה שנאמר, *as it says,* is used, and not simply שנאמר, *for it says.* כמה שנאמר means that the same idea exists elsewhere. שנאמר means that a proof exists to the idea stated. In its exposition of these four verses, only in three places does the Haggadah bring a proof and state שנאמר — in צא ולמד (p. 72), וירד מצרימה (p. 76), and ויוציאנו ה׳ ממצרים (p.102); in those three instances the Sages would not have been able to derive the intended meaning from the verses in Devarim alone, and, therefore, they cited other verses which reveal the subtle messages.

107

meaning is, *an exiled Aramean was my father*[31]; the word "Aramean" refers to Yaakov.

Although this seems to be the simplest meaning of the words, it contradicts the previous sentence in which Lavan is called the Aramean.

The purpose of this paragraph is to prove that Lavan *sought to uproot all.* The proof is from Pharaoh. Pharaoh's decree to kill the male children is not labeled with the harsh word "destroy" by the Torah. This word *is* used, however, to describe Lavan's intentions. This reveals to us that his intentions were worse than Pharaoh's, and the only decree worse than killing the male children is killing all the children. This is the proof that *Lavan sought to uproot all.*[32]

Since the Haggadah proves the wickedness of Lavan from the language used to describe Pharaoh, the paragraph begins *Go out and learn* — that is, go out from the present subject of Lavan to another section in the Torah, to that of Pharaoh, and from there you will learn *what Lavan the Aramean planned to do to our father Yaakov.*[33]

Without the proof from Pharaoh we would have thought that Lavan plotted only against the males, and they were the

---

31. One of the meanings of אבד is *exiled* (*Rashbam* on Devarim 26:5), as in ובאו האבדים בארץ אשור, *...and they who were exiled in the land of Ashur shall come* (Yeshayahu 27:13).

32. This form of proof — learning what Lavan planned to do from what the Torah states regarding Pharaoh — is used later in the Haggadah, in the paragraph beginning *Rabbi Yose the Galilean said* (see page 153).

33. See *Kiddushin 37a, Chagigah 9b,* and *Kesuvos 64b* for this use of the phrase "Go out and learn".

וַיֵּרֶד מִצְרַיְמָה. אָנוּס עַל פִּי הַדִּבּוּר:

וַיָּגָר שָׁם. מְלַמֵּד שֶׁלֹּא יָרַד יַעֲקֹב אָבִינוּ
לְהִשְׁתַּקֵּעַ בְּמִצְרַיִם אֶלָּא לָגוּר שָׁם. שֶׁנֶּאֱמַר וַיֹּאמְרוּ
אֶל פַּרְעֹה לָגוּר בָּאָרֶץ בָּאנוּ כִּי אֵין מִרְעֶה לַצֹּאן
אֲשֶׁר לַעֲבָדֶיךָ כִּי־כָבֵד הָרָעָב בְּאֶרֶץ כְּנָעַן וְעַתָּה יֵשְׁבוּ
נָא עֲבָדֶיךָ בְּאֶרֶץ גֹּשֶׁן:

object of his intention to "destroy". However, once the Torah
tells us that Pharaoh also wanted to kill only the males, yet the
Torah does not say that Pharaoh wanted to "destroy", we can
infer that Lavan intended to do far greater evil — *to uproot all.*

The Targum Unkelos on this verse (Devarim 26:5) translates as we have explained: "Lavan the Aramean sought to
destroy my father". Unkelos did not explain "the Aramean" to
refer to Yaakov and translate, "An exiled Aramean was my
father", because then there would be two contradictory terms
describing Yaakov: first, that he was "an Aramean", implying
that he had settled and become a citizen of Aram, and second,
that he was אבד, "exiled", a term which applies only to a
stranger in a foreign land.

And he went down to Egypt — compelled by Divine decree.

And sojourned there as a stranger — this teaches that our father Yaakov did not go down to settle permanently in Egypt, but to stay there temporarily, for it says: "And they [the sons of Yaakov] said to Pharaoh: 'We have come to sojourn in the land, as there is no pasture for your servants' sheep, because the famine is severe in the land of Canaan; and now, please, let your servants dwell in the land of Goshen'" (*Bereishis* 47:4).

Furthermore, Unkelos refrained from explaining that "Aramean" refers to Yaakov, because from Avraham onwards, the forefathers were called עברים, *Hebrews*. Why should the Torah refer to Yaakov with a different nationality?

וירד מצרימה — **And he went down to Egypt**

The Questions

1 וירד מצרימה אנוס על פי הדיבור *And he went down to Egypt — compelled by Divine decree.*

The Haggadah teaches that the word וירד implies that Yaakov went down to Egypt against his will, *compelled by Divine decree*. However, וירד actually implies the exact opposite. וירד implies

that the subject went of his own volition.[34] The word that should have been used to imply that he went compelled is והורד.[35]

2 Why was the phrase *this teaches* omitted? The Haggadah should have been consistent with the sentences that follow and said, *And he went down to Egypt —**this teaches** that he went compelled by Divine decree.*

3 ויגר שם *And sojourned there as a stranger — this teaches that our father Yaakov did not go down to settle permanently in Egypt, but to stay there temporarily.*

The Torah tells us that Yaakov sojourned there as a stranger *after* he moved to Egypt; that is, once he moved there, he chose not to settle permanently but to reside temporarily. The Haggadah, however, uses this sentence to indicate Yaakov's initial intention in moving to Egypt, *before* he moved. How does the Haggadah learn this from the verse which describes Yaakov's thoughts only after he arrived?

Upon close examination of the source of these two teachings, a new understanding emerges (see footnote for the source and full discussion).[36] This is what the Haggadah says:

---

34. For example, see Shoftim 14:5, וירד שמשון...תמנתה, *And Shimshon...went down to Timna.*

35. For example, see Bereishis 39:1, ויוסף הורד מצרימה, *And Yosef was brought down to Egypt.*

36. To understand these two teachings, we must look at their source — the *Sifri* (*Parshas Ki Savo* 26:15; the *Sifri* is the oldest commentary on the Books of Bamidbar and Devarim, written by the Talmudic sage, Rav [circa 220 C.E.].)

The *Sifri* has a slightly different reading than the Haggadah. The reason underlying this difference is the key to resolving our questions.

The *Sifri* says, *"And he went down to Egypt"* — *this teaches that he did not go down to settle permanently, but to stay there temporarily.*

The *Sifri* is identical to the Haggadah except for two changes.

First, the teaching that Yaakov went down to Egypt *compelled by Divine decree* is entirely omitted by the *Sifri*.

Second, the Haggadah learns from the words ויגר שם, *And he sojourned there*

111

as a stranger, that Yaakov did not go down to settle permanently. The *Sifri*, however, learns the same teaching from the words וירד מצרימה, *And he went down to Egypt.*

Why does the *Sifri* (1) omit the teaching that Yaakov went compelled by Divine decree, and (2) derive from the words וירד מצרימה and not simply from ויגר שם that Yaakov went down to Egypt only to live temporarily?

The reason for the first difference is that, in fact, there is *no* indication in this verse that Yaakov went down compelled by Divine decree. On the contrary, the word וירד implies that Yaakov went down by his own free will. For this reason the *Sifri* leaves out this detail of Yaakov's descent to Egypt.

If the verse does not imply that Yaakov went down against his will, then how does the Haggadah infer such a fact from the verse?

In truth, the Haggadah is not learning from the verse that Yaakov went down to Egypt against his will. The Haggadah is merely inserting an important fact of the story into its appropriate chronological place. That is, when the verse tells us that Yaakov went down, the Haggadah adds that he went down compelled by Divine decree; it is only an addition — we do not learn this fact from the verse.

If he went down compelled by Divine decree, then why does the verse imply that he *went down* of his own volition?

Yaakov *thought* that he was going to Egypt by his own decision. However, it had already been decreed many years earlier, in the time of Yaakov's grandfather, Avraham, that Avraham's offspring would go down to Egypt, and Yaakov's descent was merely a fulfillment of this Divine decree, albeit he thought he was going of his own accord.

The very next part of the verse, ויגר שם, from which the Haggadah derives that Yaakov went down to Egypt only to dwell temporarily, proves that we cannot infer from this verse that Yaakov went against his will. The fact that Yaakov went down with the intention to stay only for a short time while waiting for the famine in Canaan to pass and for the situation there to improve proves that he went down freely and not compelled by Divine decree; he chose to go for his own welfare. Therefore, the *Sifri* does not derive from the verse that he went down against his will, because the verse tells the exact opposite. Nonetheless, since in God's scheme of history it was necessary for the descendants of Avraham to go down to Egypt, God brought about a series of circumstances which would force Yaakov to make the decision which he made. Therefore, the Haggadah adds this fact and inserts that Yaakov went down compelled by Divine decree.

The second difference between the *Sifri* and the Haggadah is actually no difference at all. We pointed out that the Haggadah derives from *And*

בְּמְתֵי מְעָט. כְּמָה שֶׁנֶּאֱמַר בְּשִׁבְעִים נֶפֶשׁ יָרְדוּ אֲבֹתֶיךָ מִצְרָיְמָה וְעַתָּה שָׂמְךָ יהוה אֱלֹהֶיךָ כְּכוֹכְבֵי הַשָּׁמַיִם לָרֹב:

ויִּרֶד מצרימה אנוס על פי הדיבור *And he went down to Egypt — compelled by Divine decree.* The Haggadah is not *teaching* that he went down compelled by Divine decree, but is merely adding this fact to the story of Yaakov's descent to Egypt, as

---

sojourned there as a stranger that Yaakov went to live in Egypt only temporarily, while the *Sifri* learns the same from *And he went down to Egypt.*

In truth, both the *Sifri* and the Haggadah have the same source for this teaching: the two words together, ויִּרֶד and ויִּגֶר, teach that Yaakov went down only to dwell temporarily. Thus, the Torah says, ויִּרֶד מצרימה ויִּגֶר שם — at the moment of ויִּרֶד, *and he went down,* he ויִּגֶר — *sojourned as a stranger.*

The next phrase in the verse clearly proves that ויִּגֶר, *and he sojourned as a stranger,* refers to Yaakov's intention *before* his arrival in Egypt. The verse states, *And he went down to Egypt and sojourned there few in number....* Does the phrase *few in number* describe the number that travelled to Egypt, or how many sojourned there? The simple understanding is that it refers to how many travelled to Egypt (the Haggadah itself points out that the phrase *few in number* refers to the number that *travelled* to Egypt by citing Devarim 10:22). If so, the order of the verse should have read, *And he went down to Egypt few in number and sojourned there.* Since the Torah places *and sojourned there* before *few in number,* it must be that *and sojourned there* is part of *and he went down,* teaching us that ויִּרֶד, Yaakov left for Egypt with the intention of ויִּגֶר, of going only to dwell temporarily.

Nevertheless, the word ויִּגֶר and its proximity to the word ויִּרֶד is still not enough to tell us that Yaakov went down to dwell temporarily. The word ויִּגֶר has two meanings, depending upon the context in which it is used. It can mean, as we have explained it until now, to dwell temporarily, as in the word גֵּרוּת, the state of being a stranger. It can also mean to settle permanently, as in the word לָגוּר, to live in a place permanently (see, for example, Bereishis 47:7).

113

Few in number — as it says: "With seventy souls, your forefathers went down to Egypt, and now Hashem your God has made you as the stars of the heavens for multitude" (*Devarim* 10:22).

the omission of the phrase *this teaches* confirms. The Torah tells us, *And he went down,* and the Haggadah adds, *compelled by Divine decree.*

ויגר שם *And sojourned there as a stranger* — *this teaches that our father Yaakov did not go down to settle permanently in Egypt, but to stay there temporarily.* This part of the verse, ויגר שם, *and sojourned there,* is connected to the first phrase of the verse, וירד מצרימה, *and he went down to Egypt,* and modifies it. *And he went down to Egypt* — how did he go down? *And sojourned there as a stranger* — he went down with no intention to settle, but to stay temporarily.

במתי מעט — **Few in number**

The Questions

1 במתי מעט *Few in number* — as it says: *"With seventy souls, your forefathers went down to Egypt, and now Hashem your God has*

Because of the ambiguity of the meaning of ויגר, the Haggadah cites another verse to prove what the correct interpretation of it is in our context. *As it says: "And they [the sons of Yaakov] said to Pharaoh: 'We have come to sojourn in the land, as there is no pasture for your servants' sheep, because the famine is severe in the land of Canaan; and now, please, let your servants dwell in the land of Goshen'"* (Bereishis 47:4). They intended to stay only until the famine passed. ויגר, therefore, in our context means to stay temporarily.

וַיְהִי שָׁם לְגוֹי. מְלַמֵּד שֶׁהָיוּ יִשְׂרָאֵל מְצֻיָּנִים שָׁם:

made you as the stars of the heavens for multitude" (Devarim 10:22).

Why does the Haggadah cite a verse from the Book of Devarim, from a section of the Torah which is not even discussing the descent to Egypt? The Haggadah should have referred to the verse in the section of the Torah which describes the descent to Egypt, *And all the souls that were descended from Yaakov were seventy souls, and Yosef was already in Egypt* (Shemos 1:5).

2 Why does the Haggadah cite the end of the verse, *and now Hashem your God has made you as the stars of the heavens for multitude,* which has nothing to do with the point at hand?

במתי מעט *Few in number.* These few words convey an important element of the descent to Egypt. They are significant alone and need no support to prove the idea which they teach. Nevertheless, the Haggadah cites a verse which conveys the same idea, not to *prove* that they went down few in number, but merely to show that the idea expressed by these two words is mentioned elsewhere. Therefore, the verse is not preceded by the word שנאמר, *for it says,* which precedes a proof, but with כמה שנאמר, *as it says;* that is, *this is an idea that we find elsewhere: With seventy souls, your forefathers went down to Egypt.*

ועתה שמך *And now Hashem your God has made you as the stars of the heavens for multitude.* The Haggadah cites the end of the verse, even though it has no relevance to the present

115

There he became a nation — this teaches that Israel were distinctive people there.

subject, because of the principle that *any verse which Moshe did not divide, we are not permitted to divide* (Megillah 22a; see footnote on p. 83 for full discussion).

This principle also explains why the Haggadah cites this verse from the Book of Devarim and overlooks the verse in Shemos. Whichever verse the Haggadah cites, it must be quoted until its end. The verse in Shemos concludes, *and Yosef was already in Egypt.* The Haggadah, obligated to cite the verse until its end, prefers a verse which concludes with words of blessing and encouragement: *and now Hashem your God has made you as the stars of the heavens for multitude.*

ויהי שם לגוי — **There he became a nation**

The Questions

1 This part of the verse, ויהי שם לגוי גדול, *There he became a great nation,* is one, indivisible phrase. Why, then, does the Haggadah split it into two parts, ויהי שם לגוי and גדול?

2 What indication is there from ויהי שם לגוי, *There he became a nation,* that the people of Israel became a *distinctive* people?

3 Why does the Haggadah add the word *there* in, *this teaches that Israel were distinctive people there*? It is obvious that they became a distinctive people *there*, in Egypt, because that is the subject of the verse!

גָּדוֹל עָצוּם. כְּמָה שֶׁנֶּאֱמַר וּבְנֵי יִשְׂרָאֵל פָּרוּ וַיִּשְׁרְצוּ וַיִּרְבּוּ וַיַּעַצְמוּ בִּמְאֹד מְאֹד וַתִּמָּלֵא הָאָרֶץ אֹתָם:

ויהי שם לגוי *There he became a nation.* The verse which the Haggadah is presently expounding reads, *And he went down to Egypt and sojourned there as a stranger, few in number; and there he became a nation, great, strong, and numerous.*

Why does the verse repeat the word *there*? Since the Torah already states, *and sojourned **there** as a stranger,* it is obvious that **there** *he became a nation,* and thus the second *there* is unnecessary. The verse should read, ויהי לגוי גדול, *and he became a nation.*

The Haggadah learns, therefore, that the extra word שם, *there,* comes to teach us to read the phrase *There he became a nation* separate from the words *great, strong, and numerous,* and indicates to us that *Israel were distinctive people there.*

How do we know from the extra word *there* that the people of Israel were distinctive people?

The Haggadah tells us.

The word *there* refers to a certain place. If the Torah meant to tell us that there — in Egypt — the people of Israel became a great, strong, and numerous nation, it would not have to write the word *there.* The attributes "great, strong, and numerous" do not require comparison to a particular place in order to convey meaning. The attribute "distinctive", however, is only meaningful when relative to another entity. Therefore, in

Great, strong — as it says: "And the Children of Yisrael were fruitful, and they increased abundantly and multiplied and became exceedingly strong and the land was filled with them" (*Shemos* 1:7).

order to say that our nation was a distinctive people, we must compare our nation with the nation which surrounded it. If Israel was different from Egypt, then our nation was, indeed, distinctive. If Israel was not different from Egypt, then our nation was not distinctive.

The use of the word *there*, a word which focuses on a place (in our case, Egypt), indicates an attribute that only has meaning when compared with another place. Therefore, it is the extra word *there* that *teaches that Israel were distinctive people there*. The Haggadah emphasizes this point by writing the word *there* again: *this teaches that Israel were distinctive people there*.

The Haggadah cites no verse for this idea, because the attribute of being "distinctive people" is found only in this verse and nowhere else.

גדול עצום *Great, strong*. The word גדול, *great*, refers to the size of the nation in numbers. The word עצום, *strong*, refers to the strength of the nation. The Haggadah quotes a verse (Shemos 1:7) which expresses these two qualities of the nation of Israel in Egypt. *As it says: "And the Children of Israel were fruitful, and they increased abundantly, and multiplied"* — this refers to the large numbers; *"and became exceedingly*

וָרָב. כְּמָה שֶׁנֶּאֱמַר רְבָבָה כְּצֶמַח הַשָּׂדֶה נְתַתִּיךְ
וַתִּרְבִּי וַתִּגְדְּלִי וַתָּבֹאִי בַּעֲדִי עֲדָיִים שָׁדַיִם נָכֹנוּ
וּשְׂעָרֵךְ צִמֵּחַ וְאַתְּ עֵרֹם וְעֶרְיָה: וָאֶעֱבֹר עָלַיִךְ
וָאֶרְאֵךְ מִתְבּוֹסֶסֶת בְּדָמָיִךְ וָאֹמַר לָךְ בְּדָמַיִךְ חֲיִי
וָאֹמַר לָךְ בְּדָמַיִךְ חֲיִי:

strong" — this refers to their physical strength.[37]

ורב — **And numerous**

ורב *And numerous.* The Haggadah wants to know what
these words add to the description of the condition of the
people of Israel in Egypt. *And numerous* cannot mean that the
nation was large in number, because the verse already teaches
this when it says that they were *great*. Therefore, the Haggadah
tells us that *and numerous* has another meaning.

Although the word ורב, *and numerous,* usually refers to
the large size of the subject, here it alludes to the *way* in which
they grew so large, referring to the prodigious rate of repro-

---

37. Again, the Haggadah quotes the verse not to prove the idea derived from
the two words, but merely to demonstrate that the idea can be found
elsewhere.

119

And numerous — as it says: "I let you become as myriads, like the plants of the field, and you increased and grew big; and you came of age to wear jewelry of outstanding beauty, your breasts properly formed and your hair grown, but you were naked and bare" (*Yechezkel* 16:7). "And I passed over you and saw you wallowing in your blood; and I said to you: 'In your blood, live!' and I said to you: 'In your blood, live!' " (*ibid.*, 6).

duction of the Jewish people[38]. The Medrash records the miracle that the Jewish women in Egypt bore six children at each birth (*Medrash Tanchuma* and *Yalkut Shimoni* on Shemos 1:7).

The Haggadah relates this allusion to us by quoting a verse which uses a form of the word ורב in its comparison of the growth of the Jewish people to the growth of vegetation: רבבה כצמח השדה, *I let you become as myriads, like the plants of the field...* (Yechezkel 16:7). The Jewish people multiplied like plants which germinate rapidly and produce many shoots from a single root.

Since the Haggadah cites the beginning of the verse, it also cites the rest of the verse in compliance with the rule that a verse must be quoted until its end, even though the second

---

38. This also explains why the Haggadah did not cite the aforementioned verse (Shemos 1:7) that contains the word וירבו, another form of the word ורב. There, וירבו means *they multiplied.*

וַיָּרֵעוּ אֹתָנוּ הַמִּצְרִים וַיְעַנּוּנוּ וַיִּתְּנוּ עָלֵינוּ
עֲבֹדָה קָשָׁה:

וַיָּרֵעוּ אֹתָנוּ הַמִּצְרִים. כְּמָה שֶׁנֶּאֱמַר הָבָה
נִתְחַכְּמָה לוֹ פֶּן יִרְבֶּה וְהָיָה כִּי תִקְרֶאנָה מִלְחָמָה
וְנוֹסַף גַּם הוּא עַל שֹׂנְאֵינוּ וְנִלְחַם בָּנוּ וְעָלָה מִן
הָאָרֶץ:

part of the verse is not relevant to the Haggadah's point (see footnote on p. 83 for full discussion).

ואעבור עליך *"And I passed over you... and I said to you: 'In your blood, live!' and I said to you: 'In your blood, live!'"* (Yechezkel 16:6). Having quoted *but you were naked and bare* (ibid. 16:7), which alludes to the Jews' lack of merit at the time of the Exodus (cf. *Rashi*, Shemos 12:6; *Mechilta Parshas Bo ch. 5*), the Haggadah also cites the previous verse in Yechezkel. The repetition of, *In your blood, live!* alludes to the two mitzvos which God gave to the Jewish people in Egypt so that they would be worthy of salvation — the blood of the Pesach sacrifice and the blood of circumcision (*Shemos Rabbah 17:3*).

"And the Egyptians ill-treated us, and they afflicted us and laid upon us hard bondage" (*Devarim* 26:6).

And the Egyptians ill-treated us — as it says: "Come, let us deal wisely with them, lest they multiply, and then, when circumstances bring about war, they too will join our enemies, or they will also fight against us, and move up out of the land" (*Shemos* 1:10).

ויַרעו אותנו — **And the Egyptians ill-treated us**

The Questions

1 ויַרעו אותנו *And the Egyptians ill-treated us — as it says: "Come, let us deal wisely with them...".*

Why does the Haggadah cite this verse, *"Come, let us deal wisely with them...",* to show how the Egyptians ill-treated us?

And the Egyptians ill-treated us refers to abuse *in action*; that is, what the Egyptians actually did. *"Come, let us deal wisely with them..."* merely represents as yet unfulfilled intention; that is, what the Egyptians planned to do.

2 Many of the commentators have asked why the verse says ויַרעו אותנו (literally, "and they acted with evil us") and not the more grammatically appropriate ויַרעו לנו (literally, "and they acted with evil towards us"), and they have offered novel expla-

nations which do not fit the simple meaning of the words.[39]

וירעו אותנו המצרים *And the Egyptians ill-treated us — as it says: "Come, let us deal wisely with them...".* The Haggadah's intention in this paragraph is not to *teach us the meaning* of the phrase, *And the Egyptians ill-treated us,* but to explain that a connection exists between the preceding sentence, *There he became a nation, great, strong, and numerous,* with this verse, *And the Egyptians ill-treated us,* and what that connection is.

In other words, what was it that caused the Egyptians' maltreatment of us (verse 6)? Our development into a considerable people (verse 5).

And what was it about the phenomenal increase of the Jewish population that caused the Egyptians to persecute us? The fear that the large Jewish nation would wage war against them (Shemos 1:10).

The Haggadah shows that this cause and effect relationship exists in the Book of Shemos in the actual account of the Exodus. When the Egyptians saw that the Children of Israel "were fruitful, and they increased abundantly and multipled and became exceedingly strong and the land was filled with them" (Shemos 1:7), they conspired, "Come, let us deal wisely

---

39. The most common explanation given is that וירעו אותנו does not mean, *And the Egyptians acted badly towards us,* but that it means, *And the Egyptians made us into bad people.* The verse, *"Come, let us deal wisely with them... lest they join our enemies, or... fight against us",* is then cited to show how the Egyptians viewed us as potential enemies.

This explanation is unsound because in Hebrew grammar the act of judging someone in one's thoughts as evil does not take the form of the verb of the word "evil", and, therefore, וירעו אותנו can only mean, *And the Egyptians ill-treated us* (or, more accurately, *And the Egyptians became evil towards us*).

with them, lest they multiply" (Shemos 1:10). These consecutive verses in Shemos express the reason (Shemos 1:7) for the evil which the Egyptians planned to do (Shemos 1:10)[40]. Similarly, the consecutive verses here in Devarim express the same cause and effect: Because "there he became a nation, great, strong, and numerous" (Devarim 26:5), the Egyptians, in response, "ill-treated us, and they afflicted us and laid upon us hard bondage" (Devarim 26:6).

Thus, the Haggadah is not explaining how the Egyptians ill-treated us, but rather what connects their ill-treatment of us to our remarkable increase in size.

The second question, the question of the commentators that וירעו אתנו should instead read וירעו לנו poses no problem, for both forms of the direct object are grammatically acceptable.[41]

An alternative approach, although not the simple meaning of the text can be learned as follows:

The word וירעו is related to the word רעיון, *idea* or *thought*, as in בנתה לרעי מרחוק, *You understand my thought from afar* (Tehillim 139:2), and ולי מה יקרו רעיך קל, *How precious are your thoughts to me, O God!* (Tehillim 139:17)

With this definition of וירעו, the sentence וירעו אתנו המצרים

---

40. Although the Haggadah's objective is to show that the Jews' growth in size was the reason for their ill-treatment by the Egyptians (Shemos 1:10), the Haggadah nevertheless quotes until the end of that verse, even though its contents are not relevant to the topic, in compliance with the rule, *any verse which Moshe did not divide, we are not permitted to divide* (see footnote on p. 83 for full discussion).

41. For example, ולא הרעתי את אחד מהם, *I have not ill-treated any of them"* (Bamidbar 16:15), and not ולא הרעתי לאחד מהם.

124

וַיְעַנּוּנוּ. כְּמָה שֶׁנֶּאֱמַר וַיָּשִׂימוּ עָלָיו שָׂרֵי מִסִּים
לְמַעַן עַנֹּתוֹ בְּסִבְלֹתָם וַיִּבֶן עָרֵי מִסְכְּנוֹת לְפַרְעֹה אֶת
פִּתֹם וְאֶת רַעַמְסֵס:
וַיִּתְּנוּ עָלֵינוּ עֲבֹדָה קָשָׁה. כְּמָה שֶׁנֶּאֱמַר וַיַּעֲבִדוּ
מִצְרַיִם אֶת בְּנֵי יִשְׂרָאֵל בְּפָרֶךְ:

means, *And the Egyptians thought about us [to ill-treat us]*. It would then be an expression of the Egyptians' intention and not their action, and thus the verse, *Come, let us deal wisely with them...* is appropriate.

Of course, the first explanation is the simple and straightforward meaning of the Haggadah.

ויענונו — **And they afflicted us**

The Question

1 *And laid upon us hard bondage — as it says: "And the Egyptians put to work the Children of Israel, with crushing harshness"* (*Shemos 1:13*).

Why does the Haggadah bring the verse, *And the Egyptians put to work the Children of Israel...* (Shemos 1:13) to illustrate how they laid upon us hard bondage when it could have brought the very next verse (Shemos 1:14), which uses that phrase explicitly, *And they made their lives bitter with hard bondage*?

The verse (Devarim 26:6) which the Haggadah is expounding

125

And they afflicted us — as it says: "And they set over them fiscal officers in order to afflict them with their burdens, and they built storage cities for Pharaoh, Pisom and Raamses" (*Shemos* 1:11).

And laid upon us hard bondage — as it says: "And the Egyptians put to work the children of Israel, with crushing harshness" (*Shemos* 1:13).

distinguishes between two forms of persecution: (1) עינוי, affliction, and (2) עבודה קשה, hard bondage.

עינוי, affliction, denotes causing others to suffer for no aim other than the suffering. The pain suffered by the victim is the sole goal of the perpetrator. To demonstrate this type of persecution the Haggadah brings the verse, *And they set over them fiscal officers in order to afflict them with their burdens* (Shemos 1:11)[42]. The officers' only aim was to afflict them with their burdens. Their goal was not to make the Jews work, but to make the Jews suffer.

עבודה קשה, hard bondage, refers to persecution with a goal — the Egyptians wanted the Jews to work hard in order to

---

42. Although the end of the verse seems to imply that the goal of the Egyptians was the productivity of the Jews — ויבן ערי מסכנות לפרעה, ...*and they built storage houses for Pharaoh...*, closer inspection reveals that this is not the case. First, the verse states, ויבן, "and they built" (literally, "and he [the nation of Israel] built"), and not לבנות, "to build", which is what the verse should have said had the building of the storehouses been the goal of the Egyptians' persecution of the Jews. Second, the last word of the phrase למען ענתו בסבלותם, *in order to afflict them with their burdens*, bears the disjunctive note of an אתנחתא, which separates this phrase from the phrase, *And they built*. (Eds.)

126

וַנִּצְעַק אֶל יהוה אֱלֹהֵי אֲבֹתֵינוּ וַיִּשְׁמַע יהוה
אֶת־קֹלֵנוּ וַיַּרְא אֶת־עָנְיֵנוּ וְאֶת עֲמָלֵנוּ וְאֶת־לַחֲצֵנוּ:

וַנִּצְעַק אֶל־יהוה אֱלֹהֵי אֲבֹתֵינוּ. כְּמָה שֶׁנֶּאֱמַר
וַיְהִי בַיָּמִים הָרַבִּים הָהֵם וַיָּמָת מֶלֶךְ מִצְרַיִם וַיֵּאָנְחוּ
בְנֵי־יִשְׂרָאֵל מִן־הָעֲבֹדָה וַיִּזְעָקוּ וַתַּעַל שַׁוְעָתָם אֶל־
הָאֱלֹהִים מִן־הָעֲבֹדָה:

increase their productivity. The Haggadah, therefore, cites the verse which expresses this form of persecution, *And the Egyptians put to work the Children of Israel, with crushing harshness* (*Shemos* 1:13).

The emphasis of the verse is on what the Egyptians did to the Children of Israel — they put them to work. This was the goal of the Egyptians' crushing harshness.

This sort of persecution is not evident in the verse that follows, *And they made their lives bitter with hard bondage* (Shemos 1:14), which implies that the aim of the hard bondage was to make their lives bitter (which is actually עינוי and not עבודה קשה). However, once the Haggadah has cited the previous verse (verse 13), it is understood that this verse (verse 14) is a continuation of the verse before it, and the "hard bondage" mentioned here was indeed goal-oriented, and not

"And we cried out to Hashem, the God of our fathers, and Hashem heard our voice and saw our affliction and our misery and our oppression" (*Devarim* 26:7).

And we cried out to Hashem, the God of our fathers — as it says: "And it came to pass in the course of those many days that the king of Egypt died and the Children of Iisrael sighed from the slavery, and they cried, and their cry for help rose up to God from the slavery" (*Shemos* 2:23).

solely for the intent of making the Jews suffer.

ונצעק — **And we cried**

ונצעק אל ה׳ *And we cried out to Hashem, the God of our fathers* — *as it says* in the Book of Shemos (2:23) in the story of our slavery: *"And it came to pass in the course of those many days"*, days of suffering, *"that the king of Egypt died and"* then the Children of Israel had no more reason to repress their misery at their condition, for until now they feared that expressing their discontent would result in severe repercussions from the despotic monarch. But as soon as he died *"the Children of Israel sighed from the slavery, and they cried."* אנחה, *sighing*, is an internal emotion concealed within the depths of one's heart, while זעקה, *crying*, is the outward expression of that emotion.

וַיִּשְׁמַע יהוה אֶת־קֹלֵנוּ. כְּמָה שֶׁנֶּאֱמַר וַיִּשְׁמַע
אֱלֹהִים אֶת־נַאֲקָתָם וַיִּזְכֹּר אֱלֹהִים אֶת־בְּרִיתוֹ אֶת־
אַבְרָהָם אֶת־יִצְחָק וְאֶת־יַעֲקֹב:
וַיַּרְא אֶת־עָנְיֵנוּ. זוֹ פְּרִישׁוּת דֶּרֶךְ אֶרֶץ. כְּמָה
שֶׁנֶּאֱמַר וַיַּרְא אֱלֹהִים אֶת־בְּנֵי יִשְׂרָאֵל וַיֵּדַע אֱלֹהִים:

The Children of Israel sighed *from the slavery,* and only they knew that their deep feelings of desperation were due to the gruelling toil that the Egyptians had demanded of them. The Egyptians, however, did not perceive the *sighing;* they were not aware of the real reason for the Jews' outcry. All they heard was the *crying,* and they assumed that the crying was no more than the Jews' expression of their grief at the death of the king. Consequently, the Children of Israel were able to cry out to Hashem without fear of Egyptian retribution.

ותעל שועתם *"and their cry for help rose up to God from the slavery".* God, Who knows the thoughts and feelings hidden within the innermost recesses of every heart, knew that the cry of the Jews was *from the slavery* and recognized their plea to be saved. However, at this point their cry only *rose up to God;* there is no indication that He had decided to respond to it.

And Hashem heard our voice — as it says: "And God heard their groaning, and God remembered His covenant with Avraham, with Yitzchak and with Yaakov" (*ibid.*, 24).

And saw our affliction — this refers to the enforced disruption of normal family relations, as it says: "And God saw the Children of Israel, and God took note of it" (*ibid.*, 25).

וישמע — **And Hashem heard**

וישמע ה' And Hashem heard our voice and accepted our prayer — *as it says: "And God heard their groaning,"* their prayer to be saved, *"and God remembered His covenant with Avraham, with Yitzchak and with Yaakov" (ibid., 24)*. In response to their prayer, God set forth the course of events which would ultimately culminate in the redemption, the redemption which He promised to the forefathers. וישמע ה', *And Hashem heard*, tells us that He responded to their outcry, whereas the previous verse, ותעל שועתם, *and their cry for help rose up*, does not.

וירא את ענינו — **And saw our affliction**

וירא את ענינו זו פרישות דרך ארץ *And saw our affliction — this refers to the enforced disruption of normal family relations*. The

130

וְאֶת עֲמָלֵנוּ. אֵלּוּ הַבָּנִים. כְּמָה שֶׁנֶּאֱמַר כָּל־
הַבֵּן הַיִּלּוֹד הַיְאֹרָה תַּשְׁלִיכֻהוּ וְכָל־הַבַּת תְּחַיּוּן:

Egyptians forced the Jewish husbands to separate from their wives. This is indicated in the verse by the word עינינו, *our affliction*, which is often used to describe the involuntary separation between man and wife[43], *as it says: "And God saw the Children of Israel"*, but the verse does not say what God saw. This reticence informs us that the verse is referring to marital relations but, in the spirit of modesty, refrained from stating so explicitly. The words *And God saw* also imply that it was something that *only* God saw; that is, the private and personal relations between husband and wife revealed only to the Omnipresent. *"And God took note of it"*, literally, *"And God knew"*; He knew of their affliction regarding those concealed matters known only to Him — the suffering caused by the separation between husband and wife.[44]

---

43. For example, אם תענה את בנתי, *If you will afflict my daughters* (Bereishis 31:50), which refers to the deprivation of marital relations (*Rashi; Yoma 77a*).

44. The words וידע אלקים, *and God knew*, also allude to the disruption of marital relations. The word ידע, *to know*, is an idiomatic expression for marital relations. See, for example, Bereishis 4:1, *And Adam knew his wife*. This would apply here in the sense that God caused the wives of Israel to allure their husbands to them when the Egyptians had forced their separation (see *Rashi*, Shemos 38:8).

And our labor — these are the children, as it says: "...every son that is born, you shall throw into the river, and every daughter you shall let live" (*Shemos* 1:22).

ואת עמלנו — **And our labor**

The Questions

1 ואת עמלנו *And our labor — these are the children.*

How does the Haggadah see any allusion to the children from the words *and our labor?*

2 *...as it says: "...every son that is born, you shall throw into the river, and every daughter you shall let live" (Shemos 1:22).*

Why does the Haggadah mention Pharaoh's command to let the daughters live? Why should the Haggadah mention what appears to be a good deed of Pharaoh, as if to partially exonerate him from his guilt?

ואת עמלנו *And our labor.* עמל, *labor,* has two distinct characteristics. First, it refers to toil undertaken for one's benefit. Second, it refers to toil done in vain.[45]

Since עמל, *labor,* refers to work done for one's own benefit, the verse is telling us about the work the Jews performed voluntarily, for their own benefit, but for which the effort turned out to be in vain. *These are the children* for which the

---

45. For example, *What profit has a man of all of his labor* (בכל עמלו) *in which he labors under the sun* (Koheles 1:3) and *And this was my portion from all of my labor* (מכל עמלי)*... and the labor that I had labored* (ובעמל שעמלתי) *to do, and behold — all was vanity* (ibid. 2:10-11).

וְאֶת לַחֲצֵנוּ. זֶה הַדְּחַק. כְּמָה שֶׁנֶּאֱמַר וְגַם־
רָאִיתִי אֶת־הַלַּחַץ אֲשֶׁר מִצְרַיִם לֹחֲצִים אֹתָם:

Jews exerted themselves, but in vain, because Pharaoh had decreed their deaths, *as it says: "...every son that is born you shall throw into the river"* (Shemos 1:22)

The Haggadah cites the end of the verse, "and every daughter you shall let live", not to mitigate Pharaoh's treachery, but merely in compliance with the rule not to cite a verse without quoting it until the end (see footnote on p. 83 for full discussion of this rule). Alternatively, *"and every daughter you shall let live"* itself incriminates Pharaoh even more, for Pharaoh, in all of his evil, intended to spare the lives of the daughters only to exploit them for immoral purposes (*Medrash Lekach Tov* on Shemos 1:16).

ואת לחצנו — And our oppression

The Questions

1 ואת לחצנו זה הדחק *And our oppression — this is the pressure.* What "pressure" is this?

2 *...as it says: "...and I have also seen the oppression with which the Egyptians oppress them"* (ibid. 3:9).
Why is this verse cited? It makes no mention of "pressure", and there is no indication that the "oppression" the Jews experienced was "pressure".

133

And our oppression — this is the pressure, as it says: "...and I have also seen the oppression with which the Egyptians oppress them" (*ibid.* 3:9).

The word לחץ, *oppression*, has two meanings. First, לחץ denotes a lack of basic necessities[46]. Second, it denotes being physically pressed into a tight space[47].

In the context of the verse describing the situation of the Jews in Egypt, לחצנו cannot refer to the lack of basic necessities, because we know that the Jews had an ample supply, as they said during their journey through the wilderness, *We remember the fish that we ate for nothing in Egypt, the cucumbers, melons, leeks, onions, and garlic* (Bamidbar 11:5).

Accordingly, לחצנו here follows the second definition — being pressed into a tight space. This is what the Haggadah means when it says, ואת לחצנו זה הדחק, *and our oppression — this is the pressure*; that is, the Egyptians denied us adequate living space and confined us to a scanty area in the region of Goshen.

The Haggadah cites a verse not to prove that לחצנו refers to this type of pressure, but merely to point out that לחץ is mentioned in the actual account of the slavery[48].

---

46. For example, *...bread of adversity and water of hardship* (ומים לחץ) (Yeshayahu 30:20).

47. For example, *...and she crushed* (ותלחץ) *Bilam's foot against the wall* (Bamidbar 22:25).

48. For this reason the verse is introduced with כמה שנאמר, the phrase used when bringing an example, and not שנאמר, the phrase used when bringing a proof. (See footnote on p. 73).

134

וַיּוֹצִאֵנוּ יהוה מִמִּצְרַיִם בְּיָד חֲזָקָה וּבִזְרֹעַ
נְטוּיָה וּבְמֹרָא גָדֹל וּבְאֹתוֹת וּבְמֹפְתִים:

וַיּוֹצִיאֵנוּ יהוה מִמִּצְרַיִם. לֹא עַל־יְדֵי מַלְאָךְ
וְלֹא עַל־יְדֵי שָׂרָף וְלֹא עַל־יְדֵי שָׁלִיחַ. אֶלָּא הַקָּדוֹשׁ
בָּרוּךְ הוּא בִּכְבוֹדוֹ וּבְעַצְמוֹ. שֶׁנֶּאֱמַר:

וְעָבַרְתִּי בְאֶרֶץ־מִצְרַיִם בַּלַּיְלָה הַזֶּה וְהִכֵּיתִי כָל־בְּכוֹר בְּאֶרֶץ
מִצְרַיִם מֵאָדָם וְעַד בְּהֵמָה וּבְכָל אֱלֹהֵי מִצְרַיִם אֶעֱשֶׂה
שְׁפָטִים אֲנִי יהוה:

And Hashem brought — וַיוֹצִיאֵנוּ
us out

The Question

1 שנאמר...וַיוֹצִיאֵנוּ *And Hashem brought us out from Egypt...for it says....*

We have learned that the Haggadah uses the word שנאמר, *for it says*, when it needs to bring a proof for the inference it has just made from a verse. When there is no need to prove the intent of the verse, the Haggadah says כמה שנאמר, *as it says*.

Here, why does the Haggadah need to say שנאמר, to bring a proof that God alone brought us out from Egypt, when the verse

135

25

"And Hashem brought us out from Egypt with a mighty hand and with an outstretched arm and with great awesomeness, and with instructive signs and with punishing miracles" (*Devarim* 26:8).

And Hashem brought us out from Egypt - not through an angel, not through a seraph, and not through a messenger. But it was the Holy One, Blessed be He, Himself in all His glory, for it says:

"And I will pass through the land of Egypt in this night, and I will smite every firstborn in the land of Egypt, from man to beast, and against all the gods of Egypt I will execute judgment, I, Hashem" (*Shemos* 12:12).

itself says so explicitly — *And Hashem brought us out from Egypt?*[49]

ויציאנו... *And Hashem brought us out from Egypt* (Devarim 26:8). The verse emphasizes that *Hashem* brought us out from Egypt. There was no need to mention Hashem's name in this verse, since it is clear that Hashem is the subject of this verse just as Hashem is the subject of the previous verse, *and Hashem heard our voice and saw our affliction and our labor and our oppression* (Devarim 26:7). It would have sufficed to

---

49. We have slightly modified the question which appears in the 5654/1894 edition. In the 5643/1883 edition, there is no question at this point. (Eds.)

וְעָבַרְתִּי בְאֶרֶץ־מִצְרַיִם בַּלַּיְלָה הַזֶּה. אֲנִי וְלֹא מַלְאָךְ.
וְהִכֵּיתִי כָל־בְּכוֹר בְּאֶרֶץ מִצְרַיִם. אֲנִי וְלֹא שָׂרָף.
וּבְכָל־אֱלֹהֵי מִצְרַיִם אֶעֱשֶׂה שְׁפָטִים. אֲנִי וְלֹא הַשָּׁלִיחַ.
אֲנִי יהוה. אֲנִי הוּא וְלֹא אַחֵר:

בְּיָד חֲזָקָה. זוֹ הַדֶּבֶר. כְּמָה שֶׁנֶּאֱמַר הִנֵּה יַד
יהוה הוֹיָה בְּמִקְנְךָ אֲשֶׁר בַּשָּׂדֶה בַּסּוּסִים בַּחֲמוֹרִים
בַּגְּמַלִּים בַּבָּקָר וּבַצֹּאן דֶּבֶר כָּבֵד מְאֹד:

say, ויוציאנו ממצרים, *And He brought us out from Egypt.*

It must be that the repetition of Hashem's name here is to
teach that Hashem Himself brought us out, *not through an
angel, not through a seraph, and not through a messenger. But
it was the Holy One, Blessed be He, Himself in all His glory.*
However, we cannot exclude *all* of these possibilities from the
single extra word "Hashem" in the verse.

Therefore, the Haggadah cites Shemos 12:12 as the source for
excluding these possible saviors. Since these exclusions could not
have been made merely from the verse ויוציאנו ה׳ ממצרים, *And
Hashem brought us out from Egypt* (Devarim 26:8), it was
necessary for the Haggadah to bring, as proof, Shemos 12:12,

And I will pass through the land of Egypt in this night — I, and no angel.

And I will smite every firstborn in the land of Egypt — I, and no seraph.

And against all the gods of Egypt I will execute judgments — I, and no messenger.

I, Hashem — it is I, and no other.

With a mighty hand — this refers to the pestilence, as it says: "Behold, the hand of Hashem will be upon your property which you have in the fields, on the horses, on the asses, on the camels, on the cattle, and on the sheep, a very severe pestilence" (*Shemos* 9:3).

and accordingly introduced the verse with שנאמר.

שנאמר... *as it says: "And I will pass..."*. This verse contains several seemingly superfluous statements, but since there are no unnecessary words in the Torah, these words must have been included to teach something. Our Sages, therefore, deduced from these statements the sources for teaching that Hashem alone brought us out from Egypt, and not angel, seraph, or messenger. The Haggadah enumerates these sources.

ביד חזקה — **With a mighty hand**

ביד חזקה *with a mighty hand — this refers to the pestilence.* The verse mentions two seemingly synonymous phrases,

וּבִזְרֹעַ נְטוּיָה. זוֹ הַחֶרֶב. כְּמָה שֶׁנֶּאֱמַר וְחַרְבּוֹ שְׁלוּפָה בְּיָדוֹ נְטוּיָה עַל־יְרוּשָׁלָיִם:

וּבְמֹרָא גָדֹל. זֶה גִּלּוּי שְׁכִינָה. כְּמָה שֶׁנֶּאֱמַר אוֹ הֲנִסָּה אֱלֹהִים לָבוֹא לָקַחַת לוֹ גוֹי מִקֶּרֶב גּוֹי בְּמַסֹּת בְּאֹתֹת וּבְמוֹפְתִים וּבְמִלְחָמָה וּבְיָד חֲזָקָה וּבִזְרוֹעַ נְטוּיָה וּבְמוֹרָאִים גְּדֹלִים כְּכֹל אֲשֶׁר־עָשָׂה לָכֶם יהוה אֱלֹהֵיכֶם בְּמִצְרַיִם לְעֵינֶיךָ:

יד חזקה and זרוע נטויה, a mighty hand and an outstretched arm. The Haggadah explains the different meanings of the two phrases.

With a mighty hand refers to pestilence, since the "hand" of Hashem is mentioned in the account of the plague of pestilence, *as it says: "Behold, the hand of Hashem will be upon your property... a very severe pestilence"* (Shemos 9:3).

The plague of pestilence deserves to be mentioned in these verses of *Parshas Bikkurim* because, in one respect, it was the greatest of all the plagues, since it is the only plague which is referred to as *the hand of God*. In what respect was it the

And with an outstretched arm — this is the sword, as it says: "...and his drawn sword in his hand, outstretched over Yerushalayim" (*Divrei Hayamim* I, 21:16).

And with great awesomeness — this is the revelation of the Divine Presence, as it says: "Or has a god proved himself, to come to take a nation unto himself from out of the midst of another nation, with proofs of might, with signs and with instructive miracles, and with war and with a strong hand and with an outstretched arm and with great awesomeness, comparable to all that Hashem your God did for you in Egypt before your eyes?" (*Devarim* 4:34).

---

greatest of all the plagues? The Medrash teaches that pestilence accompanied all of the other plagues that afflicted Egypt (*Shemos Rabbah* 10:2).

ובזרוע נטויה *And with an outstretched arm* — *this is the sword.* "The sword" metaphorically refers to the smiting of the Egyptian firstborn. The word נטויה, *outstretched,* alludes to the sword, for we find elsewhere that the two terms are used together, *as it says: "...and his drawn sword in his hand, outstretched over Yerushalayim"* (Divrei Hayamim I, 21:16). One who fights with a sword *stretches out* his arm to attack his foe.

140

The killing of the firstborn also deserves to be mentioned in *Parshas Bikkurim* because it, like pestilence, was the greatest of all the plagues in one respect, in that it was the climactic culmination of all the plagues[50].

ובמרא גדל — **And with great awesomeness**

ובמרא גדל זה גלוי שכינה *And with great awesomeness — this is the revelation of the Divine Presence.* How does the Haggadah know that these words refer to the revelation of the Divine Presence? The word מורא, *awesomeness*, is related to the word מראה, *appearance*, and thus we read the words *and with a great appearance*, referring to the revelation of the Divine Presence[51].

זה גילוי שכינה *And with great awesomeness — this is the revelation of the Divine Presence.* The signs and wonders that occurred in Egypt demonstrated unequivocally the existence and presence of the all-powerful God who governs the world

---

50. In the Hebrew commentary, the author's reason why pestilence deserved to be mentioned in *Parshas Bikkurim* is divided into two reasons by an "א" and a "ב". However, this is apparently a printer's error, because the first reason for both pestilence and for the smiting of the firstborn is "because it was the greatest of all the plagues", which is obviously a contradiction — only one of them could have been the greatest. A careful reading will suggest that the author means that pestilence and the smiting of the firstborn were each the greatest plague in a different respect, and reading the text without the "א" and "ב" will show this quite clearly. (Eds.)

51. *Targum Unkelos* also translates ובמרא גדל as ובחזונא רבא, *a great appearance.*

as its supreme Controller, leaving no possibility to dismiss them as prodigies of the forces of nature.

This supernatural process was vital for the welfare of the Children of Israel who had been wallowing in the prevalent idolatry and moral depravity of the surrounding Egyptian environment, as our Sages teach, לקחת לו גוי מקרב גוי *"to come to take a nation unto himself from out of the midst of another nation"* (Devarim 4:34) — *[this teaches that] these [the Egyptians] were idol-worshippers and these [the Israelites] were idol-worshippers* (cf. *Vayikra Rabbah* 23:2; *Shir Hashirim Rabbah* 2:6). But when God revealed His presence through signs and wonders and arrested the laws of nature, the Children of Israel recognized Who the true God is. They extracted themselves from the quagmire of idolatry, they recognized the worthlessness of the Egyptian gods, and they returned to their faith and trust in the Almighty.

This was the primary reason why God persistently hardened the heart of Pharaoh. After all, God could have let Pharaoh submit to His demand, "Let my people go" (Shemos 5:1), after the first plague — or even *before* any plague — was wrought upon Egypt. Alternatively, God could have simply crushed Egypt with a single bow, or petrified the people rendering them immobile, thereby allowing the Children of Israel to calmly walk out of Egypt. Why did God have to initiate a prolonged process of miracle after miracle?

Because without the signs and wonders, the Children of Israel would not have gained the most important requisite for their redemption. The process of redemption had to be prolonged in order to include miraculous manifestations of the

וּבְאֹתֹת. זֶה הַמַּטֶּה. כְּמָה שֶׁנֶּאֱמַר וְאֶת־ הַמַּטֶּה הַזֶּה תִּקַּח בְּיָדֶךָ אֲשֶׁר תַּעֲשֶׂה בּוֹ אֶת־הָאֹתֹת:

presence of God to effectively extirpate the last remnants of idolatrous beliefs from their hearts. The process had to be a long one in order to draw them gradually from depravity to purity, from corruption to holiness. A single isolated, spectacular plague followed by an immediate departure from Egypt would not have been enough to uproot the seeds of idolatry which had been planted and had sprouted for many years in the hearts of the people. To achieve a permanent change a progression of successive events was necessary; the gradual process, along with the different lessons which each plague taught, would effectively eradicate the last vestiges of idolatry from their hearts and minds until they fully regained concrete knowledge of God and resolute faith in Him.

כמה שנאמר *as it says: "Or has a god proved himself, to come to take a nation unto himself from out of the midst of another nation...".* As the Medrash says, the Children of Israel had assimilated into "the midst of another nation" so that *these [the Egyptians] were idol-worshippers and these [the Israelites] were idol-worshippers*, yet God still succeeded in separating them. And what motivated the Jewish people to reject the idolatry which they had been so steeped in and to embrace belief in God?

It was במסת באתת ומופתים, *with proofs of might, with signs and with instructive miracles, and with war and with a strong hand and with an outstretched arm and with great awesome-*

And with instructive signs — this is the staff, as it says: "and this staff shall you take in your hand, with which you should perform the signs" (*Shemos* 4:17).

ness, comparable to all that Hashem your God did for you in Egypt; that is, specifically *for you*, for *your* sake did God perform all of these miracles in Egypt. He revealed His presence with unprecedented clarity *before your eyes*, so that your own eyes would witness Him; only by seeing for yourselves the manifold miracles of God would you be able to be taken *from out of the midst* of a nation of idol-worshippers. It was the miracles which you saw, the manifestation of the Divine Presence, that enabled you to extract yourselves from the evil ways of Egypt to become a holy people to God, to become the people that you are today.

ובאתות — **And with instructive signs**

ובאתות *And with instructive signs — this is the staff.* We might have thought that אותות and מופתים, *instructive signs* and *punishing miracles*, refer to the plagues with which God afflicted Egypt, some having the characteristics of "signs" and some having the characteristics of "miracles". Our Sages, however, understood these words differently.

Had these two words included all of the plagues, there would have been no need for the Torah to include the plague

וּבְמֹפְתִים זֶה הַדָּם. כְּמָה שֶׁנֶּאֱמַר וְנָתַתִּי מוֹפְתִים בַּשָּׁמַיִם וּבָאָרֶץ.

One dips his finger into the cup and dabs a bit of wine onto his plate when saying each of the words "blood and fire and pillars of smoke," as well as when reciting each of the ten plagues and pronouncing "detzach, adash beachav," for a total of 16 times. Some have the custom of pouring from the cup rather than dabbing their finger. The cups are then refilled.

דָּם וָאֵשׁ וְתִמְרוֹת עָשָׁן:

of pestilence and the smiting of the firstborn in the first part of the verse (*With a mighty hand — this refers to the pestilence; And with an outstretched arm — this is the sword*); they would have been included anyway with the rest of the plagues under "signs" and "miracles". It must be that "signs" and "miracles" are not intended to include the plagues.

Therefore, ובאתות, *and with instructive signs*, must refer to the staff of Moshe, with which the signs were executed[52]. Alternatively, *instructive signs* refers to the staff because upon it were etched the letters דצ״ך עד״ש באח״ב, the mnemonic of the Hebrew initials of the ten plagues[53].

כמה שנאמר *as it says: "and this staff shall you take in your hand, with which you should perform the signs"* (Shemos 4:17).

---

52. See, for example, Shemos 7:19, 8:1, 8:12, 9:23, and 10:13.
53. *Shemos Rabbah 5:6, 8:3.*

145

And with punishing miracles — this is the blood, as it says: "I will do miracles in heaven and on earth:

One dips his finger into the cup and dabs a bit of wine onto his plate when saying each of the words "blood and fire and pillars of smoke," as well as when reciting each of the ten plagues and pronouncing "detzach, adash beachav," for a total of 16 times. Some have the custom of pouring from the cup rather than dabbing their finger. The cups are then refilled.

blood and fire and pillars of smoke" (*Yoel* 3:3).

This verse is not brought as proof that ובאתות, *and with instructive signs*, refers to the staff, but merely to show that in the Torah's account of the Exodus the staff was used to carry out the signs. The verse is, therefore, introduced with the phrase כמה שנאמר, *as it says* (see footnote on p. 73).

ובמופתים — **And with punishing miracles**

ובמופתים זה הדם *And with punishing miracles — this is the blood.* Why is the blood referred to as *miracles*, in the plural form?[54]

---

54. A more basic question, one which the Commentary does not explicitly address, is how the word *miracles* alludes to blood to begin with. The verse in Yoel is not the source, because if it was the source the Haggadah would

דָּבָר אַחֵר. **בְּיָד חֲזָקָה** שְׁתַּיִם. **וּבִזְרֹעַ נְטוּיָה**
שְׁתַּיִם. **וּבְמֹרָא גָדֹל** שְׁתַּיִם. **וּבְאֹתוֹת** שְׁתַּיִם.
וּבְמֹפְתִים שְׁתַּיִם: אֵלּוּ עֶשֶׂר מַכּוֹת שֶׁהֵבִיא הַקָּדוֹשׁ
בָּרוּךְ הוּא עַל־הַמִּצְרַיִם בְּמִצְרַיִם וְאֵלּוּ הֵן:

---

have introduced it with שנאמר and not כמה שנאמר.

It could be that the word *miracles* alludes to blood for the following reason. First, we know that it cannot refer to all of the plagues for the same reason that the previous word, ובאתות, cannot refer to all of the plagues (see above). Second, because of its adjacency to the word ובאתות in the verse, which we know refers to the staff, *miracles* must allude to one of the wonders performed by the staff. The verse in Yoel helps determine to which of the wonders it alludes. Since three things are called מופתים in the verse in Yoel, and only one of them appeared in Egypt, that must be the one to which the word מופתים alludes. Since the proof is not entirely from the verse in Yoel, the Haggadah did not introduce the verse with the word שנאמר, since the verse is not a proof on its own.

An alternative explanation could be that the plural form of the word *miracles* implies that it was a phenomenon which occurred more than once. The only phenomenon which occurred more than once was blood. Hence, the verse in Yoel is not necessary to prove that *miracles* refers to blood. However, the Commentary in the following paragraph admits that had the verse stated מופת, in the singular form, we would still have known that it was blood. But how? To answer, we would then need the verse in Yoel as a proof. But again, we would have a problem, to which of the three things referred to in Yoel as *miracles* does the word מופתים here refer? We would then have to rely on the adjacency of the word מופתים to the word ובאתות, which would return us to the previous answer (that is, since we only know that *miracles* refers to blood from a combination of factors, the Haggadah did not say שנאמר). (Eds.)

An alternative explanation: **with a MIGHTY HAND** — two (Hebrew words imply two plagues); **and with an OUTSTRETCHED ARM — two; and with GREAT AWESOMENESS** - two; **and with instructive SIGNS** — two (plural); **and with punishing MIRACLES** - two (plural). These are the ten plagues which the Holy One, Blessed be He, brought upon the Egyptians in Egypt. And they are as follows:

The word *miracles* alludes to the two miracles which were performed with blood. The first occurred when Moshe presented a sign to the Children of Israel to prove that he had been sent by God to redeem them: *And you shall take river water and pour it on the ground... and it shall become blood on the ground* (Shemos 4:9).

The second occurred when the Nile River was turned to blood (Shemos 7:14-25). This particular plague merits mention in *Parshas Bikkurim* because it was the first of all the plagues.

The word מופתים, *miracles*, refers to blood, as we find in the Book of Yoel (3:3), *I will do miracles* (מופתים) *in heaven and on earth: blood and fire and pillars of smoke.*

דבר אחר — **An alternative explanation**

דבר אחר *An alternative explanation.* This *alternative ex-*

דָּם. צְפַרְדֵּעַ. כִּנִּים. עָרוֹב.
דֶּבֶר. שְׁחִין. בָּרָד. אַרְבֶּה. חֹשֶׁךְ.
מַכַּת בְּכוֹרוֹת:

planation does not discard the previous explanation of the verse, but merely adds that the language of the verse also alludes to the ten plagues.

The *alternative explanation* addresses the extra words in the verse which the previous explanation did not explain. For the verse to include everything that the previous explanation mentioned, it would have sufficed to say,

ביד נטויה ובמורא ובאות ובמופת

With an outstretched hand and with awesomeness and with an instructive sign and a punishing miracle.

From "hand" we would have derived pestilence; from "outstretched", the sword; from "awesomeness", the revelation of the Divine Presence; from "an instructive sign", the staff; and from "a punishing miracle", the blood.

The extra words, "*mighty* hand", "outstretched *arm*", and "*great* awesomeness", and the plural form of "signs" and "miracles" in the verse contain within them additional teachings. The doubled wording of each phrase implies two plagues. Hence, from the five phrases which are doubled, ten plagues are hinted to in this verse.

The Haggadah lists each doubled phrase from which we infer two plagues, and then summarizes and says, *These are*

Blood, Frogs, Vermin, Wild Beasts, Pestilence, Boils, Hail, Locusts, Darkness, Smiting of the Firstborn.

the ten plagues which the Holy One, Blessed be He, brought upon the Egyptians in Egypt.

If we look in other editions of the Haggadah, we will find that many have made a mistake in the punctuation of this paragraph. They consider אלו עשר מכות, *These are the ten plagues*, the start of a new statement. In truth, though, it is the final part of the previous statement, ובאתות שתים ובמופתים שתים ... אלו עשר מכות שהביא הקדוש ברוך היא על המצרים במצרים *and with instructive SIGNS — two (plural); and with punishing MIRACLES — two (plural); these are the ten plagues which the Holy One, Blessed be He, brought upon the Egyptians in Egypt.* The next statement proceeds to list the ten plagues by name and begins, ואלו הן, *And they are as follows.*

This explains the apparent redundancy, *These are the ten plagues... and they are as follows.* If *These are the ten plagues* is the beginning of a new sentence, then there is no need to repeat, *and they are as follows.* According to our explanation, however, there is no redudancy. *These are the ten plagues* expresses the total of the five pairs derived from the verse; whereas *And they are as follows*, the beginning of a new sentence, is an introduction to the list of those ten plagues.

ואלו הן *And they are as follows: Blood, Frogs.* צפרדע is literally *frog*, in the singular form, unlike כנים, *lice*, which is in

רַבִּי יְהוּדָה הָיָה נוֹתֵן בָּהֶם סִמָּנִים:
דְּצַ"ךְ עַדַ"שׁ בְּאַחַ"ב:
רַבִּי יוֹסֵי הַגְּלִילִי אוֹמֵר. מִנַּיִן אַתָּה אוֹמֵר
שֶׁלָּקוּ הַמִּצְרִים בְּמִצְרַיִם עֶשֶׂר מַכּוֹת וְעַל הַיָּם לָקוּ
חֲמִשִּׁים מַכּוֹת. בְּמִצְרַיִם מַה הוּא אוֹמֵר. וַיֹּאמְרוּ

the plural. The Haggadah refers to this plague in the singular form echoing the verse, *And the frog came up* (Shemos 8:2)[55].

מכת בכורות *Smiting of the Firstborn.* None of the first nine plagues is preceded by the word מכת, *the plague of* or *the smiting of.* Why is the smiting of the firstborn preceded by מכת, *the smiting of,* and not merely referred to as בכורות, *Firstborn?*

The answer is simple. The names of all the other plagues describe their roles as plagues. The word "firstborn", however, does not convey any meaning of affliction or punishment, and therefore the word מכת precedes it.

The word מכת, *the smiting of,* was used instead of מיתת, *the death of,* echoing the verse which does not say that God *killed* all the firstborn, but that *God smote all the firstborn* (Shemos 12:29). Similarly, the Psalmist writes, *and He smote all the firstborn* (Tehillim 105:36).

---

55. For an explanation why the verse uses the singular form, see *Rashi ad loc.*; *Shemos Rabbah 10:4*; *Sanhedrin 67b.*

151

Rabbi Yehudah made a mnemonic of their Hebrew initials, as follows:

DETZACH, ADASH, BEACHAV

Rabbi Yose the Galilean said: From what passage
can you infer that the Egyptians were smitten with
ten plagues in Egypt and with fifty plagues at the
Sea? Of the plagues in Egypt, it says: "And those

רבי יהודה — **Rabbi Yehudah**

רבי יהודה היה נותן בהם סימנים *Rabbi Yehudah made a
mnemonic.* Having mentioned the ten plagues, the compiler
of the Haggadah cites the words of Rabbi Yehudah on the
subject. His source is the Medrash: *Rabbi Yehudah said, "The
staff weighed forty se'ah... and the ten plagues were inscribed
upon it in mnemonic form:* דצ"ך עד"ש באח"ב (*Shemos Rabbah
8:3*), and therefore he cites the statement in the name of Rabbi
Yehudah.

Why did Rabbi Yehudah arrange the initials in his mnemonic in this order?

An examination of the account of the plagues (Shemos,
chapters 7-12) shows that they were divided into three groups
of three. The first two plagues of each group were preceded
by warnings, while the third plague in each group came with
no warning. Rabbi Yehudah's acronym divides the plagues into

הַחַרְטֻמִּם אֶל־פַּרְעֹה אֶצְבַּע אֱלֹהִים הוּא. וְעַל־הַיָּם מַה הוּא אוֹמֵר. וַיַּרְא יִשְׂרָאֵל אֶת־הַיָּד הַגְּדֹלָה אֲשֶׁר עָשָׂה יְהוָה בְּמִצְרַיִם וַיִּירְאוּ הָעָם אֶת־יְהוָה וַיַּאֲמִינוּ בַּיהוָה וּבְמֹשֶׁה עַבְדּוֹ. כַּמָּה לָקוּ בְּאֶצְבַּע עֶשֶׂר מַכּוֹת. אֱמֹר מֵעַתָּה בְּמִצְרַיִם לָקוּ עֶשֶׂר מַכּוֹת וְעַל־הַיָּם לָקוּ חֲמִשִּׁים מַכּוֹת:

these three groups (the tenth plague, which was not included in the three groups, is appended to the end of the acronym).

Rabbi Yose the Galilean said — רבי יוסי הגלילי אומר

The Questions

1 כמה לקו באצבע *How many plagues were visited on them by a finger? Ten plagues.*

What proof is there from the word אצבע, the *finger* of God, that the Egyptians were smitten with ten plagues? The statement *It is a finger of God* was made in reference to the plague of lice, the third plague.

2 ועל הים מה הוא אומר *While at the sea, it is said: "And Israel saw the great hand which Hashem had used upon Egypt...".*

How does Rabbi Yose learn from the word *hand* that God smote

153

knowledgeable of the writings said to Pharaoh: 'It is a finger of God'..." (*Shemos* 8:15), while at the Sea, it is said: "And Yisrael saw the great hand which Hashem had used upon Egypt; and the people feared Hashem and trusted in Hashem and in Moshe, His servant" (*ibid.* 14:31). How many plagues were visited on them by a *finger?* Ten plagues. Thus, in Egypt the Egyptians were smitten with ten plagues, wile at the Sea they were smitten [by the *hand*], with fifty plagues.

the Egyptians with fifty plagues at the sea? The word *hand* is also found in reference to a single plague — that of pestilence (Shemos 9:3). Perhaps at the sea God smote the Egyptians with pestilence!

רבי יוסי הגלילי אומר *Rabbi Yose the Galilean said: From what passage can you infer* from the fact that *the Egyptians were smitten with ten plagues in Egypt* that they were smitten *with fifty plagues at the sea?* Explains Rabbi Yose,

Of the plagues in Egypt, it says: "And those knowledgeable of the writings said to Pharaoh: 'It is a finger of God'..." (Shemos 8:15). Rabbi Yose does not mean that the word *finger* refers to ten plagues, because, after all, it is the singular form and cannot refer to more than one plague. Rather, Rabbi Yose means that *every plague alone* can be described as the *finger of God.*

From where, though, does he learn that the word *finger* refers to each plague?

He learns this from the plague of כנים, lice, which the advisors of Pharaoh called the *finger of God* (Shemos 8:15). Similarly, each of the other nine plagues was the *finger of God*.

If so, why is the plague of lice the only plague referred to as the *finger of God?*

Only when the third plague struck Egypt did Pharaoh's advisors realize that these plagues were the handiwork of God, or the *finger of God*. In reality, though, all of the plagues were the acts of God, and the advisors only called the third plague as such because it was with this plague that they realized the Divine source of all the plagues. Hence, each plague was in fact the *finger of God*.

Therefore, Rabbi Yose teaches, since each of the ten plagues brought upon Egypt was the work of God's *finger,* when the Torah says that God used His *great hand* upon Egypt at the Sea, it must mean that He brought fifty plagues upon them. If there are five fingers on a hand, and each finger signifies the ten plagues (since the finger of God caused each plague), then there must have been fifty plagues at the sea.

ועל הים מה הוא אומר... *...while at the Sea, it is said: "And Israel saw the great hand which Hashem had used upon Egypt..."* (Shemos 8:15). There, at the sea, the plagues were like a hand, five times as numerous as they had been in Egypt.

כמה לקו באצבע עשר מכות *How many plagues were visited on them by a finger? Ten plagues. Thus,* it follows that if *in Egypt the Egyptians were smitten with ten plagues,* then *at the sea they were smitten [by the hand] with fifty plagues.*

If this, however, is the meaning of the word *hand* (i.e. five times ten plagues), what does the Torah mean when it refers

to the plague of pestilence as *the hand of God: Behold, the hand of God will be upon your property... a very severe pestilence* (Shemos 9:3)?

The word *hand* has two meanings. When used to describe the plague of pestilence, יד ה', means מכת ה', *God's striking*. When used to describe all of the plagues, it means, literally, the hand of God (in an anthropomorphic sense, of course).

We must logically explain the two instances of God's *hand*, one by the plague of pestilence and one by the Sea, as having two different connotations. Otherwise, the Torah could not say that "Israel saw the great hand" at the Sea, implying that they saw the hand for the first time. If this "hand" is the same "hand" they saw during the plague of pestilence, then they saw nothing new at the Sea. Therefore, when they saw the "hand" at the Sea while it afflicted the Egyptians with fifty plagues, it was the first time they had seen the hand of God (i.e. five times ten plagues) in action.[56]

רבי אליעזר אומר — **Rabbi Eliezer said**

The Question

1 רבי אליעזר אומר *Rabbi Eliezer said....* Why does Rabbi Eliezer ignore the first phrase, *the glow of His anger*, and start counting from the second phrase, *excess of wrath*? (Compare with Rabbi Akiva, who does count *the glow of His anger*.)

רבי אליעזר אומר *Rabbi Eliezer said: From what passage can it be inferred that each plague which the Holy One, Blessed be*

---

56. The different meanings of the word "hand" may be explained by the different grammatical structures, יד and היד הגדולה. The latter includes the adjective "great" as well as the definite article "the". (Eds.)

רַבִּי אֱלִיעֶזֶר אוֹמֵר. מִנַּיִן שֶׁכָּל מַכָּה וּמַכָּה
שֶׁהֵבִיא הַקָּדוֹשׁ בָּרוּךְ הוּא עַל הַמִּצְרִים בְּמִצְרַיִם
הָיְתָה שֶׁל אַרְבַּע מַכּוֹת. שֶׁנֶּאֱמַר יְשַׁלַּח־בָּם חֲרוֹן
אַפּוֹ עֶבְרָה וָזַעַם וְצָרָה מִשְׁלַחַת מַלְאֲכֵי רָעִים.
עֶבְרָה אַחַת. וָזַעַם שְׁתַּיִם. וְצָרָה שָׁלֹשׁ. מִשְׁלַחַת
מַלְאֲכֵי רָעִים אַרְבַּע. אֱמֹר מֵעַתָּה בְּמִצְרַיִם לָקוּ
אַרְבָּעִים מַכּוֹת וְעַל־הַיָּם לָקוּ מָאתַיִם מַכּוֹת:

*He, brought upon the Egyptians in Egypt was actually a
fourfold one? For it says: "He lets break forth against them the
glow of His anger: excess of wrath, and condemnation, and
distress; a mission of messengers of evil" (Tehillim 78:49)....*

Rabbi Eliezer does not include the glow of His anger in his
count of the magnitude of each plague for two reasons.

First, חרון אפו, *the glow of His anger*, is written in the
possessive form, unlike the other four phrases. Had the verse
read, חרון אף, *the glow of anger*, consistent with the other four
phrases, then Rabbi Eliezer would have included it in his count.
Likewise, had the other phrases been written in the possessive
case (for example, עברתו, *excess of his wrath*, instead of עברה,
excess of wrath), consistent with the first phrase, then Rabbi Eliezer

Rabbi Eliezer said: From what passage can it be inferred that each plague which the Holy One, Blessed be He, brought upon the Egyptians in Egypt was actually a fourfold one? For it says: "He lets break forth against them the glow of His anger: excess of wrath, and condemnation, and distress; a mission of messengers of evil" (*Tehillim* 78:49). [Excess of] wrath — one, condemnation — two, distress — three, a mission of messengers of evil — four. Thus, in Egypt the Egyptians were smitten with forty plagues, while at the Sea they were smitten with two hundred plagues (see above).

would have included all five in his count. The difference in form reveals that *the glow of his anger* is not to be included in the count, that it is merely a general statement which the other four phrases come to describe more specifically.

Second, if *the glow of His anger* was meant to be included in the count, then the following word would have had the prefix "and" — *the glow of His anger **and** excess of wrath*. Since *excess of wrath* is not preceded by "and", Rabbi Eliezer understands this to be a sign that this phrase is the first in the count, and not *the glow of His anger* [57].

---

57. Although the phrase, *a mission of messengers of evil*, does not begin with the prefix "and", since there is no ambiguity regarding its inclusion in the count of plagues, the lack of "and" is not significant. (Eds.)

רַבִּי עֲקִיבָא אוֹמֵר. מִנַּיִן שֶׁכָּל מַכָּה וּמַכָּה
שֶׁהֵבִיא הַקָּדוֹשׁ בָּרוּךְ הוּא עַל הַמִּצְרִים בְּמִצְרַיִם
הָיְתָה שֶׁל חָמֵשׁ מַכּוֹת. שֶׁנֶּאֱמַר יְשַׁלַּח־בָּם חֲרוֹן אַפּוֹ
עֶבְרָה וָזַעַם וְצָרָה מִשְׁלַחַת מַלְאֲכֵי רָעִים. חֲרוֹן אַפּוֹ
אַחַת. עֶבְרָה שְׁתַּיִם. וָזַעַם שָׁלֹשׁ. וְצָרָה אַרְבַּע.
מִשְׁלַחַת מַלְאֲכֵי רָעִים חָמֵשׁ: אֱמֹר מֵעַתָּה בְּמִצְרַיִם
לָקוּ חֲמִשִּׁים מַכּוֹת וְעַל הַיָּם לָקוּ חֲמִשִּׁים וּמָאתַיִם
מַכּוֹת:

אמר מעתה *Thus,* it follows that if *in Egypt the Egyptians were smitten with forty plagues,* then *at the Sea they were smitten with two hundred plagues.* Rabbi Eliezer agrees with Rabbi Yose the Galilean's reasoning that at the Sea the Egyptians were smitten with five times the number of plagues they received in Egypt, but argues that in Egypt each of the ten plagues was fourfold.

רבי עקיבא אומר — **Rabbi Akiva said**

רבי עקיבא אומר *Rabbi Akiva said.* Rabbi Akiva argues with Rabbi Eliezer's logic that *the glow of His anger* does not allude to any addition to the plagues. Rabbi Akiva maintains that the very presence of the phrase shows that it is coming to add to

Rabbi Akiva said: From what passage can it be inferred that each plague which the Holy One Blessed be He, brought upon the Egyptians in Egypt was actually a fivefold one? For it says: "He lets break forth against them the glow of His anger, excess of wrath, and condemnation, and distress; a mission of messengers of evil" (*ibid.*) [The glow of His] anger — one, [excess of] wrath — two, condemnation — three, distress — four, a mission of messengers of evil — five. Thus, in Egypt the Egyptians were smitten with fifty plagues, while at the Sea they were smitten with two-hundred-and-fifty plagues.

the plagues, because the verse could well have been written without it: *He lets break forth against them excess of wrath, and condemnation...,* or at least without the extra word חרון, *the glow of: He lets break forth against them his anger, excess of wrath, and condemnation....* Rabbi Akiva learns, therefore, that the extra phrase indicates an additional plague.

אמר מעתה *Thus,* it follows that if *in Egypt the Egyptians were smitten with fifty plagues,* then *at the Sea they were smitten with two hundred and fifty plagues.* Rabbi Akiva, like Rabbi Eliezer, agrees with Rabbi Yose the Galilean's reasoning that at the Sea the Egyptians were smitten with five times the number of plagues they received in Egypt, but argues that in Egypt each of the ten plagues was fivefold.

כַּמָּה מַעֲלוֹת טוֹבוֹת לַמָּקוֹם עָלֵינוּ:

אִלּוּ הוֹצִיאָנוּ מִמִּצְרַיִם

וְלֹא־עָשָׂה בָהֶם שְׁפָטִים דַּיֵּנוּ:

אִלּוּ עָשָׂה בָהֶם שְׁפָטִים

וְלֹא־עָשָׂה בֵאלֹהֵיהֶם דַּיֵּנוּ:

אִלּוּ עָשָׂה בֵאלֹהֵיהֶם

וְלֹא־הָרַג אֶת־בְּכוֹרֵיהֶם דַּיֵּנוּ:

אִלּוּ הָרַג אֶת־בְּכוֹרֵיהֶם

וְלֹא־נָתַן לָנוּ אֶת־מָמוֹנָם דַּיֵּנוּ:

אִלּוּ נָתַן לָנוּ אֶת־מָמוֹנָם

וְלֹא־קָרַע לָנוּ אֶת־הַיָּם דַּיֵּנוּ:

אִלּוּ קָרַע לָנוּ אֶת־הַיָּם

וְלֹא־הֶעֱבִירָנוּ בְתוֹכוֹ בֶּחָרָבָה דַּיֵּנוּ:

אִלּוּ הֶעֱבִירָנוּ בְתוֹכוֹ בֶּחָרָבָה

וְלֹא־שִׁקַּע צָרֵינוּ בְּתוֹכוֹ דַּיֵּנוּ:

אִלּוּ שִׁקַּע צָרֵינוּ בְּתוֹכוֹ

וְלֹא־סִפֵּק צָרְכֵּנוּ בַּמִּדְבָּר אַרְבָּעִים שָׁנָה דַּיֵּנוּ:

אִלּוּ סִפֵּק צָרְכֵּנוּ בַּמִּדְבָּר אַרְבָּעִים שָׁנָה

וְלֹא־הֶאֱכִילָנוּ אֶת־הַמָּן דַּיֵּנוּ:

אִלּוּ הֶאֱכִילָנוּ אֶת־הַמָּן

וְלֹא־נָתַן לָנוּ אֶת־הַשַּׁבָּת דַּיֵּנוּ:

161

How Many Stages of Benevolence Did the Omnipresent Grant Us!

Had He brought us out of Egypt and not executed judgment on the Egyptians	Dayenu.*
Had He executed judgment on them and not upon their idols	Dayenu.
Had He destroyed their idols and not slain their firstborn	Dayenu.
Had He slain their firstborn and not given us their wealth	Dayenu.
Had He given us their wealth and not split the Sea for us	Dayenu.
Had He split the Sea for us and not led us through it on dry land	Dayenu.
Had He led us through it on dry land and not drowned our tormentors in it	Dayenu.
Had He drowned our tormentors in it and not provided our needs in the desert for forty years	Dayenu.
Had He provided our needs in the desert for forty years and not fed us with mannah	Dayenu.
Had He fed us with mannah and not given us Shabbos	Dayenu.

* Dayenu — it would have sufficed for us

אִלּוּ נָתַן לָנוּ אֶת־הַשַּׁבָּת
וְלֹא־קֵרְבָנוּ לִפְנֵי הַר־סִינַי דַּיֵּנוּ:
אִלּוּ קֵרְבָנוּ לִפְנֵי הַר־סִינַי
וְלֹא־נָתַן לָנוּ אֶת־הַתּוֹרָה דַּיֵּנוּ:
אִלּוּ נָתַן לָנוּ אֶת הַתּוֹרָה
וְלֹא הִכְנִיסָנוּ לְאֶרֶץ יִשְׂרָאֵל דַּיֵּנוּ:
אִלּוּ הִכְנִיסָנוּ לְאֶרֶץ יִשְׂרָאֵל
וְלֹא בָנָה לָנוּ אֶת בֵּית הַבְּחִירָה דַּיֵּנוּ:

How many stages of benevolence — כמה מעלות טובות

The Questions

1 כמה מעלות טובות למקום עלינו *How many stages of benevolence did the Omnipresent grant us!*

The literal translation is, *How many stages of benevolence **to the Omnipresent on us***. What does *to the Omnipresent on us* mean? If the Haggadah means, *did the Omnipresent grant us*, it should have said, ממקום, *from the Omnipresent*, for we are speaking of kindness *from* Him *to* us[58].

Furthermore, the use of the word עלינו, literally — *upon us*, is inappropriate. The Haggadah should have said, לנו, *to us*, if it was speaking about the benevolence which the Omnipresent granted to us.

---

58. In addition, this interpretation would not make sense where the phrase למקום עלינו appears again at the end of this paragraph: על אחת כמה וכמה טובה כפולה ומכפלת למקום עלינו, which would mean, *How much more so are the many and repeated kindnesses the Omnipresent granted us*. על אחת כמה וכמה is a phrase used as a logical argument, an *a fortiori* statement. But here it is merely stating that many acts of kindness are greater than few acts of kindness, which is obvious!

Had He given us Shabbos and not brought
us near to Mount Sinai Dayenu.

Had He brought us near to Mount Sinai
and not given us the Torah Dayenu.

Had He given us the Torah and not
brought us into the land of Israel Dayenu.

Had He brought us into land of Israel and
not built the Holy Temple for us Dayenu.

2 Many of the kindnesses enumerated in this paragraph were indispensable to our physical survival, such as the splitting of the Sea and the provision of our needs in the wilderness. Others were indispensable to our spiritual condition, such as the giving of the Torah at Sinai, the land of Israel, the building of the Holy Temple, and the gift of Shabbos; without them we would have no unique identity nor purpose as God's chosen people. Moreover, to say that it would have been enough for us without the Torah and without Shabbos seems heretical.

How, then, can we say that had God not bestowed those kindnesses upon us, דינו, *it would have sufficed for us?*

כמה מעלות טובות *How many stages of benevolence.* This paragraph points out that a single act of kindness would have been sufficient to oblige us to praise and thank the Almighty beyond the extent of our abilities, and that how much more so are we obliged to praise and thank Him when we consider the innumerable kindnesses which He has done for us. There exists no limit to the gratitude which we owe Him, and, therefore, we must thank Him with every form of praise and

עַל אַחַת כַּמָּה וְכַמָּה טוֹבָה כְפוּלָה וּמְכֻפֶּלֶת
לַמָּקוֹם עָלֵינוּ. שֶׁהוֹצִיאָנוּ מִמִּצְרַיִם. וְעָשָׂה בָהֶם
שְׁפָטִים. וְעָשָׂה בֵאלֹהֵיהֶם. וְהָרַג אֶת־בְּכוֹרֵיהֶם.
וְנָתַן לָנוּ אֶת־מָמוֹנָם. וְקָרַע לָנוּ אֶת־הַיָּם. וְהֶעֱבִירָנוּ

exaltation we are capable of expressing. We read this paragraph now in preparation for the recital of Hallel with the
appropriate feelings of gratitude and reverence.

The word מעלות does not mean *stages* as most commentators interpret it. Rather, the word מעלות means *praises*[59], as
in, לעלה ולקלס, *to extol and to praise*[60]. The Haggadah is driving
home the point that for every one of God's kindnesses alone
we would have been obligated to extol and praise Him with
even the last vestige of our strength; how much more so for
all of His kindnesses combined.

Furthermore, the phrase דינו, *it would have sufficed for us*,
does not mean that this kindness would have sufficed for us, for
our physical and spiritual wellbeing, as most commentators
interpret it. Rather, דינו means that each kindness *would have
sufficed for us* to oblige us to extol and to praise God with all
of our strength.

This idea is clearly expressed in the *Nishmas* passage of

---

59. From the root עלה, to raise up.

60. From the Shabbos and festival morning prayers, and from the Haggadah
after Hallel. The same use of עלה appears in Kaddish: ויתעלה, *and may He be
extolled*.

Thus, we owe the Omnipresent a debt of gratitude, not for one, but for many and repeated benefits. For He brought us out of Egypt. And executed judgment on them. And destroyed their idols. And slew their firstborn. And gave us their wealth. And split the Sea for us. And led us through

the Shabbos and festival morning prayers: *Were our mouths full with song as the sea, and our tongues with joy's outpouring as the swell of its waves, and our lips with praise as the expanse of heaven... we would still be unable to thank You sufficiently, Hashem our God and God of our forefathers, and to bless Your name for even one of the thousand thousand, thousands of thousands and myriad of myriads of favors which You have bestowed upon our fathers and upon us.*

We now understand this paragraph. כמה מעלות טובות למקום עלינו; *How many praises for the kindnesses do we owe to the Omnipresent.* עלינו *is the fitting word here, for it means it is upon us as an obligation*[61].

אלו הוציאנו ממצרים *Had he brought us out of Egypt* and not performed any other kindness for us, *and not executed judgement on the Egyptians it would have sufficed for us* — to oblige us to exalt and to praise God with all of our might for this single act of kindness.

Similarly, אלו קרבנו לפני הר סיני, *Had he brought us near to*

---

61. As in the *Aleinu* prayer we say three times each day, עלינו לשבח לאדון הכל, *It is upon us as an obligation to praise the Master of all.*

166

בְּתוֹכוֹ בֶּחָרָבָה. וְשִׁקַּע צָרֵינוּ בְּתוֹכוֹ. וְסִפֵּק צָרְכֵּנוּ בַּמִּדְבָּר אַרְבָּעִים שָׁנָה. וְהֶאֱכִילָנוּ אֶת הַמָּן. וְנָתַן לָנוּ אֶת הַשַּׁבָּת. וְקֵרְבָנוּ לִפְנֵי הַר־סִינַי. וְנָתַן לָנוּ אֶת־הַתּוֹרָה. וְהִכְנִיסָנוּ לְאֶרֶץ יִשְׂרָאֵל. וּבָנָה לָנוּ אֶת בֵּית הַבְּחִירָה לְכַפֵּר עַל־כָּל־עֲוֹנוֹתֵינוּ:

Mount Sinai and not given us to the Torah it would have suffaced for us. We asked how this could have sufficed — without the Torah we would be no different from any other nation! In truth, however, we are not saying that this kindness would have sufficed for our development. We are saying that bringing us to Mount Sinai, even without giving us the Torah, would have sufficed to oblige us to praise and thank God. But to become the beloved nation of God, it certainly would not have sufficed without the Torah.

After listing examples of God's benevolence to us, the Haggadah summarizes the theme of this paragraph and states, עַל אַחַת כַּמָּה וְכַמָּה טוֹבָה כְפוּלָה וּמְכֻפֶּלֶת לַמָּקוֹם עָלֵינוּ, *How much more [are the praises that] we owe to the Omnipresent for many and repeated benefits.*

This description of our obligation to praise God culminates in the paragraph לְפִיכָךְ, *Therefore we are obligated to give thanks, to praise His mighty acts, to laud, glorify, exalt....* That is, since we would be obligated to praise God for a single kindness, how much more so are we obligated to praise God for the many kindnesses which He has bestowed upon us, and

it on dry land. And drowned our tormentors in it. And provided our needs in the desert for forty years. And fed us with mannah. And gave us Shabbos. And brought us near to Mount Sinai. And gave us the Torah. And brought us into the land of Israel. And built for us the Holy Temple to atone for all our sins.

therefore we are obligated.... The Haggadah uses many types of expressions of praise to emphasize our obligation to praise God with every means that exists, despite the inevitability that even if we manage to do so, we will still fall short of adequately thanking God for even one of His kindnesses.

If these paragraphs, על אחת כמה וכמה and כמה מעלות טובות, are the prelude to לפיכך, why are they not immediately followed by לפיכך[62]? Why do the paragraphs פסח, רבן גמליאל, מרור ,מצה and בכל דור ודור interrupt?

These two paragraphs were placed after the account of the departure from Egypt because they mention events which occurred following the Exodus but which were not mentioned earlier in the Haggadah. These events include giving us the Egyptian wealth, splitting the Sea and leading us through on dry land, drowning our tormentors, providing our needs in the desert, feeding us with mannah, and bringing us into the land

---

62. These two paragraphs are not mentioned in the Mishnah in *Pesachim* (ch. 10), the source for the order of the Haggadah. They were added later to introduce the paragraph לפיכך, as we have explained. Why, then, were they not inserted immediately prior to לפיכך?

רַבָּן גַּמְלִיאֵל הָיָה אוֹמֵר. כָּל שֶׁלֹּא־אָמַר שְׁלֹשָׁה דְבָרִים אֵלּוּ בַּפֶּסַח לֹא־יָצָא יְדֵי חוֹבָתוֹ. וְאֵלּוּ הֵן.

פֶּסַח. מַצָּה. וּמָרוֹר:

of Israel. These paragraphs also include events essential to our spiritual development, including giving us the Sabbath, bringing us near to Mount Sinai, giving us the Torah, and building the Holy Temple. Since these paragraphs conclude our account of the Exodus, they were placed at this point in the Haggadah.

But still — why does the paragraph לפיכך not come immediately after these two paragraphs?

The compiler of the Haggadah could not have placed לפיכך here for the following reason:

As we have explained (see *Overview*), the six sections of the Haggadah were established according to the sequence of the six phrases in the verse, והגדת לבנך ביום ההוא לאמר בעבור זה עשה ה׳ לי בצאתי ממצרים (Shemos 13:8). We know that the paragraph לפיכך introduces Hallel, as its concluding words state, *Let us therefore recite before him: Halleluyah!*

The recitation of Hallel, in which we declare בצאת ישראל ממצרים, corresponds to the last phrase of Shemos 13:8, בצאתי ממצרים. The recounting of the Exodus story — the section of the Haggadah we are presently discussing — corresponds to

169

✤RABBAN Gamliel used to say: Whoever does not explain the following three things at the Pesach festival has not fulfilled his obligation, namely:

PESACH, MATZAH, and MAROR.

the phrase לאמר in Shemos 13:8. Between לאמר and בצאתי ממצרים are two phrases: בעבור זה, to which the teaching of Rabban Gamliel corresponds; and עשה ה׳ לי, to which the paragraph בכל דור ודור corresponds.

Therefore, כמה מעלות טובות and על אחת כמה וכמה (which conclude the recounting of the Exodus) could not have been followed by לפיכך (which must precede Hallel) without upsetting the order of the Haggadah as based upon the verse, והגדת.

רבן גמליאל היה אומר — Rabban Gamliel used to say

The Questions

1 What is special about these three mitzvos — *pesach, matzah,* and *maror,* which obligates us to explain their purpose and reasons? No other mitzvah requires that we explain its purpose and reason in order to fulfill our obligation.

2 Why does the Haggadah say, רבן גמליאל היה אומר, *Rabban Gamliel used to say,* and not רבן גמליאל אומר, *Rabban Gamliel*

170

פֶּסַח שֶׁהָיוּ אֲבוֹתֵינוּ אוֹכְלִים בִּזְמַן שֶׁבֵּית הַמִּקְדָּשׁ הָיָה קַיָּם עַל־שׁוּם מָה. עַל־שׁוּם שֶׁפָּסַח הַקָּדוֹשׁ בָּרוּךְ הוּא עַל בָּתֵּי אֲבוֹתֵינוּ בְּמִצְרָיִם. שֶׁנֶּאֱמַר וַאֲמַרְתֶּם זֶבַח־פֶּסַח הוּא לַיהוה אֲשֶׁר פָּסַח עַל־בָּתֵּי בְנֵי־יִשְׂרָאֵל בְּמִצְרַיִם בְּנָגְפּוֹ אֶת־מִצְרַיִם וְאֶת־בָּתֵּינוּ הִצִּיל וַיִּקֹּד הָעָם וַיִּשְׁתַּחֲווּ:

says, as we saw just a few paragraphs earlier, רבי עקיבא אומר, *Rabbi Akiva says*?

3 Why was this paragraph placed at this point in the Haggadah?

4 Why must we say, מצה זו, *this* matzah which we eat, and מרור זה, *this* maror which we eat? It would suffice to say *Matzah which we eat* and *Maror which we eat*.

רבן גמליאל היה אומר *Rabban Gamliel used to say*. That is, he used to say this on Seder night. The source for Rabban Gamliel's ruling is the verse which commands us to recount the Exodus story on Seder night:

והגדת לבנך ביום ההוא לאמר בעבור זה עשה ה׳ לי בצאתי ממצרים

PESACH the Paschal lamb that our fathers used to eat
at the time when the Holy Temple was still standing
— for what reason? Because the Holy One, Blessed
be He, passed over the houses of our fathers in
Egypt, as it says: "And you shall say: 'It is a meal of
a salvation performed through a hesitating pass-
over, dedicated to Hashem Who hesitated as He
passed over the houses of the Children of Yisrael in
Egypt when He mortally smote the Egyptians and
our houses He saved.' And the people bowed and
prostrated themselves" (*Shemos* 12:27).

*And you shall relate to your child on that day, saying, "It
is because of this that Hashem acted for me when I came forth
out of Egypt".*

The phrase *because of this* alludes to these three items —
the Paschal lamb, the matzah, and the maror — the three items
(or the two items when the Holy Temple is not standing and
we do not have the Paschal lamb) which are on the table in front
of us on Seder night. We saw this allusion to the matzah and
maror earlier in the Haggadah in the paragraph יכול מראש חדש
which states, *Therefore, the text specifies "it is because of this."
I can say "it is because of this" only at such a time when the*

The leader of the Seder lifts the broken middle matzah
for all the participants to see.

מַ**צָה** זוֹ שֶׁאָנוּ אוֹכְלִים עַל שׁוּם מָה. עַל שׁוּם שֶׁלֹּא הִסְפִּיק בְּצֵקָם שֶׁל אֲבוֹתֵינוּ לְהַחֲמִיץ עַד שֶׁנִּגְלָה עֲלֵיהֶם מֶלֶךְ מַלְכֵי הַמְּלָכִים הַקָּדוֹשׁ בָּרוּךְ הוּא וּגְאָלָם. שֶׁנֶּאֱמַר וַיֹּאפוּ אֶת־הַבָּצֵק אֲשֶׁר הוֹצִיאוּ מִמִּצְרַיִם עֻגֹת מַצּוֹת כִּי לֹא חָמֵץ כִּי גֹרְשׁוּ מִמִּצְרַיִם וְלֹא יָכְלוּ לְהִתְמַהְמֵהַּ וְגַם־צֵדָה לֹא־עָשׂוּ לָהֶם:

matzah and the maror are in front of you.

When the Torah commands the father to tell his son *it is because of this*, it is commanding him to give the reason for *this*, as if the verse reads, *this is because of*. The father must explain to his son that the reason for *this* (the Paschal lamb, matzah, and maror) ultimately finds its source in the departure from Egypt. Thus, Rabban Gamliel teaches that it is not enough to simply say the words "it is because of this", but one must teach one's child why we have each of these three features of

173

The leader of the Seder lifts the broken middle matzah
for all the participants to see.

❧MATZAH unleavened bread — this matzah

which we eat — for what reason? Because the dough of our fathers did not have time to become leavened before the King of kings, the Holy One, Blessed be He, revealed Himself to them and redeemed them. As it says: "And they baked the dough which they had brought forth from Egypt into unleavened cakes, for it was not leavened, because they had been driven out of Egypt and could not tarry, and even provisions they had not prepared for themselves" (*ibid.* 12:39).

Pesach night and what each one commemorates.

The Haggadah alludes to the source of Rabban Gamliel's ruling by writing, ***This** matzah*, and ***This** maror*, echoing the phrase in Shemos 13:8, *it is because of **this**.* (We do not refer to the Paschal lamb as *this* Paschal lamb because we do not have it in front of us.)

This paragraph comes at this point in the Haggadah because, as we have explained (see *Overview*), the compiler of the Haggadah organized each section according to the order

of phrases in Shemos 13:8. Since this section corresponds to the phrase בעבור זה, *it is because of this*, which follows the phrase לאמר, *saying*, to which the recounting of the Exodus story corresponds, this section was logically placed after the recounting of the Exodus story.

פסח — The Paschal Lamb

The reason for the Pesach sacrifice is written explicitly in the verse, *And you shall say: "It is a meal of a salvation performed through a hesitating pass-over, dedicated to Hashem"* because it was He *"Who hesitated as He passed over the houses of the Children of Israel"* (Shemos 12:27). Since the reason for the Pesach sacrifice is stated in the verse, it is introduced by the phrase שנאמר, which indicates a proof (see footnote on p. 106).

מצה זו — This matzah

The Questions

1. What was the kindness that God granted by not allowing time for the dough of our fathers to become leavened? Why are we commanded to commemorate this "kindness"?

2. What is so important about the unleavened bread that this festival is called, חג המצות, *the Festival of Matzah*, as if the matzah was the essence of the festival?

3. The Almighty brought us forth from Egypt by compelling Pharaoh to drive us out in haste. Why did the Almighty not compel Pharaoh to let us leave at a more relaxed pace, rather than drive us out in haste?

4 *...because they had been driven out of Egypt and could not tarry.* *And could not tarry* implies that the Children of Israel were intrinsically unable to stay in Egypt, and not merely that the Egyptians would not let them stay. In other words, *they could not tarry* says that even if the Egyptians had not expelled them, the Children of Israel still would have been unable to stay in Egypt. Why not?

מצה זו *This matzah.* The alacrity with which we left Egypt — which the matzah symbolizes — was the primary component of our miraculous departure as we see from the central role it plays in the festival of Pesach. What was so important, though, about leaving Egypt in haste?

Our Sages tell us that our ancestors in Egypt were deeply immersed in the abominations of their hosts, thoroughly assimilated in their evil deeds and corrupt customs. The Medrash says, *These [the Egyptians] were idol-worshippers and these [the Israelites] were idol-worshippers* (cf. *Vayikra Rabbah 23:2; Shir Hashirim Rabbah 2:6*). The people of Israel were so steeped in the immorality of Egypt that had they lingered there for even one more moment, they would have become irreversibly engulfed in the lifeless existence of the Egyptians, sinking to the fiftieth level of impurity[63]. Had our fathers tarried and allowed that moment to come, redemption would have been meaningless, for with or without the shackles of slavery, we would have remained like any other idol-worshipping

---

63. This concept of the fiftieth and final level of impurity is found in the name of the *Arizal* (see *Beis Halevi* on *Parshas Bo*, p. 23). The existence of this level is a matter of dispute (see *Leshem Shevo VeAchlama, Derushei Olam Hatohu, Part II, Derush V, Anaf 2, ch. 5*). (Eds.)

The leader of the Seder lifts the maror for all the participants to see.

מָרוֹר זֶה שֶׁאָנוּ אוֹכְלִים עַל־שׁוּם מָה. עַל־שׁוּם שֶׁמֵּרְרוּ הַמִּצְרִים אֶת־חַיֵּי אֲבוֹתֵינוּ בְּמִצְרָיִם. שֶׁנֶּאֱמַר וַיְמָרְרוּ אֶת חַיֵּיהֶם בַּעֲבֹדָה קָשָׁה בְּחֹמֶר וּבִלְבֵנִים וּבְכָל עֲבֹדָה בַּשָּׂדֶה אֵת כָּל־עֲבֹדָתָם אֲשֶׁר עָבְדוּ בָהֶם בְּפָרֶךְ:

nation. The haste with which we left Egypt was vital to our existence as the holy nation of God.

Therefore, God caused the Egyptians to expel us speedily, not allowing us to remain an instant longer.

When we commemorate the departure from Egypt we must concentrate on the haste with which it occurred in order to remember its true purpose — our spiritual metamorphosis into the nation of God. For this reason we are commanded to eat matzah — to remind us of the haste with which we left Egypt. Our Sages further highlighted this idea by naming the festival חג המצות, *the Festival of Matzah.*

177

The leader of the Seder lifts the maror for all the participants to see.

MAROR the bitter herbs — this maror which we eat — for what reason? Because the Egyptians embittered the lives of our fathers in Egypt, as it says: "And they [the Egyptians] embittered their lives with hard labor, with mortar and bricks and with all manner of work in the field; they embittered all their work which they made them do, with harshness" (*ibid.* 1:14).

מרור זה — **This maror**

מרור זה *This maror which we eat — for what reason? Because the Egyptians embittered the lives of our fathers in Egypt, as it says: "And they [the Egyptians] embittered their lives with hard labor...".* This verse tells us that the Egyptians embittered the lives of our fathers, but it does not provide the reason why we eat bitter herbs. Similarly, the verse cited in the previous paragraph, מצה זו, does not provide an explicit reason why we eat matzah; it merely tells us that the dough of our fathers did not have time to rise.

Nevertheless, once we know that the Egyptians embittered the lives of our fathers in Egypt, we can logically assume that the command to eat bitter herbs is to remember that bitterness.

בְּכָל דּוֹר וָדוֹר חַיָּב אָדָם לִרְאוֹת אֶת־עַצְמוֹ
כְּאִלּוּ הוּא יָצָא מִמִּצְרַיִם. שֶׁנֶּאֱמַר וְהִגַּדְתָּ לְבִנְךָ בַּיּוֹם
הַהוּא לֵאמֹר בַּעֲבוּר זֶה עָשָׂה יהוה לִי בְּצֵאתִי
מִמִּצְרָיִם. לֹא אֶת־אֲבוֹתֵינוּ בִּלְבָד גָּאַל הַקָּדוֹשׁ בָּרוּךְ
הוּא אֶלָּא אַף אוֹתָנוּ גָּאַל עִמָּהֶם. שֶׁנֶּאֱמַר וְאוֹתָנוּ
הוֹצִיא מִשָּׁם לְמַעַן הָבִיא אֹתָנוּ לָתֶת לָנוּ אֶת הָאָרֶץ
אֲשֶׁר נִשְׁבַּע לַאֲבוֹתֵינוּ:

The matzos are covered and the cup is lifted and held
until the closing sentence "Who has redeemed Yisrael"
(according to some customs it is put down after
"Halleluyah" and the matzos are uncovered, then
lifted again for the berachah "Who redeemed us..."
and the matzos covered once again).

Similarly, once we know that our fathers left Egypt in haste,
we can infer that the reason for eating matzah is to remember
that haste.

In every single generation one is obligated to look upon himself as if he personally had gone forth out of Egypt, as it says: "And you shall relate to your child on that day, saying: 'It is because of this that Hashem acted for me when I came forth out of Egypt'" (*ibid.* 13:8). Not only our fathers did the Holy One, Blessed be He, redeem, but us, too, He redeemed together with them, as it says: "And He brought us out from there that He might bring us home to give to us the land which He had sworn to our fathers" (*Devarim* 6:23).

The matzos are covered and the cup is lifted and held until the closing sentence "Who has redeemed Yisrael" (according to some customs it is put down after "Halleluyah" and the matzos are uncovered, then lifted again for the berachah "Who redeemed us..." and the matzos covered once again).

בכל דור ודור — In every single generation

The Questions

1 Why does the Haggadah cite two verses to support this obligation? It would have sufficed to cite Shemos 13:8, without Devarim 6:23, to tell us that every person is obligated to look upon himself as if he personally had gone forth out of Egypt.

180

2 This idea, that we, ourselves, went forth out of Egypt, was already mentioned at the beginning of the Haggadah in the paragraph עבדים היינו: *And if the Holy One, Blessed be He, had not taken our fathers out of Egypt, then we, our children, and our children's children would still have been subjugated to Pharaoh in Egypt,* where we view ourselves as having been taken out of Egypt. Why is it repeated here in different words?

בכל דור ודור *In every single generation.* Having concluded Rabban Gamliel's teaching from the phrase בעבור זה, *because of this,* in Shemos 13:8, the Haggadah moves on to the next phrase in that verse, עשה ה' לי, *Hashem acted for me* (see *Overview*).

חיב אדם לראות את עצמו *One is obligated to look upon himself as if he personally had gone forth out of Egypt, as it says: "And you shall relate to your child on that day, saying: 'It is because of this that Hashem acted for me when I came forth out of Egypt' ".* This verse clearly commands us to relate the account of the departure from Egypt as though we, personally, had experienced it.

The Haggadah adds that the command is not merely to pretend or to imagine oneself leaving Egypt, but to know that in truth *not only our fathers did the Holy One, Blessed be He, redeem, but us, too, He redeemed together with them, as it says: "And He brought us out from there that He might bring us home to give to us the land which He had sworn to our fathers"* (Devarim 6:23); that is, *we* actually participated in the redemption[64].

---

64. The word *us* in this verse cannot refer to those who lived at the time of the Exodus, because this verse comes in response to the son's question, *When your son will ask you in time to come, saying: "What are the testimonies, the statutes, and the social ordinances which Hashem our God has commanded you?"* (Devarim 6:20). *In time to come* refers to a future age, a time when there will be no one alive who actually witnessed the departure from Egypt, and yet the prescribed response is, *and He brought us out from there.*

181

We see that the command is not merely to imagine ourselves leaving Egypt, but to know that we, indeed, were redeemed, for *if the Holy One, Blessed be He, had not taken our fathers out of Egypt, then we, our children, and our children's children would still have been subjugated to Pharaoh in Egypt.*

Why does the Haggadah cite two verses to show the obligation of viewing ourselves as if we personally had gone forth out of Egypt?

From Shemos 13:8 we learn the obligation to *relate* the Exodus story, as it says, *And you shall relate to your child.* In the second verse, Devarim 6:23, there is no mention of an obligation to *relate* the story[65].

From Devarim 6:23 we learn the obligation to know and tell our children that we, too, were redeemed from Egypt, as it says, *And He brought us out*, and *us* must be referring to those of us who did not actually witness the Exodus, because the previous verse (Devarim 6:22) states, *in time to come*, a time when no one who was there will be alive.

Why does the Haggadah also mention this obligation earlier, in the paragraph עבדים היינו?

There, the statement that had the Almighty *not taken our fathers out of Egypt, then we, our children, and our children's children would still have been subjugated to Pharaoh in Egypt*

---

65. Although the verses in Devarim also mention an obligation to relate the story, as it says, *When your son will ask you... And you shall tell your son, "We were slaves to Pharaoh in Egypt, and Hashem brought us out from Egypt with a mighty hand"* (Devarim 6:20-21), nevertheless Shemos 13:8 is the only verse which can be used as the source for the obligation to relate the Exodus story, because it applies even without a question from the son (see *Overview*).

לְפִיכָךְ אֲנַחְנוּ חַיָּבִים לְהוֹדוֹת לְהַלֵּל לְשַׁבֵּחַ לְפָאֵר לְרוֹמֵם לְהַדֵּר לְבָרֵךְ לְעַלֵּה וּלְקַלֵּס לְמִי שֶׁעָשָׂה לַאֲבוֹתֵינוּ וְלָנוּ אֶת־כָּל הַנִּסִּים הָאֵלֶּה הוֹצִיאָנוּ מֵעַבְדוּת לְחֵרוּת מִיָּגוֹן לְשִׂמְחָה מֵאֵבֶל לְיוֹם טוֹב וּמֵאֲפֵלָה לְאוֹר גָּדוֹל וּמִשִּׁעְבּוּד לִגְאֻלָּה וְנֹאמַר לְפָנָיו שִׁירָה חֲדָשָׁה הַלְלוּיָהּ:

does *not* come to teach us the obligation to view ourselves as having personally left Egypt. Rather, it comes for a different purpose altogether — to show why *even if we were all wise... we would nevertheless be obligated to recount the story of the departure from Egypt.*

This obligation is not mentioned until this point in the Haggadah because this paragraph corresponds to the phrase עשה ה׳ לי — *Hashem acted for me* in Shemos 13:8, the verse upon which the order of the Haggadah is based (see *Overview*).

183

❧THEREFORE we are obliged

to give thanks, to praise His mighty acts, to laud, glorify, exalt, proclaim His might, bless, extol and celebrate Him Who wrought all these miracles for our fathers and for us. He brought us forth from slavery into freedom, from sorrow into joy, from mourning into festivity, and from darkness into great light, and from subjugation into redemption. Let us therefore recite before Him (a new song): Halleluyah!

לפיכך — **Therefore**

The Questions

1 Why does the Haggadah use so many different expressions of praise in this paragraph?

2 Why was this paragraph placed here?

3 את כל הנסים האלה *All these miracles.* Why does the Haggadah say *all these miracles* when it does not mention any miracles at all? *He brought us forth from slavery into freedom, from sorrow into joy, from mourning into festivity* and so on are all just different descriptions of the redemption. Where is the list of *all these miracles?*

לפיכך *Therefore.* After recounting the story of the Exodus from Egypt in detail according to the order of the relevant verses in the Torah, the Haggadah now turns to Hallel, the joyful

expression of praise to God for His benevolence. The recitation of Hallel corresponds to the words בצאתי ממצרים, *when I came forth out of Egypt* in Shemos 13:8, because it features the paragraph בצאת ישראל ממצרים, *When Israel went forth from Egypt*. It was, therefore, placed at this point in the Haggadah, parallel to the sequence of the six phrases in Shemos 13:8.

The role of the paragraph לפיכך is to tie together everything we have read in the Haggadah up to this point with the praises of Hallel. In view of the inexpressible kindnesses which God bestowed upon us and the many miracles He wrought on our behalf, *therefore we are obliged to give thanks, to praise His mighty acts, to laud, glorify, exalt, proclaim His might, bless, extol, and praise Him.*

We explained earlier that the paragraphs כמה מעלות טובות and על אחת כמה וכמה are intended to introduce the paragraph לפיכך. Those two paragraphs convey the idea that we would be obligated to feel and to express infinite praises and thanks to God for any single act of kindness He performed for us — how much more so for all of His acts of kindness combined. *Therefore we are obliged to give thanks, to praise His mighty acts, to laud, glorify, exalt, proclaim His might, bless, extol, and praise Him.*

Many different expressions of praise are listed to emphasize our endless obligation to praise and thank with all our ability, with every form of praise that exists, *Him Who wrought all these miracles for our fathers and for us;* that is, the miracles specified in the paragraphs כמה מעלות טובות and על אחת כמה וכמה, through

---

66. The text in the Mishnah does not include these two paragraphs. If so, to what does the phrase *all these miracles* refer? It refers to the miracles specified in the verses from *Parshas Bikkurim*, read earlier in the Haggadah.

185

which *He brought us forth from slavery into freedom.*[66]

From slavery into freedom, from sorrow into joy, from mourning into festivity, and from darkness into great light, and from subjugation into redemption. The different phrases, which apparently are only illustrative descriptions of the delivery from slavery into freedom, actually refer to several events[67]. The Vilna Gaon explains:

From slavery into freedom — this is the departure from Egypt.

From sorrow into joy — this is the splitting of the Sea, for the Children of Israel were saved from the onslaught of the approaching Egyptian army.

From mourning into festivity — *mourning* refers to the Jewish people's remorse after the sin of the Golden Calf, as it says, *And the people mourned* (Shemos 33:4).

Festivity refers to Yom Kippur, the day when Moshe descended from Mount Sinai with the second set of tablets, a sign that God had forgiven the Jewish people for their sin. *There were never in Israel greater days of joy than the fifteenth of Av and Yom Kippur (Taanis 26b; Bava Basra 121a).*

From darkness into great light — from the wilderness, a place of foreboding darkness, to the land of Israel, a land radiant with spiritual light.

From subjugation into redemption — from subjugation under the rule of foreign forces in the time of the Judges (as described in the Book of Judges), to redemption in the time

---

67. Consequently, the phrase *all these miracles* refers not to the miracles listed in the previous paragraphs, but to the miracles to which these five phrases allude.

הַלְלוּיָהּ הַלְלוּ עַבְדֵי יהוה הַלְלוּ אֶת־שֵׁם
יהוה: יְהִי שֵׁם יהוה מְבֹרָךְ מֵעַתָּה וְעַד־עוֹלָם:
מִמִּזְרַח שֶׁמֶשׁ עַד־מְבוֹאוֹ מְהֻלָּל שֵׁם יהוה: רָם עַל־
כָּל־גּוֹיִם יהוה. עַל הַשָּׁמַיִם כְּבוֹדוֹ: מִי כַּיהוה
אֱלֹהֵינוּ. הַמַּגְבִּיהִי לָשָׁבֶת. הַמַּשְׁפִּילִי לִרְאוֹת
בַּשָּׁמַיִם וּבָאָרֶץ: מְקִימִי מֵעָפָר דָּל. מֵאַשְׁפֹּת יָרִים
אֶבְיוֹן: לְהוֹשִׁיבִי עִם־נְדִיבִים. עִם נְדִיבֵי עַמּוֹ:
מוֹשִׁיבִי עֲקֶרֶת הַבַּיִת אֵם־הַבָּנִים שְׂמֵחָה הַלְלוּיָהּ:

of David and Solomon, who secured complete autonomy for
the Jewish nation enabling it to freely pursue its spiritual goals.

The paragraph concludes, *Let us therefore recite before Him:
Halleluyah!*[68] to usher in the purpose of these passages — the
joyous recitation of Hallel.

---

68. The author points out that since the sentence, *Let us therefore recite before
Him*, introduces Hallel, the words "a new song" which appear in some texts
should be omitted, because Hallel is not a new song. The words "a new song"
are also omitted in the text of this paragraph found in the Mishnah (*Pesachim
10:5*). The Haggadahs of Rav Amram Gaon, Rav Saadiah Gaon, the Rambam,
and the Rashbatz also omit these words. The *Mishnah Brurah*, however,
justifies their inclusion in the Haggadah (*Mishnah Brurah 473:71*). (Eds.)

Halleluyah! Praise, o' servants of God, praise the Name of God. Blessed be the Name of Hashem from now until eternity. From the place in the east where the sun rises to the place in the west where it sets, let the Name of Hashem be praised. For Hashem is high above all nations, His glory is beyond the heavens. But who is like Hashem our God, Who, though enthroned on high, looks down so low, into the heavens and upon the earth? He raises out of the dust the poor man, and lifts the destitute up from the dunghill. To set him next to princes, next to the princes of his people. He causes the barren woman of the house to sit as a joyous mother of children; Halleluyah! (*Tehillim* 113).

הללויה — **Halleluyah**

הללויה *Halleluyah!* The word *Halleluyah*[69] serves the same purpose as the words *Mizmor* and *Michtam*, which come at the beginning of a chapter of Tehillim — it describes the nature of the Psalm which it introduces.

Halleluyah comes at the beginning of a Psalm which

---

69. Halleluyah is a contraction of the two words, *Hallelu* (praise) and *Y-ah*, (God's name). The Talmud calls it the greatest single statement of praise to God in all of Tehillim since it contains both the name of God and the concept of praise (*Pesachim 117a*).

expresses general praises of God and His might. This is in contrast to the word *Mizmor*, which comes at the beginning of a Psalm which expresses praise or prayer to God for a specific kindness.

The Psalm which we are about to recite does not praise God for any specific event; rather it is a song of general praise of God, the heart's outpouring of love and exaltation to Him. The following Psalm, בצאת ישראל, on the other hand, deals specifically with praises for the miracles which God wrought when He took our nation out of Egypt, including the splitting of the Sea and the Revelation at Mount Sinai.

Therefore, this set of Psalms is known as *Hallel HaMitzri, the Egyptian Hallel.* We say it at the Seder before the meal while we are still involved in telling the story of the Exodus from Egypt. The second half of Hallel, beginning with Psalm 115, לא לנו, is not recited until after the meal, because it does not contain praises of God for the Exodus from Egypt, but praises of God for the future redemption from our present exile. The meal serves as an interruption in Hallel to remind us of the two different topics which Hallel addresses in order that we have the proper intentions when reciting each part of Hallel.

הללו עבדי ה׳ הללו את שם ה׳ *Praise, o'servants of God, praise the Name of God.* After the declaration *Halleluyah*, the Psalmist explains the intent of that declaration. The word *Hallelu, praise,* of *Halleluyah* invites the servants of God to open their hearts in unrestrained praise. This is what the Psalmist means by the first half of his declaration, *Praise, o'servants of God.* The word *Y-ah* of *Halleluyah* directs them to the subject of

their praise, *the Name of God.* This is what the Psalmist means by the second half of his declaration, *praise the Name of God.*

יהי שם ה׳ מבורך *Blessed be the Name of Hashem from now until eternity.* After calling upon us to praise God in the present, the Psalmist extends his exhortation to us to praise God in the future. The Psalmist continues and, not limiting his summons to praise God to the boundaries of temporal existence, beckons us to praise God not only throughout all of time but throughout all of space as well, from one end of the world to the other: *From the place in the east where the sun rises to the place in the west where it sets, let the Name of Hashem be praised.*

רם על כל גוים *For Hashem is high above all nations, His glory is beyond the heavens.* The Psalmist proceeds to describe Israel's elevated stature over all the other peoples of the world.

For Hashem is high above all nations, and He does not administer to them directly, but controls their lives only via the *mazalos,* forces which mediate between the controlling powers of God and their worldly counterparts. The fate of the people of Israel, however, is directly controlled by the hands of God. Furthermore, *His glory is beyond the heavens;* that is, in the existence of the nations of the world, things seem so random that it appears that God is not involved, as if He were far removed from their mundane existence. But God's relationship with Israel is different —

מי כה׳ אלקינו המגביהי לשבת *But who is like Hashem our God, Who, though enthroned on high, looks down so low, into the heavens and upon the earth?* Although He is *enthroned on high,* the omnipotent One Whose greatness is infinite, immeasurable, incomprehensible, He nevertheless comes down, as it

בְּצֵאת יִשְׂרָאֵל מִמִּצְרָיִם בֵּית יַעֲקֹב מֵעַם לֹעֵז:
הָיְתָה יְהוּדָה לְקָדְשׁוֹ יִשְׂרָאֵל מַמְשְׁלוֹתָיו: הַיָּם רָאָה
וַיָּנֹס. הַיַּרְדֵּן יִסֹּב לְאָחוֹר: הֶהָרִים רָקְדוּ כְאֵילִים.
גְּבָעוֹת כִּבְנֵי צֹאן: מַה לְּךָ הַיָּם כִּי תָנוּס. הַיַּרְדֵּן תִּסֹּב
לְאָחוֹר: הֶהָרִים תִּרְקְדוּ כְאֵילִים. גְּבָעוֹת כִּבְנֵי־צֹאן:
מִלִּפְנֵי אָדוֹן חוּלִי אָרֶץ. מִלִּפְנֵי אֱלוֹהַּ יַעֲקֹב: הַהֹפְכִי
הַצּוּר אֲגַם־מָיִם. חַלָּמִישׁ לְמַעְיְנוֹ־מָיִם:

were, and *looks so low, into the heavens* which, despite their
loftiness compared to where we stand, are immensely lower
than the throne of God, and He even goes so far as to look
upon the earth, intimately involving Himself in our day-to-day
lives. The Psalmist proceeds to describe two parables of God's
providence: the poor and the barren —

מקימי מעפר דל *He raises out of the dust the poor man, and
lifts the destitute up from the dunghill*. Not only does God assist
the poor man in the dust, but God even comes to the aid of
the one who is worse off — the destitute man in the dunghill.
And not only does he lift him up out of his poverty, but —

להושיבי עם נדיבים עם נדיבי עמו *To set him next to princes,
next to the princes of his people*. He raises up the destitute and

191

When Yisrael went forth from Egypt, the House of Yaakov from a people of alien tongue. Yehudah became His sanctuary, Yisrael His sphere of dominion. The Sea saw it and fled, the Jordan sought to turn backward. The mountains skipped like rams, the hills like young sheep. What ails you, o' Sea, that you flee, o' Jordan, that you turn backward; o' mountains, that you skip like rams, o' hills, like young sheep? Before the Master, the Creator of the earth, before the God of Yaakov. Who turns the rock into a pool of water, flint into a fountain of water (*ibid.* 114).

even sets him *next to princes*. And not only next to princes, but *next to the princes of his people* — an additional display of Divine providence, for, under normal circumstances, one who rises up from such an ignominious condition can sit only amongst princes who never knew him, who are unaware of his former lowly status. Were they to know how poor he had once been, they would be ashamed to sit with him. But God, in His infinite wisdom, places the once poor man amongst *princes of his people*, princes who recognize him and remember his former wretched state of existence, and nevertheless they feel no shame when he joins their company.

מושיבי עקרת הבית *He causes the barren woman of the house to sit as a joyous mother of children.* This is another allegory

of God's providence and involvement in the life of the Jewish people. Both of these examples of Divine assistance — changing the fortune of the poor man, and giving children to the barren woman — symbolize God's special relationship with His children, Israel.

בצאת ישראל ממצרים — When Israel went forth from Egypt

בצאת ישראל ממצרים בית יעקב מעם לעז *When Israel went forth from Egypt, the House of Yaakov from a people of alien tongue. Yehudah became His holy sanctuary, Israel, His sphere of dominion.* The Psalmist now specifies one particularly awesome act of God, one of the most extraordinary events in the history of mankind — the Exodus from Egypt.

When Israel went forth refers to the members of the upper caste of inherited spiritual status[70], the Levites, and *the House of Yaakov* refers to the rest of the nation, whom God brought forth from *a people of alien tongue,* a miraculous delivery from the grips of a mighty people[71], and elevated them to the responsibility of serving as *his holy sanctuary,* the nation amidst whom the presence of God dwells, and *His sphere of dominion,* the nation privileged to be the subjects of the King of Kings.

הים ראה וינס *The Sea saw it and fled.* The Psalmist uses

---

70. God changed the name of our forefather, Yaakov, to Israel (Bereishis 32:29). The name Israel, therefore, signifies a superior state to the name of Yaakov.

71. The Commentary understands the word לעז, a word which denotes a person who speaks an alien tongue, to be related to עז, *mighty.*

anthropomorphic imagery to describe the awesome effect which the event of the Exodus had upon the world. The Sea saw the holy nation of Israel and the miracles which God performed for His people and it fled in awe.

הירדן תסוב לאחור *the Jordan sought to turn backward.* This refers to the miraculous splitting of the Jordan River which occurred when Yehoshua led the Jewish people into the land of Israel forty years after the Exodus.

ההרים רקדו כאילים *The mountains skipped like rams, the hills like young sheep.* The excited movement of the mountains is an allusion to the giving of the Torah on Sinai, as it says *Why do you skip, o' peaked mountains.... the Lord is among them, Sinai in holiness* (Psalms 68:17-18).

מה לך הים כי תנוס *What ails you, o' Sea, that you flee, o' Jordan, that you turn backward; o' mountains, that you skip like rams, o' hills, like young sheep?* The Psalmist poetically puts the question to these features of nature, inquiring as to the cause of their strange behavior. And, in his song, they respond to him, מלפני אדון חולי ארץ *Before the Master, the Creator of the earth, before the God of Yaakov.* Their response refers to three features of God's authority over the physical elements of the world. First, He is their *Master.* Second, He is their מחולל, their generator, the One Who gives power to and creates the earth[72]. Third, He is *the God of Yaakov,* who commanded the Sea, the river, the mountains and the hills to do whatever they could

---

72. The Commentary understands the word חולי to mean מחולל, *creator,* a noun. The common translation, however, understands the phrase חולי ארץ to mean *tremble o' earth,* an imperative. See *Rashi* and *Metzudas Tzion* on the verse who both interpret חולי as מחולל, *creator.*

בָּרוּךְ אַתָּה יהוה אֱלֹהֵינוּ מֶלֶךְ הָעוֹלָם אֲשֶׁר גְּאָלָנוּ וְגָאַל אֶת אֲבוֹתֵינוּ מִמִּצְרַיִם וְהִגִּיעָנוּ הַלַּיְלָה הַזֶּה לֶאֱכָל בּוֹ מַצָּה וּמָרוֹר. כֵּן יהוה אֱלֹהֵינוּ וֵאלֹהֵי אֲבוֹתֵינוּ יַגִּיעֵנוּ לְמוֹעֲדִים וְלִרְגָלִים אֲחֵרִים הַבָּאִים לִקְרָאתֵנוּ לְשָׁלוֹם שְׂמֵחִים בְּבִנְיַן עִירֶךְ וְשָׂשִׂים בַּעֲבוֹדָתֶךְ וְנֹאכַל שָׁם מִן הַזְּבָחִים וּמִן הַפְּסָחִים (יֵשׁ אוֹמְרִים בְּמוֹצָאֵי שַׁבָּת: מִן הַפְּסָחִים וּמִן הַזְּבָחִים) אֲשֶׁר יַגִּיעַ דָּמָם עַל קִיר מִזְבַּחֲךָ

for the benefit of His nation, the children of Yaakov.

ההפכי הצור אגם מים *Who turns the rock into a pool of water, flint into a fountain of water.* In addition to the movement of the Sea, the river, the mountains and the hills on behalf of His nation,

---

73. Why does the Psalmist express the miracle that God brought forth water from rock twice? The Psalmist may be referring to the two episodes described in the Torah in which Moshe was commanded by God to supply the people with water from rocks. In the first incident (Shemos 17:1-7), the rock is called צור, and the amount of water which comes from it is modest — *and water will come out from it.* Alluding to this incident the Psalmist writes ההפכי הצור אגם מים , referring to the rock as צור and to the water as *a pool of water,* suggesting a small supply.

✤BLESSED be You, Hashem our God, King of

the universe, Who redeemed us and redeemed our fathers from Egypt and enabled us to attain this night, on which to eat matzah and maror. So Hashem, our God and God of our fathers, enable us to attain other festivals of assembly and of pilgrimage which approach us in peace, rejoicing in the building of Your city and joyful in Your sacrificial service; and we shall eat there from the sacrifices and from the Pesach offerings (on *Motzai Shabbos* some say: from the Pesach offerings and from the sacrifices) whose blood will be sprinkled on the

God caused the rock to turn into a pool of water and flint into a fountain of water, giving them water from solid stone.[73]

In the second episode (Bamidbar 20:7-11), the rock is called סלע and the amount of water which comes forth is significant — *and a lot of water came forth*. The Psalmist alludes to this second incident by writing חלמיש למעינו מים, referring to the rock as חלמיש, another word for סלע, and to the water as למעינו מים, *a fountain of water*, suggesting a large amount of water. This may be the intention of the author when he comments on the words חלמיש למעינו מים: "שנתן להם מים מסלע." (Eds.)

לְרָצוֹן וְנוֹדֶה לְךָ שִׁיר חָדָשׁ עַל גְּאֻלָּתֵנוּ וְעַל
פְּדוּת נַפְשֵׁנוּ. בָּרוּךְ אַתָּה יהוה גָּאַל יִשְׂרָאֵל:

One should intend to fulfill the requirement of
drinking the second of the four cups of wine.

בָּרוּךְ אַתָּה יהוה אֱלֹהֵינוּ מֶלֶךְ הָעוֹלָם
בּוֹרֵא פְּרִי הַגָּפֶן:

The required amount of the second cup is drunk,
within the required period of time,
while reclining to the left.

Who redeemed us ~~~ אשר גאלנו

אשר גאלנו *Who redeemed us.* We bless God for having redeemed us and our fathers from Egypt. By doing so we fulfill the obligation to look upon ourselves as if we personally had gone forth from Egypt.

וגאל את אבותינו ממצרים *and redeemed our fathers from Egypt and enabled us to attain this night.* We do not merely acknowledge that God gave us life, but that He gave us the opportunity to fulfill the commandments of this night, *to eat matzah and maror.*

After giving thanks for reaching this night, we make a request for the future: כן ה'...יגיענו למועדים ולרגלים אחרים *So, Hashem our God and God of our fathers, enable us to attain*

sacrifices) whose blood will be sprinkled on the sides of Your altar for gracious acceptance, and we shall thank You with a new song for our redemption and for the deliverance of our souls. Blessed be You, Hashem, Who has redeemed Yisrael.

One should intend to fulfill the requirement of drinking the second of the four cups of wine.

Blessed be You, Hashem our God, King of the universe, Who creates the fruit of the vine.

The required amount of the second cup is drunk, within the required period of time, while reclining to the left.

other festivals of assembly, such as Rosh Hashana and Yom Kippur, when there is no pilgrimage to Jerusalem, as well as festivals *of pilgrimage*, Pesach, Shavuos, and Sukkos — *which approach us in peace.*

We pray that we should be worthy of ascending to Jerusalem where we will be *rejoicing in the building of Your city and joyful in Your sacrificial service; and we shall eat there* on this night of the year *from the sacrifices* — the קרבן חגיגה, the Festival Offering, which we eat before the Pesach offering in order to eat the Pesach offering while satiated, *and from the Pesach offerings*[74]. We pray for the restoration of the Temple

---

74. In the 5654/1894 edition, the author includes a footnote at this point regarding the source for the alternate wording, *from the Pesach offerings and from the sacrifices*, which some customarily say when Seder night falls on

198

offerings not because we relish the flavor of their meat, but because we desire offerings *whose blood will be sprinkled on the sides of Your altar for gracious acceptance.*

When this time will come *we shall thank You with a new song for our redemption,* that is, the redemption from the forces which threaten our physical well-being, *and for the deliverance of our souls,* that is, the deliverance from the forces which threaten our spiritual well-being.

ברוך אתה ה׳ גאל ישראל *Blessed be You, Hashem, Who has redeemed Israel* from the Egyptian exile[75].

Motzai Shabbos. His point is the subject of dispute between several other authorities (see *Pardes Yosef, Parshas Bo, 12:11,* the comment thereon of Rav Avraham Mordechai Alter zt"l, the former Admor of Gur and author of *Imrei Emes,* comment 33 on p. 14 of *Sefer Shemos; Haggadah Shleimah,* p. 143 n.10). (Eds.)

75. The Halacha requires that the final words of a lengthy prayer, such as this one, resemble the closing blessing which follows these words (*Pesachim 104a*). Before the closing blessing, *Blessed be You, Hashem, Who has redeemed Israel,* we express our desire to thank God *for our redemption and for the deliverance of our souls.* The problem is that the redemption mentioned here refers to the future redemption, while the closing blessing refers to the past redemption from Egypt.

The answer is that the future redemption is indeed rooted in the redemption from Egypt, as God said to the prophet Michah concerning the future redemption, *As in the days of your departure from the land of Egypt I will show him [the Jewish nation] wonders* (Michah 7:15). Therefore, the last few words do indeed resemble the closing blessing.

רָחְצָה

From the time the hands are washed until after eating the korech, no unnecessary speaking is allowed. Therefore, the leader of the Seder should now explain to all the participants (especially children) all the instructions they will need to know concerning the eating of the matzah and the maror.

It is unlikely that there will be enough matzah on the Seder plate for all of the assembled. Furthermore, since the leader of the Seder is required to distribute from his matzah to those assembled, to have to measure and distribute the required amount after the blessing would constitute an unnecessary lapse of time between the berachah and the fulfilling of the mitzvah. Therefore, it is advisable that everyone have the measured, required amount of matzah from other, shemurah matzos before him (see Required Measurements and Amounts, page 21), before he goes to wash his hands. After the leader of the Seder will have recited the berachah and have measured the required amount for himself, he will easily and quickly be able to distribute bits of the leftover matzah to all assembled to eat together with their portions.

All present wash their hands (a washbasin is brought to the leader of the Seder) and recite the following berachah (one who washed his hands before the karpas and is sure that they have been kept clean, should first contaminate them by touching his shoe or the like):

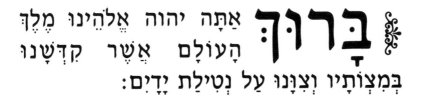

בָּרוּךְ אַתָּה יהוה אֱלֹהֵינוּ מֶלֶךְ הָעוֹלָם אֲשֶׁר קִדְּשָׁנוּ בְּמִצְוֹתָיו וְצִוָּנוּ עַל נְטִילַת יָדָיִם:

Rochtzah

From the time the hands are washed until after eating the korech, no unnecessary speaking is allowed. Therefore, the leader of the Seder should now explain to all the participants (especially children) all the instructions they will need to know concerning the eating of the matzah and the maror.

It is unlikely that there will be enough matzah on the Seder plate for all of the assembled. Furthermore, since the leader of the Seder is required to distribute from his matzah to those assembled, to have to measure and distribute the required amount after the blessing would constitute an unnecessary lapse of time between the berachah and the fulfilling of the mitzvah. Therefore, it is advisable that everyone have the measured, required amount of matzah from other, shemurah matzos before him (see Required Measurements and Amounts, page 21), before he goes to wash his hands. After the leader of the Seder will have recited the berachah and have measured the required amount for himself, he will easily and quickly be able to distribute bits of the leftover matzah to all assembled to eat together with their portions.

All present wash their hands (a washbasin is brought to the leader of the Seder) and recite the following berachah (one who washed his hands before the karpas and is sure that they have been kept clean, should first contaminate them by touching his shoe or the like):

BLESSED be You, Hashem our God, King of the universe, Who has sanctified us by His commandments and commanded us concerning the washing of the hands.

מוֹצִיא

*If the leader of the Seder is to make the berachos over
the matzah and maror for all assembled (as is the
custom in many homes), then he and they must have
that in mind while the berachos are being made, and
everyone should have in mind that it is his intention to
fulfill his duty to eat matzah on Pesach night.*

*The leader of the Seder, of each participant, if he is to
make his own berachos, takes all three matzos in his
hand (the two whole ones for lechem mishneh and the
broken one between them for lechem oni) and says the
following berachah:*

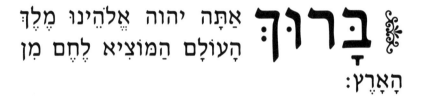

בָּרוּךְ אַתָּה יהוה אֱלֹהֵינוּ מֶלֶךְ
הָעוֹלָם הַמּוֹצִיא לֶחֶם מִן
הָאָרֶץ:

Motzi

*If the leader of the Seder is to make the berachos over
the matzah and maror for all assembled (as is the
custom in many homes), then he and they must have
that in mind while the berachos are being made, and
everyone should have in mind that it is his intention to
fulfill his duty to eat matzah on Pesach night.*

*The leader of the Seder, of each participant, if he is to
make his own berachos, takes all three matzos in his
hand (the two whole ones for lechem mishneh and the
broken one between them for lechem oni) and says the
following berachah:*

BLESSED be You, Hashem,
our God, King of
the universe, Who brings forth bread from the earth.

*He now releases the bottom matzah from his grip and
says the following berachah, with the intention that it
refer also to the matzah of the korech and afikoman
which will be eaten later on:*

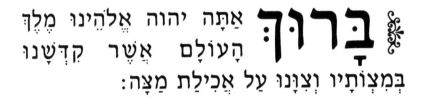

בָּרוּךְ אַתָּה יהוה אֱלֹהֵינוּ מֶלֶךְ
הָעוֹלָם אֲשֶׁר קִדְּשָׁנוּ
בְּמִצְוֹתָיו וְצִוָּנוּ עַל אֲכִילַת מַצָּה:

*In some communities the matzah is dipped in salt, but
in most it is not.*

*The required amounts of matzah (see Required
Measurements and Amounts, page 21) are then eaten
by all of the participants, while reclining on the left
side, within the required period of time.*

205

Matzah

*He now releases the bottom matzah from his grip and
says the following berachah, with the intention that it
refer also to the matzah of the korech and afikoman
which will be eaten later on:*

BLESSED be You, Hashem our God, King of the universe, Who has sanctified us by His commandments and commanded us concerning the eating of matzah.

*In some communities the matzah is dipped in salt, but
in most it is not.*

*The required amounts of matzah (see Required
Measurements and Amounts, page 21) are then eaten
by all of the participants, while reclining on the left
side, within the required period of time.*

*The leader of the Seder then takes a kezayis of maror
(see Required Amounts and Measurements, page 22),
dips it briefly in charoses, and shakes off the excess
charoses. After putting aside one such kezayis for
himself, he proceeds to distribute similar portions to all
present. Everyone should have in mind that it is his
intention to fulfill the requirement of eating maror on
Pesach night. The leader, or each participant if he is
making his own berachos, then says the following
berachah with the intention that it refer also to the
maror of the korech which will be eaten later on:*

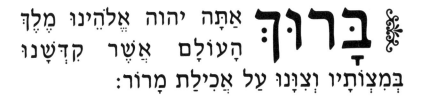

*All the assembled eat their portions of maror, not
reclining, within the required period of time.*

Maror

*The leader of the Seder then takes a kezayis of maror
(see Required Amounts and Measurements, page 22),
dips it briefly in charoses, and shakes off the excess
charoses. After putting aside one such kezayis for
himself, he proceeds to distribute similar portions to all
present. Everyone should have in mind that it is his
intention to fulfill the requirement of eating maror on
Pesach night. The leader, or each participant if he is
making his own berachos, then says the following
berachah with the intention that it refer also to the
maror of the korech which will be eaten later on:*

BLESSED be You, Hashem our God, King of the universe, Who has sanctified us by His commandments and commanded us concerning the eating of maror.

*All the assembled eat their portions of maror, not
reclining, within the required period of time.*

The leader of the Seder takes a kezayis of the third
unbroken matzah, places upon it a kezayis of maror,
dips it in the charoses (some shake off the charoses and
some do not), and distributes similar portions to the
other participants. Before eating the korech the
following is said:

זֵכֶר לְמִקְדָּשׁ כְּהִלֵּל. כֵּן עָשָׂה הִלֵּל בִּזְמַן שֶׁבֵּית
הַמִּקְדָּשׁ הָיָה קַיָּם. הָיָה כּוֹרֵךְ (פֶּסַח) מַצָּה וּמָרוֹר
וְאוֹכֵל בְּיַחַד. לְקַיֵּם מַה שֶּׁנֶּאֱמַר עַל־מַצּוֹת וּמְרֹרִים
יֹאכְלֻהוּ:

Everyone eats his portion, while reclining to the left,
within the required period of time.

209

Korech

*The leader of the Seder takes a kezayis of the third
unbroken matzah, places upon it a kezayis of maror,
dips it in the charoses (some shake off the charoses and
some do not), and distributes similar portions to the
other participants. Before eating the korech the
following is said:*

This is in remembrance of the Temple, according to
the custom of Hillel. Thus did Hillel at the time when
the Temple was standing: He would combine (the
Paschal lamb,) the matzah and the maror and eat
them together in order to fulfill what is written:
"...with unleavened bread and bitter herbs shall they
eat it" (*Bemidbar* 9:11).

*Everyone eats his portion, while reclining to the left,
within the required period of time.*

שֻׁלְחָן עוֹרֵךְ

*It is customary to eat eggs at the beginning of the meal
and not to eat roasted meat of any kind. Some do not
dip any food. Although one may not drink wine
between the first and second cups or between the third
and fourth, at the meal, between the second and the
third cups, one is permitted to do so provided that he is
cautious not to become drowsy as a result. One should
recline throughout the meal unless it is uncomfortable.
One may not eat so much that he has no appetite for
the afikoman.*

*One should be careful to finish the meal early enough
for the afikoman to be eaten before midnight. The
meal is not to be considered as a "break" in the Seder,
and, consequently, as a time for levity, lightheadedness
and idle talk. On the contrary, it is a part of the service
and should be treated with the proper dignity and in
the festive yom tov spirit. It is appropriate to discuss the
Exodus and to sing zemiros of thankfulness to Hashem
during this time.*

211

Shulchan Orech

*It is customary to eat eggs at the beginning of the meal
and not to eat roasted meat of any kind. Some do not
dip any food. Although one may not drink wine
between the first and second cups or between the third
and fourth, at the meal, between the second and the
third cups, one is permitted to do so provided that he is
cautious not to become drowsy as a result. One should
recline throughout the meal unless it is uncomfortable.
One may not eat so much that he has no appetite for
the afikoman.*

*One should be careful to finish the meal early enough
for the afikoman to be eaten before midnight. The
meal is not to be considered as a "break" in the Seder,
and, consequently, as a time for levity, lightheadedness
and idle talk. On the contrary, it is a part of the service
and should be treated with the proper dignity and in
the festive yom tov spirit. It is appropriate to discuss the
Exodus and to sing zemiros of thankfulness to Hashem
during this time.*

Some families are accustomed to studying at the Seder table a portion of the laws governing the eating of the Paschal lamb. Here is the order of these laws, as arranged by Rabbi Yaakov Emden, of blessed memory, to be recited as a memorial so as to fulfill verbally the commandment to eat of the Paschal lamb on this night.

אכילת בשר הפסח בליל חמשה עשר של חודש האביב מצות עשה מן התורה, שנאמר ואכלו את הבשר בלילה הזה צלי אש ומצות על מררים יאכלוהו.

מצוה מן המובחר לאכול בשר הפסח אכילת שובע, לפיכך אם הקריב שלמי חגיגה בארבעה עשר אוכל מהם תחילה, אחר כך אוכל בשר הפסח כדי לשבוע ממנו. ואם לא אכל אלא כזית יצא ידי חובתו, ושניהם אינם נאכלים אלא צלי אש.

וצריכים ברכה לכל אחד בפני עצמו. על הפסח אומר אשר קדשנו במצותיו וצונו לאכול הפסח, ועל החגיגה, לאכול הזבח.

הפסח טעון הלל באכילתו, ואמר רב משום רבי חייא כזיתא פסחא והלילא פקע איגרא.

Some families are accustomed to studying at the Seder table a portion of the laws governing the eating of the Paschal lamb. Here is the order of these laws, as arranged by Rabbi Yaakov Emden, of blessed memory, to be recited as a memorial so as to fulfill verbally the commandment to eat of the Paschal lamb on this night.

To eat the flesh of the Paschal lamb on the night of the fifteenth day of the month of spring [Nissan] is a positive Torah commandment, as it says: "And they shall eat the flesh in that night, roasted with fire; with unleavened bread and with bitter herbs shall they eat it" (*Shemos* 12:8)

The mitzvah is best performed by eating the flesh of the Paschal lamb until satiated; hence, if a Jew offered up Festival Peace Offerings on the fourteenth, he eats of them first and then finishes with the flesh of the Paschal lamb, thereby becoming satiated. If he ate no more of the Paschal lamb than an amount the size of an olive, he has nevertheless fulfilled his obligation, and both the festival offering and the Paschal lamb are eaten only roasted by fire.

A separate blessing is mandatory for each. On the Paschal lamb one recites "...and commanded us to eat the Pesach," while on the Festival Offering one says "...to eat the sacrifice."

A requirement for the eating of the Paschal lamb is the recitation of the Hallel. Rav said in the name of Rabbi Chiyah: "an amount the size of an olive of the Paschal lamb and the Hallel 'shattered the roof' " [so large were the groups of people who ate of the Pesach together].

אין צולין את הפסח על גבי כלי אבן או כלי מתכת ולא בשפוד של מתכת. כיצד צולין אותו? מביאין שפוד של רמון — תוחבו מתוך פיו עד בין נקובתו, ותוחב כרעיו ובני מעיו בשפוד למעלה מפיו של טלה, ותולהו לתוך התנור והאש למטה.

אין הפסח נאכל נא ומבושל, ואינו נאכל בשתי חבורות ואין מוציאין מחבורה לחבורה, ולא האוכל רשאי לאכול משני פסחים, שאין נמנים על שני פסחים כאחת.

ואינו נאכל אלא למנוייו (בשעת שחיטה) ישראל מהול טהור בן ברית. וכשם שמילת בניו ועבדיו מעכבתו מלשחוט הפסח כך מעכבתו מלאכול בו.

השובר עצם בפסח הטהור לוקה, ואפילו שלא בליל פסח. לפיכך שורפין עצמות הפסח בכלל הנותר מבשרו כדי שלא יבואו בהן לידי תקלה.

אין רשאין לאכול מגדי הרך אלא מה שנאכל בשור הגדול.

הפסח אינו נאכל אלא עד חצות הלילה הזה. בשר חגיגה שעלה עם הפסח על השולחן וכן כל התבשילין העולין עמו מתבערין עמו, ואינן נאכלין אלא עד חצות כפסח.

The Paschal lamb is not roasted upon stone or metal or with a metal spit. How was it roasted? A spit of pomegranate wood was brought and thrust through the mouth to the buttocks, its legs and innards were skewered on the spit above the mouth of the sheep and the sheep was suspended in an oven with the fire burning underneath.

The Paschal lamb is eaten neither half-cooked nor cooked with water, nor in two groups. It is not taken from one group to another, and one is not permitted to eat from two lambs, since one is not permitted to be listed for two lambs at the same time.

The Paschal lamb is eaten only by those who have applied to eat from it (at the time of slaughter), by Jews who are circumcised, ritually pure, and members of the covenant. Just as a person's uncircumcised sons and uncircumcised slaves disqualify him from slaughtering a Paschal lamb, so, too, they disqualify him from eating it.

Whoever breaks a bone of a ritually pure Paschal lamb is liable for lashes, even if it is not on the night of Pesach. Hence, the bones of the lamb are burned together with the remains of its flesh, so as to avoid committing any offense.

Only what is edible in a full-grown ox may be eaten of a tender lamb.

The Paschal lamb may be eaten only until midnight [of the fifteenth]. The remaining flesh of the Festival Offering that was set on the table together with the Paschal lamb, and the remainder of all cooked foods placed on the table as well, are all burned together with the remainder of the Paschal lamb. All are eaten only until midnight, like the Paschal lamb itself.

חלוק פסח מצרים מפסח דורות בג' דברים, שהוא היה מקחו מבעשור וטעון הגעת דם באגודת אזוב על המשקוף ושתי המזוזות ושנאכל בחפזון.

זו היא מצות אכילת הפסח, הרחמן יזכנו לאכלו בעיר מקדשנו במהרה בימינו, ויקיים בנו מקרא שכתוב כי לא בחפזון תצאו ובמנוסה לא תלכון כי הולך לפניכם ה' ומאספכם אלהי ישראל. כימי צאתנו מארץ מצרים יראנו נפלאות, ודבר אלהינו יקום לעולם ימינו רוממה עושה נוראות.

All the participants should eat the required amount of the afikoman while reclining to the left and within the required period of time, having in mind that it is their intention to fulfill their duty to eat the afikoman.

After the afikoman, it is forbidden to eat or drink anything except for the last two cups of wine, and water, tea, or the like.

The Paschal lamb in Egypt differed from that of all subsequent generations in three respects: the Pesach of Egypt had to be taken on the tenth day; its blood had to be splashed by means of a bunch of hyssop on the lintel and both door posts; and it had to be eaten in haste.

This is the mitzvah of eating the Paschal lamb. May the All Merciful grant us the merit to eat it in the city of our Temple speedily and in our days, and may the Biblical prediction be fulfilled through us: "For you shall not go out in haste, neither shall you go by flight, for Hashem goes before you, and the God of Israel will be your rear guard" (*Yeshayahu* 52:12). May He show us wonders as in the days when we went forth from Egypt, and may the word of our God endure forever. His right hand is exalted, doing awesome deeds.

Tzafun

At the end of the meal, preferably before midnight, everyone must eat a kezayis of the afikoman in remembrance of the Korban Pesach. It is preferable to eat a second kezayis in remembrance of the matzah which was eaten with it.

The pieces of afikoman are broken from the larger part of the broken middle matzah which was hidden away at the beginning of the Seder for this purpose. If it is lost or there is not enough for all of the participants, any shemurah matzah may be used.

It is customary to allow the children to "steal" the afikoman at the beginning of the Seder and to "buy" it back from them now to show how precious this mitzvah is to us. However, the bargaining should not take too long, so as not to delay the eating of the afikoman before midnight.

שִׁיר הַמַּעֲלוֹת בְּשׁוּב יהוה אֶת שִׁיבַת צִיּוֹן הָיִינוּ כְּחֹלְמִים: אָז יִמָּלֵא שְׂחוֹק פִּינוּ וּלְשׁוֹנֵנוּ רִנָּה אָז יֹאמְרוּ בַגּוֹיִם הִגְדִּיל יהוה לַעֲשׂוֹת עִם אֵלֶּה: הִגְדִּיל יהוה לַעֲשׂוֹת עִמָּנוּ הָיִינוּ שְׂמֵחִים: שׁוּבָה יהוה אֶת שְׁבִיתֵנוּ כַּאֲפִיקִים בַּנֶּגֶב: הַזֹּרְעִים בְּדִמְעָה בְּרִנָּה יִקְצֹרוּ: הָלוֹךְ יֵלֵךְ וּבָכֹה נֹשֵׂא מֶשֶׁךְ הַזָּרַע בֹּא־יָבֹא בְרִנָּה נֹשֵׂא אֲלֻמֹּתָיו:

The third cup is filled for birkas hamazon. If the cup is not clean, it must first be washed and rinsed. It is customary to wash the hands with mayim acharonim. Although a guest is usually honored with leading birkas hazimun, on Pesach night it is customary for the leader of the Seder to do so, although he may appoint another participant. One should have in mind that he is fulfilling the requirement of reciting birkas hamazon. The cup is held throughout birkas hamazon and one should not recline.

If there are at least three adult males eating together at the Seder, the assembled say the following (if there are at least ten adult males, the words in parentheses are added):

Barech

A Song of Ascents. When Hashem will turn once more to the return of Tzion, we will have been like those who dream. Then our mouth will fill with laughter and our tongue with exultation; then they will say among the nations: "Hashem has done great things with these." Hashem has done great things with us at all times; we have remained glad. Turn, Hashem, to our captivity once more, as the springs in the South. Those who sow in tears will reap in exultation. Though he who bears the measure of seed goes on his way weeping, he shall surely come home with exultation, bearing his sheaves (*Tehillim* 126).

The third cup is filled for birkas hamazon. If the cup is not clean, it must first be washed and rinsed. It is customary to wash the hands with mayim acharonim. Although a guest is usually honored with leading birkas hazimun, on Pesach night it is customary for the leader of the Seder to do so, although he may appoint another participant. One should have in mind that he is fulfilling the requirement of reciting birkas hamazon. The cup is held throughout birkas hamazon and one should not recline.

If there are at least three adult males eating together at the Seder, the assembled say the following (if there are at least ten adult males, the words in parentheses are added):

Leader: רַבּוֹתַי נְבָרֵךְ:

The others respond: יְהִי שֵׁם יהוה מְבֹרָךְ מֵעַתָּה וְעַד עוֹלָם:

The leader repeats the above verse and says: בִּרְשׁוּת מָרָנָן וְרַבָּנָן וְרַבּוֹתַי נְבָרֵךְ

(אֱלֹהֵינוּ) שֶׁאָכַלְנוּ מִשֶּׁלּוֹ:

The others respond: בָּרוּךְ (אֱלֹהֵינוּ) שֶׁאָכַלְנוּ מִשֶּׁלּוֹ וּבְטוּבוֹ חָיִינוּ:

The leader repeats the above verse and says:

בָּרוּךְ הוּא וּבָרוּךְ שְׁמוֹ:

בָּרוּךְ אַתָּה יהוה אֱלֹהֵינוּ מֶלֶךְ הָעוֹלָם הַזָּן אֶת הָעוֹלָם כֻּלּוֹ בְּטוּבוֹ בְּחֵן בְּחֶסֶד וּבְרַחֲמִים הוּא נוֹתֵן לֶחֶם לְכָל־בָּשָׂר כִּי לְעוֹלָם חַסְדּוֹ. וּבְטוּבוֹ הַגָּדוֹל תָּמִיד לֹא חָסַר לָנוּ וְאַל־יֶחְסַר לָנוּ מָזוֹן לְעוֹלָם וָעֶד. בַּעֲבוּר שְׁמוֹ הַגָּדוֹל כִּי הוּא אֵל זָן וּמְפַרְנֵס לַכֹּל וּמֵטִיב לַכֹּל וּמֵכִין מָזוֹן לְכָל־בְּרִיּוֹתָיו אֲשֶׁר בָּרָא. בָּרוּךְ אַתָּה יהוה הַזָּן אֶת־הַכֹּל:

221

Leader:

Gentlemen, we wish to say Grace.

The others respond:

Blessed be the Name of Hashem from this time forth and unto eternity.

The leader repeats the above verse and says:

With your permission, let us bless Him (our God) from Whose bounty we have eaten.

The others respond:

Blessed be Him (our God) from Whose bounty we have eaten, and through Whose goodness we live.

The leader repeats the above verse and says:
Blessed be He, and Blessed be His Name.

BLESSED be You, Hashem our God, King of the universe, Who nourishes the whole world with His goodness, with favor, lovingkindness and compassion. He gives food to all flesh because His lovingkindness endures forever. And through His great goodness we have never lacked nor shall we ever lack food, for His great Name's sake. For He is God Who feeds and sustains all beings, does good to all and prepares food for all His creatures which He has created. Blessed be You, Hashem, Who gives food to all.

נוֹדֶה לְךָ יהוה אֱלֹהֵינוּ עַל שֶׁהִנְחַלְתָּ
לַאֲבוֹתֵינוּ אֶרֶץ חֶמְדָּה טוֹבָה וּרְחָבָה. וְעַל
שֶׁהוֹצֵאתָנוּ יהוה אֱלֹהֵינוּ מֵאֶרֶץ מִצְרַיִם וּפְדִיתָנוּ
מִבֵּית עֲבָדִים וְעַל בְּרִיתְךָ שֶׁחָתַמְתָּ בִּבְשָׂרֵנוּ וְעַל
תּוֹרָתְךָ שֶׁלִּמַּדְתָּנוּ וְעַל חֻקֶּיךָ שֶׁהוֹדַעְתָּנוּ וְעַל חַיִּים
חֵן וָחֶסֶד שֶׁחוֹנַנְתָּנוּ וְעַל אֲכִילַת מָזוֹן שָׁאַתָּה זָן
וּמְפַרְנֵס אוֹתָנוּ תָּמִיד בְּכָל־יוֹם וּבְכָל עֵת וּבְכָל
שָׁעָה:

וְעַל הַכֹּל יהוה אֱלֹהֵינוּ אֲנַחְנוּ מוֹדִים לָךְ
וּמְבָרְכִים אוֹתָךְ יִתְבָּרַךְ שִׁמְךָ בְּפִי כָּל־חַי תָּמִיד
לְעוֹלָם וָעֶד. כַּכָּתוּב וְאָכַלְתָּ וְשָׂבָעְתָּ וּבֵרַכְתָּ אֶת־
יהוה אֱלֹהֶיךָ עַל־הָאָרֶץ הַטֹּבָה אֲשֶׁר נָתַן־לָךְ. בָּרוּךְ
אַתָּה יהוה עַל הָאָרֶץ וְעַל הַמָּזוֹן:

רַחֵם יהוה אֱלֹהֵינוּ עַל יִשְׂרָאֵל עַמֶּךְ וְעַל
יְרוּשָׁלַיִם עִירֶךְ וְעַל צִיּוֹן מִשְׁכַּן כְּבוֹדֶךְ וְעַל מַלְכוּת
בֵּית דָּוִד מְשִׁיחֶךְ וְעַל הַבַּיִת הַגָּדוֹל וְהַקָּדוֹשׁ שֶׁנִּקְרָא
שִׁמְךָ עָלָיו. אֱלֹהֵינוּ אָבִינוּ רְעֵנוּ זוּנֵנוּ פַּרְנְסֵנוּ

We thank You, Hashem our God, because You have given as a heritage to our fathers a desirable, good and spacious land; and because You brought us forth, Hashem our God, from the land of Egypt and delivered us from the house of bondage; as well as for Your covenant which You have sealed in our flesh; and for Your Torah which You have taught us; for Your statutes which You have made known to us; and for the life, favor, and lovingkindness which You have bestowed upon us; and for the food, for You feed and sustain us constantly every day, in every season, and at every hour.

For all this, Hashem our God, we thank You and bless You, Blessed be Your Name by the mouth of all living things constantly and forever, even as it is written: "When you have eaten and are satisfied, you shall bless Hashem your God for the good land which He has given you." Blessed be You, Hashem, for the land and for the food.

Have compassion, Hashem our God, on Yisrael Your People, and on Yerushalayim Your city, and on Tzion, the Abode of Your glory, and on the kingdom of the house of David, Your Anointed, and on the great and the holy House over which Your Name was proclaimed. Our God, our Father, tend

וְכַלְכְּלֵנוּ וְהַרְוִיחֵנוּ וְהַרְוַח־לָנוּ יהוה אֱלֹהֵינוּ מְהֵרָה מִכָּל צָרוֹתֵינוּ. וְנָא אַל־תַּצְרִיכֵנוּ יהוה אֱלֹהֵינוּ לֹא לִידֵי מַתְּנַת בָּשָׂר וָדָם וְלֹא לִידֵי הַלְוָאָתָם כִּי אִם לְיָדְךָ הַמְּלֵאָה הַפְּתוּחָה הַקְּדוֹשָׁה וְהָרְחָבָה שֶׁלֹּא נֵבוֹשׁ וְלֹא נִכָּלֵם לְעוֹלָם וָעֶד:

(On Shabbos add:)

רְצֵה וְהַחֲלִיצֵנוּ יהוה אֱלֹהֵינוּ בְּמִצְוֹתֶיךָ וּבְמִצְוַת יוֹם הַשְּׁבִיעִי הַשַּׁבָּת הַגָּדוֹל וְהַקָּדוֹשׁ הַזֶּה כִּי יוֹם זֶה גָּדוֹל וְקָדוֹשׁ הוּא לְפָנֶיךָ לִשְׁבָּת־בּוֹ וְלָנוּחַ בּוֹ בְּאַהֲבָה כְּמִצְוַת רְצוֹנֶךָ וּבִרְצוֹנְךָ הָנִיחַ לָנוּ יהוה אֱלֹהֵינוּ שֶׁלֹּא תְהֵא צָרָה וְיָגוֹן וַאֲנָחָה בְּיוֹם מְנוּחָתֵנוּ וְהַרְאֵנוּ יהוה אֱלֹהֵינוּ בְּנֶחָמַת צִיּוֹן עִירֶךָ וּבְבִנְיַן יְרוּשָׁלַיִם עִיר קָדְשֶׁךָ כִּי אַתָּה הוּא בַּעַל הַיְשׁוּעוֹת וּבַעַל הַנֶּחָמוֹת:

אֱלֹהֵינוּ וֵאלֹהֵי אֲבוֹתֵינוּ יַעֲלֶה וְיָבֹא וְיַגִּיעַ וְיֵרָאֶה וְיֵרָצֶה וְיִשָּׁמַע וְיִפָּקֵד וְיִזָּכֵר זִכְרוֹנֵנוּ וּפִקְדוֹנֵנוּ וְזִכְרוֹן אֲבוֹתֵינוּ וְזִכְרוֹן מָשִׁיחַ בֶּן דָּוִד עַבְדֶּךָ וְזִכְרוֹן יְרוּשָׁלַיִם עִיר קָדְשֶׁךָ וְזִכְרוֹן כָּל עַמְּךָ בֵּית יִשְׂרָאֵל

us, feed us, sustain us, and nourish us, and relieve us, and speedily grant us relief, Hashem our God, from all our troubles. And, Hashem our God, let us not be in need of the gifts of human hands, or of their loans, but only of Your hand, which is full, open, holy and generous, so that we may not be ashamed nor blush with shame forever and ever.

(On Shabbos add:)

> Be pleased, Hashem our God, and fortify us by Your commandments and by the commandment pertaining to the seventh day, this great and holy Shabbos, for this day is great and holy before You, that we may refrain thereon from every manner of work and rest upon it in love in accordance with the commandment of Your will. In Your favor, Hashem our God, grant us rest so that there be no distress, no grief or sighing on the day of our rest, and let us, Hashem our God, behold the consolation of Tzion, Your city, and the rebuilding of Yerushalayim, the city of Your Sanctuary, for You are the Master of all salvation and the Master of all consolation.

Our God and God of our fathers, may our remembrance and the consideration of us and the remembrance of our fathers, and the remembrance of Mashiach the son of David Your servant, and the remembrance of Yerushalayim, Your holy city, and the remembrance of all Your people, the House of

לְפָנֶיךָ לִפְלֵיטָה לְטוֹבָה לְחֵן וּלְחֶסֶד וּלְרַחֲמִים לְחַיִּים וּלְשָׁלוֹם בְּיוֹם חַג הַמַּצּוֹת הַזֶּה. זָכְרֵנוּ יהוה אֱלֹהֵינוּ בּוֹ לְטוֹבָה וּפָקְדֵנוּ בּוֹ לִבְרָכָה וְהוֹשִׁיעֵנוּ בּוֹ לְחַיִּים וּבִדְבַר יְשׁוּעָה וְרַחֲמִים חוּס וְחָנֵּנוּ וְרַחֵם עָלֵינוּ וְהוֹשִׁיעֵנוּ כִּי אֵלֶיךָ עֵינֵינוּ כִּי אֵל מֶלֶךְ חַנּוּן וְרַחוּם אָתָּה:

וּבְנֵה יְרוּשָׁלַיִם עִיר הַקֹּדֶשׁ בִּמְהֵרָה בְיָמֵינוּ. בָּרוּךְ אַתָּה יהוה בּוֹנֶה בְרַחֲמָיו יְרוּשָׁלַיִם אָמֵן:

בָּרוּךְ אַתָּה יהוה אֱלֹהֵינוּ מֶלֶךְ הָעוֹלָם הָאֵל אָבִינוּ מַלְכֵּנוּ אַדִּירֵנוּ בּוֹרְאֵנוּ גּוֹאֲלֵנוּ יוֹצְרֵנוּ קְדוֹשֵׁנוּ קְדוֹשׁ יַעֲקֹב רוֹעֵנוּ רוֹעֵה יִשְׂרָאֵל הַמֶּלֶךְ הַטּוֹב וְהַמֵּטִיב לַכֹּל שֶׁבְּכָל יוֹם וָיוֹם הוּא הֵטִיב הוּא מֵטִיב הוּא יֵיטִיב לָנוּ. הוּא גְמָלָנוּ הוּא גוֹמְלֵנוּ הוּא יִגְמְלֵנוּ לָעַד לְחֵן וּלְחֶסֶד וּלְרַחֲמִים וּלְרֶוַח הַצָּלָה

Yisrael, rise and come, reach You and be seen, be accepted and heard, considered and remembered for deliverance and for well-being, for favor and lovingkindness, for compassion, for life and for peace on this day of the Festival of Unleavened Bread. Remember this day, Hashem our God, for good, be mindful of us for blessing, and save us for life; and in the promise of salvation and compassion, spare us and favor us, and be compassionate with us and save us, for our eyes look up to You; for You, o' God, are a gracious and compassionate King.

And rebuild Yerushalayim, the city of holiness, speedily in our days. Blessed be You, Hashem, Who in His compassion rebuilds Yerushalayim, Amen.

Blessed be You, Hashem our God, King of the universe, o' God, our Father, our King, our Mighty One, our Creator, our Redeemer, our Maker, our Holy One, the Holy One of Yaakov, our Shepherd, the Shepherd of Yisrael, o' King, Who is kind and Who does good to all! He alone has done good to us day after day; it is He alone Who does good; and it is He alone Who will do good to us in the future. He dealt kindly with us, He deals kindly with us, and He will deal kindly with us, for favor, and for lov-ingkindness and compassion, and for relief, rescue and

וְהַצְלָחָה בְּרָכָה וִישׁוּעָה נֶחָמָה פַּרְנָסָה וְכַלְכָּלָה
וְרַחֲמִים וְחַיִּים וְשָׁלוֹם וְכָל טוֹב וּמִכָּל טוּב לְעוֹלָם
אַל יְחַסְּרֵנוּ:

הָרַחֲמָן הוּא יִמְלוֹךְ עָלֵינוּ לְעוֹלָם וָעֶד. הָרַחֲמָן
הוּא יִתְבָּרַךְ בַּשָּׁמַיִם וּבָאָרֶץ. הָרַחֲמָן הוּא יִשְׁתַּבַּח
לְדוֹר דּוֹרִים וְיִתְפָּאַר בָּנוּ לָעַד וּלְנֵצַח נְצָחִים
וְיִתְהַדַּר בָּנוּ לָעַד וּלְעוֹלְמֵי עוֹלָמִים. הָרַחֲמָן הוּא
יְפַרְנְסֵנוּ בְּכָבוֹד. הָרַחֲמָן הוּא יִשְׁבּוֹר עֻלֵּנוּ מֵעַל
צַוָּארֵנוּ וְהוּא יוֹלִיכֵנוּ קוֹמְמִיּוּת לְאַרְצֵנוּ. הָרַחֲמָן
הוּא יִשְׁלַח לָנוּ בְּרָכָה מְרֻבָּה בַּבַּיִת הַזֶּה וְעַל שֻׁלְחָן
זֶה שֶׁאָכַלְנוּ עָלָיו. הָרַחֲמָן הוּא יִשְׁלַח לָנוּ אֶת אֵלִיָּהוּ
הַנָּבִיא זָכוּר לַטּוֹב וִיבַשֶּׂר לָנוּ בְּשׂוֹרוֹת טוֹבוֹת
יְשׁוּעוֹת וְנֶחָמוֹת.

הָרַחֲמָן הוּא יְבָרֵךְ (אֶת [אָבִי מוֹרִי] בַּעַל הַבַּיִת
הַזֶּה וְאֶת [אִמִּי מוֹרָתִי] בַּעֲלַת הַבַּיִת הַזֶּה). אוֹתִי
(וְאֶת אִשְׁתִּי / בַּעְלִי וְאֶת זַרְעִי) וְאֶת כָּל אֲשֶׁר לִי
וְאֶת כָּל הַמְסֻבִּין כָּאן. אוֹתָם וְאֶת בֵּיתָם וְאֶת
זַרְעָם וְאֶת כָּל אֲשֶׁר לָהֶם אוֹתָנוּ וְאֶת כָּל אֲשֶׁר לָנוּ

success, for blessing and salvation, for consolation, sustenance and nourishment, and for compassion, and for life, and for peace and all good. And with all the good may He never cause us to become wanting.

May the Compassionate One reign over us to all eternity. May the Compassionate One be blessed in heaven and on earth. May the Compassionate One be praised from generation to generation, glorified through us for all eternity, and garbed in majesty through us for everlasting. May the Compassionate One grant us an honorable livelihood. May the Compassionate One break our yoke from off our neck and lead us upright to our land. May the Compassionate One send abundant blessing into this house, and upon this table at which we have eaten. May the Compassionate One send us Eliyahu the Prophet, may he be remembered for good, to bring us good news of salvation and consolation.

May the Compassionate One bless ([my father, my teacher] the master of this house, and [my mother, my teacher] the mistress of this house) me, (my wife/husband and children) and all that is mine, and all that sit here, both them, their household, their children and all that belongs to them, also us and all that

כְּמוֹ שֶׁנִּתְבָּרְכוּ אֲבוֹתֵינוּ אַבְרָהָם יִצְחָק וְיַעֲקֹב בַּכֹּל מִכֹּל כֹּל כֵּן יְבָרֵךְ אוֹתָנוּ כֻּלָּנוּ יַחַד בִּבְרָכָה שְׁלֵמָה וְנֹאמַר אָמֵן:

בַּמָּרוֹם יְלַמְּדוּ עֲלֵיהֶם וְעָלֵינוּ זְכוּת שֶׁתְּהֵא לְמִשְׁמֶרֶת שָׁלוֹם. וְנִשָּׂא בְרָכָה מֵאֵת יהוה וּצְדָקָה מֵאֱלֹהֵי יִשְׁעֵנוּ וְנִמְצָא חֵן וְשֵׂכֶל טוֹב בְּעֵינֵי אֱלֹהִים וְאָדָם:

On Shabbos add:
הָרַחֲמָן הוּא יַנְחִילֵנוּ יוֹם שֶׁכֻּלּוֹ שַׁבָּת וּמְנוּחָה לְחַיֵּי הָעוֹלָמִים:

הָרַחֲמָן הוּא יַנְחִילֵנוּ יוֹם שֶׁכֻּלּוֹ טוֹב. יוֹם שֶׁכֻּלּוֹ אָרוּךְ. יוֹם שֶׁהַצַּדִּיקִים יוֹשְׁבִים וְעַטְרוֹתֵיהֶם בְּרָאשֵׁיהֶם וְנֶהֱנִים מִזִּיו הַשְּׁכִינָה וְיִהְיֶה חֶלְקֵנוּ עִמָּהֶם:

הָרַחֲמָן הוּא יְזַכֵּנוּ לִימוֹת הַמָּשִׁיחַ וּלְחַיֵּי הָעוֹלָם הַבָּא. מִגְדּוֹל יְשׁוּעוֹת מַלְכּוֹ וְעוֹשֶׂה חֶסֶד לִמְשִׁיחוֹ לְדָוִד וּלְזַרְעוֹ עַד עוֹלָם. עֹשֶׂה שָׁלוֹם בִּמְרוֹמָיו הוּא יַעֲשֶׂה שָׁלוֹם עָלֵינוּ וְעַל כָּל יִשְׂרָאֵל וְאִמְרוּ אָמֵן:

is ours, even as our fathers, Avraham, Yitzchak, and Yaakov were blessed in everything, from everything and with everything, so may He bless all of us together with a perfect blessing and let us say, Amen.

May their and our merits be pleaded on High so that it may contribute to enduring peace, and that we may receive a blessing from Hashem and kindness from the God of our salvation, and obtain worthiness of favor and understanding of the good in the sight of God and man.

On Shabbos add:

May the Compassionate One let us inherit that day which shall be all Shabbos and rest for life everlasting.

May the Compassionate One let us inherit that day which is altogether good. That everlasting day, the day when the righteous sit with crowns upon their heads, enjoying the radiance of the Divine Presence — and may our portion be among them.

May the Compassionate One make us worthy of reaching the days of the Mashiach and life everlasting; He Who is a tower of salvation to His King and shows lovingkindness to His Anointed, to David and his descendants forever. May He Who makes peace

יְראוּ אֶת יהוה קְדֹשָׁיו כִּי אֵין מַחְסוֹר לִירֵאָיו. כְּפִירִים רָשׁוּ וְרָעֵבוּ וְדֹרְשֵׁי יהוה לֹא יַחְסְרוּ כָל טוֹב. הוֹדוּ לַיהוה כִּי טוֹב כִּי לְעוֹלָם חַסְדּוֹ. פּוֹתֵחַ אֶת יָדֶךָ וּמַשְׂבִּיעַ לְכָל חַי רָצוֹן. בָּרוּךְ הַגֶּבֶר אֲשֶׁר יִבְטַח בַּיהוה וְהָיָה יהוה מִבְטַחוֹ. נַעַר הָיִיתִי גַּם זָקַנְתִּי וְלֹא רָאִיתִי צַדִּיק נֶעֱזָב וְזַרְעוֹ מְבַקֶּשׁ לָחֶם. יהוה עֹז לְעַמּוֹ יִתֵּן יהוה יְבָרֵךְ אֶת עַמּוֹ בַשָּׁלוֹם:

One should have in mind that it his intention to fulfill the requirement of drinking the third of the four cups of wine.

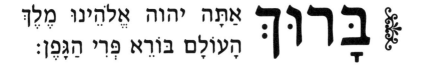

בָּרוּךְ אַתָּה יהוה אֱלֹהֵינוּ מֶלֶךְ הָעוֹלָם בּוֹרֵא פְּרִי הַגָּפֶן:

The required amount of the third cup is drunk, within the required period of time, while reclining to the left.

in His High places, make peace for us and for all of Yisrael, and let us say, Amen.

O' fear Hashem, you who are sanctified to Him, for there is no want for them that fear Him. Young lions have become poor and suffered hunger, but they who seek Hashem shall never want for any good thing. Give thanks to Hashem for He is good, for His lovingkindness endures forever. You open Your hand and satisfy the desire of every living thing. Blessed is the man who trusts in Hashem, and to whom Hashem is also the source of His trust. I was young and I have grown old, but I have never seen a righteous man forsaken whose progeny was forced to beg for bread. May Hashem grant to His people the power to be victorious over all; may Hashem bless His people with peace.

One should have in mind that it his intention to fulfill the requirement of drinking the third of the four cups of wine.

BLESSED be You, Hashem our God, King of the universe, Who creates the fruit of the vine.

The required amount of the third cup is drunk, within the required period of time, while reclining to the left.

הַלֵּל

A special cup for Eliyahu Hanavi is now poured and the door is opened to indicate that it is leil shimurim, "a night which enjoys the protection of Hashem." In some homes, the fourth cup for everyone is poured now, too, but some wait until before the recitation of Hallel. Some follow the custom of standing when they open the door.

שְׁפֹךְ חֲמָתְךָ אֶל הַגּוֹיִם אֲשֶׁר לֹא יְדָעוּךָ וְעַל מַמְלָכוֹת אֲשֶׁר בְּשִׁמְךָ לֹא קָרָאוּ: כִּי אָכַל אֶת יַעֲקֹב וְאֶת נָוֵהוּ הֵשַׁמּוּ: שְׁפָךְ עֲלֵיהֶם זַעְמֶךָ וַחֲרוֹן אַפְּךָ יַשִּׂיגֵם: תִּרְדֹּף בְּאַף וְתַשְׁמִידֵם מִתַּחַת שְׁמֵי יהוה:

שפוך חמתך — **Pour out Your wrath**[76]

אשר לא ידעוך *Pour out your wrath toward the nations that do not know you and on the kingdoms that have not proclaimed your name.* The king of the Egyptians said, *I do not know Hashem* (Shemos 5:2). We ask God to display His might and

---

76. The author includes the commentary by the *Abarbanel* from here until הודו לה׳ כי טוב. We have included the Abarbanel's commentary on the passage of שפוך חמתך, because it explains the role of this paragraph in the structure of the Haggadah. (Eds.)

Hallel

*A special cup for Eliyahu Hanavi is now poured and the
door is opened to indicate that it is leil shimurim, "a
night which enjoys the protection of Hashem." In some
homes, the fourth cup for everyone is poured now, too,
but some wait until before the recitation of Hallel. Some
follow the custom of standing when they open the door.*

Pour out Your wrath toward the nations that do not
know You and on the kingdoms that have not proclaimed Your Name. For he has devoured Yaakov, and
they have laid waste his habitation (*Tehillim* 79:6-7).
Pour out Your perceptible wrath over them, and let
the fire of Your anger overtake them (*ibid.* 69:25).
Pursue them with anger and destroy them from under
the Heavens of Hashem (*Eychah* 3:66).

crush the oppressors of Israel who *do not know You,* just as
He did to Pharaoh and the Egyptians who did not know Him.
כי אכל את יעקב ואת נוהו השמו *For he has devoured Yaakov,
and they have laid waste his habitation.* The nations that

שפוך חמתך אל הגוים *Pour out your wrath toward the nations.* These two
verses come from Tehillim 79:6-7 and also appear, with minor variations, in
Yirmiyahu 10:25. They were included in the Haggadah at this point as an
introduction to the next part of Hallel, לא לנו. In לא לנו the Psalmist beseeches
God to redeem us from our present and future oppressors just as He saved
us from the Egyptians. We introduce לא לנו with these verses of supplication
that God defeat the enemies of His people.

oppress us now have committed even greater atrocities against Your people than did the Egyptians, for *they have laid waste his habitation* — they destroyed both the first and second Holy Temples.

Introduction to Hallel[77]

The Talmud records a dispute over who authored these paragraphs of Tehillim which comprise Hallel:

Who said this Hallel? Rabbi Eliezer says that Moshe and Israel said it when they stood at the Sea.... Rabbi Yehudah says that Yehoshua and Israel said it when the kings of Canaan rose up against them.... Rabbi Elazar HaModai says that Devorah and Barak said it when Sisera rose up against them.... Rabbi Elazar ben Azaryah says that Chizkiya and his company said it when Sancheriv rose up against them.... Rabbi Akiva says that Channanya, Mishael, and Azaryah said it when the wicked Nebuchadnezzar rose up against them.... Rabbi Yosi the Galilean says that Mordechai and Esther said it when the wicked Haman rose up against them.... And the Sages say that the Prophets among the people established them for Israel to say at different times and when in distress... and when they will be redeemed, to say it upon their redemption (*Pesachim 117a*).

The *Malbim*, in his commentary, follows the opinion of Rabbi Elazar ben Azaryah that King Chizkiya authored these Psalms. He interprets parts of the Psalms to refer to Chizkiya's

---

77. This is an introduction to the *Malbim's* commentary on the chapters of Tehillim which follow. (Eds.)

illness, the attempted coup of Shevna, the defeat of Sancheriv, and the king's walk to the Holy Temple. He points out in his introduction to these Psalms that the events described herein, such as the illness, the recovery, and the salvation from the enemy, could also refer to events in the life of David, and, therefore, it is likely that David also said these verses.

The *Malbim*, in his introduction to Tehillim, addresses the apparent contradiction concerning the authorship of the Book of Tehillim. In one place the Talmud tells us,

> David wrote the Book of Tehillim by way of ten elders: Adam, Malchi-Tzedek, Avraham, Moshe, Heimon, Yedoson, Asaf, and the three sons of Korach. (*Bava Basra 14b*)

Rashi explains that when David wrote Tehillim, he included Psalms which had been said by those who lived before him, as well as by those who lived during his time. *Rashi* gives examples of Psalms which had been composed by the other great individuals, but which were only committed to writing by David. Most of Tehillim was composed by David himself.

This however, contradicts the Talmud in Pesachim, which tells us that others — who lived even after the time of David — wrote the part of Tehillim which we call Hallel.

The *Malbim* first answers it is not inconceivable that David did not write all of Tehillim. Just as the Talmud in *Bava Basra* states that some of the Psalms which David wrote were actually composed by earlier individuals, some Psalms could have been added by later individuals, as long as the era of prophecy had not yet ended. The *Malbim* says that this is the simple and obvious answer "which I have explained in order to shut the

The door is closed (and everyone is seated if they stood), and those who have not already done so pour the fourth cup. Although Hallel is usually said standing, on Pesach night we recite it while seated. However, one should not do so in a reclining position but, rather, sit respectfully, as if in the presence of a king. Some are accustomed to hold the cups in their hands throughout the recitation of Hallel and some do not. One should have in mind that it is his intention to fulfill the requirement of reciting Hallel on Pesach night.

לֹא לָנוּ יהוה לֹא לָנוּ כִּי לְשִׁמְךָ תֵּן כָּבוֹד עַל חַסְדְּךָ עַל אֲמִתֶּךָ: לָמָה יֹאמְרוּ הַגּוֹיִם אַיֵּה נָא אֱלֹהֵיהֶם: וֵאלֹהֵינוּ

mouths of the instigators and provocateurs... the group of interpreters whose only aim is to degrade the honor of the holy writings." He gives a second answer for "us, whose *emunah*, faith, is whole," and says that the Psalms were originally said by David (or by the ten individuals before David, as mentioned in *Bava Basra*) with the spirit of prophecy, but were only openly articulated when the events which they describe actually occurred. However, the *Malbim* reiterates, the first answer is sufficient for understanding the simple meaning of the verses of Psalms.

239

The door is closed (and everyone is seated if they stood), and those who have not already done so pour the fourth cup. Although Hallel is usually said standing, on Pesach night we recite it while seated. However, one should not do so in a reclining position but, rather, sit respectfully, as if in the presence of a king. Some are accustomed to hold the cups in their hands throughout the recitation of Hallel and some do not. One should have in mind that it is his intention to fulfill the requirement of reciting Hallel on Pesach night.

☙**NOT** to us, Hashem, not to us, but to Your own Name give honor, for the sake of Your lovingkindness, for the sake of Your truth. Wherefore shall the nations say: "Where now is their

לא לנו — **Not to us**

לא לנו *Not to us, Hashem, not to us* (Tehillim 115:1). In the first part of Hallel we read that when God took our fathers out of Egypt they became *His sphere of dominion* (Tehillim 114:2). This means that He dominated the forces of nature for the sake of Israel. At the time of the Exodus, the miracles and wonders which God wrought were for the sake of His nation. Now, however, when we pray for the future redemption, we recognize that we are not on the lofty level of holiness that our fathers were at the time of the Exodus, and, accordingly, we ask God to redeem us *not to us* — not for our sake, but — *to*

בַּשָּׁמַיִם כֹּל אֲשֶׁר חָפֵץ עָשָׂה: עֲצַבֵּיהֶם כֶּסֶף
וְזָהָב מַעֲשֵׂה יְדֵי אָדָם: פֶּה לָהֶם וְלֹא יְדַבֵּרוּ
עֵינַיִם לָהֶם וְלֹא יִרְאוּ: אָזְנַיִם לָהֶם וְלֹא יִשְׁמָעוּ
אַף לָהֶם וְלֹא יְרִיחוּן: יְדֵיהֶם וְלֹא יְמִישׁוּן
רַגְלֵיהֶם וְלֹא יְהַלֵּכוּ לֹא יֶהְגּוּ בִּגְרוֹנָם: כְּמוֹהֶם

Your own name give honor. At the time of the future redemption of the Jewish people, God will openly demonstrate His
omnipotence to the nations of the world, nations which will
then give honor and praise to God's name. If God does not
redeem us, though, a terrible *Chilul Hashem* will occur; the
nations will claim that the redemption of His people is beyond
His power and they will scorn His name.

We ask God to bring the redemption either *for the sake of
your lovingkindness* — out of pure lovingkindness, even if we
have no merit and You have not promised to redeem us, or
for the sake of Your truth — to remain faithful to Your word
when You promised us that You would always be our God
and our Redeemer.

למה יאמרו הגוים *Wherefore shall the nations say: "Where
now is their God?"* Since You revealed yourself when You
brought us forth from Egypt, the nations know that You are
the God of Israel and that You do miracles for them. But when

241

God?" But our God is in the Heavens; everything is as He has willed to bring it about. Their idols of silver and gold are the work of human hands; they have a mouth, but they do not speak; they have eyes, but they do not see; they have ears, but they do not hear; they have a nose, but they do not smell; [they have] their hands, but they cannot touch with them; [they have] their feet, but they do not walk; they can utter no sound with their throat. They who

they see Israel lingering in exile, they will say that You have lost Your power. They will desecrate Your holy name.

But we remain aware of the truth. *But our God* even though He *is in the Heavens*, nevertheless *everything is as He has willed to bring it about* — He directs, controls, and supervises everything in the universe as He wills. *Their idols*, on the other hand, although they do not abide in the heavens and are physically quite close to their worshippers who can look directly at them, are still useless to them. Their idols are merely *of silver and gold*, of metals which are inferior even to trees, which at least are living organisms. Not only are their idols inferior beause of their material, but also because of their makers, for they *are the work of human hands*. Furthermore, they do not even have the abilities of humans — *they have a mouth, but do not speak*. They also have no faculties of sensation — *they have eyes, but they do not see; they have ears, but they do not hear; they have a nose, but they do not smell;*

יִהְיוּ עֹשֵׂיהֶם כֹּל אֲשֶׁר בֹּטֵחַ בָּהֶם: יִשְׂרָאֵל
בְּטַח בַּיהוה עֶזְרָם וּמָגִנָּם הוּא: בֵּית אַהֲרֹן
בִּטְחוּ בַיהוה עֶזְרָם וּמָגִנָּם הוּא: יִרְאֵי יהוה
בִּטְחוּ בַיהוה עֶזְרָם וּמָגִנָּם הוּא:

[they have] their hands, but they cannot touch with them. They
may have all the external instruments of human senses, but
are still lifeless. They also have *their feet, but they do not walk.*
They cannot even utter a weak, inward sound, or think an
effortless thought (the medium between silence and speech)
— *they can utter no sound with their throat.* They fail to fulfill
the purpose for which they were created. *They who make them
shall become like them.*

But we, *O' Israel, trust in Hashem,* even though His abode
may be in the heavens, we nevertheless trust in Him. *He is their
help* to save us from trouble, *and their shield* to subdue our
enemies. And according to the degree of one's trust in God, so
God helps him. *O' house of Aharon,* whose trust in God is greater
than that of the rest of Israel's, *He is their help and their shield* to
a greater degree than He is to the house of Israel. So, too, those
who fear Hashem, whose trust is on an even higher level, will
merit even more specific Divine assistance.

ה׳ זכרנו יברך *Hashem, Who has been mindful of us* because
we trust in Him, *He will bless* us anew, and the magnitude of
His blessing will be directly proportional to the level of our

make them shall become like them; indeed, everyone who trusts in them. O' Yisrael, trust in Hashem;
He is their help and their shield. O' house of Aharon,
trust in Hashem; He is their help and their shield.
O' you who fear Hashem, trust in Hashem; He is
their help and their shield (*Tehillim* 115:1-11).

trust in Him, so that *He will bless the House of Israel* according
to their level of trust, *He will bless the House of Aharon*
according to their higher level of trust, and *He will bless those who
fear Hashem* according to their even higher level of trust in Him.
Furthermore, He will bless *the small together with the great*, for
when God bestows His generous blessing upon the great, the
small also benefit from it. Thus, when God bestows His blessing
upon *those who fear Him*, all of Israel benefits from it.

If the small benefit from the blessing meant for the great,
what distinguishes the great from the small? God, therefore,
will give you increase, He will add more and more to the
blessing that the great individuals deserve in order to distin-
guish them from the small. But still, the small ones receive
benefit from the added blessing which the great ones receive!
The added blessing directed towards the great actually go both
to you and to your children, to you, the great, righteous ones,
and to your children, the small, less righteous ones. Therefore
God must constantly increase the blessing to the great, and the
result is an endless cycle of increased blessing.

In addition to the blessing we merit when God recalls our

יהוה זְכָרָנוּ יְבָרֵךְ יְבָרֵךְ אֶת בֵּית יִשְׂרָאֵל יְבָרֵךְ
אֶת בֵּית אַהֲרֹן: יְבָרֵךְ יִרְאֵי יהוה הַקְּטַנִּים עִם
הַגְּדֹלִים: יֹסֵף יהוה עֲלֵיכֶם עֲלֵיכֶם וְעַל בְּנֵיכֶם:

trust in Him, *Blessed are you for Hashem, Who makes the heaven and earth* — we are in constant receipt of the blessing with which He has always blessed us. We acknowledge that God is the Maker of heaven and earth, unlike the nations of the world — whom the Psalmist mentioned above — who believe that the heaven and earth always existed and are not at all managed by God. We, on the other hand, know that God is the Maker of heaven and earth. We say that He *makes* the heaven and earth, and not that he *made* them, because He is constantly renewing the work of Creation. He is in complete control of every facet of the heaven's and earth's existence. He causes the skies to act in accordance with the natural laws He established at Creation, while he directs the earth to operate in accordance with the level of virtue of the deeds of its inhabitants. Thus, *the heavens are the heavens of Hashem*, since their activity does not depend on the deeds of man, *but He has given the earth to the children of men*, since the productivity of the earth depends upon the virtue of man's deeds. This is what the Psalmist meant when he wrote in the preceding paragraph, *everything is as He has willed to bring it about* — He directs, controls, and supervises everything — including

Hashem, Who has been mindful of us, He will bless. He will bless the House of Yisrael; He will bless the House of Aharon; He will bless those who fear Hashem, the small together with the great; Hashem will give you increase, to you and to your children.

the heavens and the earth — as He wills.

The Psalmist proceeds to recount a personal experience, telling how he became hopelessly ill, but how — through sincere prayer — he aroused God's mercy Who returned him to his health. He introduces his experience and says, *It is not the dead that proclaim God's might, and not all those who go down into silence;* God created man in order to serve Him and acknowledge Him, and man cannot fulfill this purpose after he dies. *But as for us, we will bless the mighty God from this time forth and forever,* we not only praise Him, but we bless Him.

How do we bless God? What can we possibly add to His infinite greatness?

To "bless" God is to give Him reason to bless us. We give Him reason to bless us by doing His will and abiding by His word. Thus, when our deeds are meritorious, we "cause" God to bless us. And by giving God reason to bless us, we have "blessed" God.

God, therefore, does not desire the death of His righteous servants, but that they should live and bless Him and sing praise to Him. With that introduction, the Psalmist continues.

אהבתי *I loved* (Tehillim 116). Even when I was not in

בְּרוּכִים אַתֶּם לַיהוה עֹשֵׂה שָׁמַיִם וָאָרֶץ: הַשָּׁמַיִם
שָׁמַיִם לַיהוה וְהָאָרֶץ נָתַן לִבְנֵי אָדָם: לֹא הַמֵּתִים
יְהַלְלוּ־יָהּ וְלֹא כָּל יֹרְדֵי דוּמָה: וַאֲנַחְנוּ נְבָרֵךְ יָהּ
מֵעַתָּה וְעַד עוֹלָם הַלְלוּיָהּ:

אָהַבְתִּי כִּי יִשְׁמַע יהוה אֶת קוֹלִי תַּחֲנוּנָי: כִּי
הִטָּה אָזְנוֹ לִי וּבְיָמַי אֶקְרָא: אֲפָפוּנִי חֶבְלֵי מָוֶת
וּמְצָרֵי שְׁאוֹל מְצָאוּנִי צָרָה וְיָגוֹן אֶמְצָא: וּבְשֵׁם יהוה

distress, I loved my supplications, because *Hashem will hear*.
I love to supplicate and pray unto God, because He always
answers my prayers. Moreover, He not only answers when I
call out, but *He has inclined His ear to me*, like a father who
turns his ear towards his beloved son hoping to hear his voice,
for the sound of his voice is sweet to him and he desires to
listen to his son's requests.

I will, therefore, call out to God not only in times of distress,
but *I will call [upon Him] in my days*, days of security and
well-being[78]. How much more so when I am in need, when
the pains of death oppressed me, and even more so *when the straits*

---

78. The word "days", with no modifier, refers to good days.

Blessed are you for Hashem, Who makes heaven and earth. The heavens are the heavens of Hashem, but He has given the earth to the children of men. It is not the dead that proclaim God's might, and not all those who go down into silence. But as for us, we will bless the mighty God from this time forth and forever. Halleluyah! (*ibid.* 12-18).

I loved my supplications because Hashem will always hear my voice. For He has inclined His ear to me in the past, and I will call [upon Him] in my days. [When] the pains of death oppressed me, when the straits of the grave gained hold of me, when I faced trouble and sorrow, [when] I call upon the

of the grave gained hold of me (the straits of the grave come after death), and *when I faced trouble and sorrow,* I certainly *call upon the Name of Hashem* and implore, *"I beseech You, o' Hashem, deliver my soul"* from the agony of eternal punishment.

Hashem listens to my prayer, and *then Hashem deals graciously with me,* for He gives gratuitously even when the recipient is undeserving, *and is just* to reward the righteous according to his righteous deeds, *and our God takes pity* on the destitute and oppressed. These are three levels of God's kindness: He always answers one's prayers because He is (1) gracious and (2) just. In addition, when one is in distress He answers out of (3) compassion.

אֶקְרָא אָנָּא יהוה מַלְּטָה נַפְשִׁי: חַנּוּן יהוה וְצַדִּיק
וֵאלֹהֵינוּ מְרַחֵם: שֹׁמֵר פְּתָאים יהוה דַּלּוֹתִי וְלִי
יְהוֹשִׁיעַ: שׁוּבִי נַפְשִׁי לִמְנוּחָיְכִי כִּי יהוה גָּמַל עָלָיְכִי:
כִּי חִלַּצְתָּ נַפְשִׁי מִמָּוֶת אֶת עֵינִי מִן דִּמְעָה אֶת רַגְלִי
מִדֶּחִי: אֶתְהַלֵּךְ לִפְנֵי יהוה בְּאַרְצוֹת הַחַיִּים:
הֶאֱמַנְתִּי כִּי אֲדַבֵּר אֲנִי עָנִיתִי מְאֹד: אֲנִי אָמַרְתִּי
בְחָפְזִי כָּל הָאָדָם כֹּזֵב:

שומר פתאים ה׳ *Hashem protects the unaware; I had been brought low* — I was *unaware* of my sins and the need to repent. God, however, protects the unaware — He brought illness upon me in order to protect me from sinning and to rouse me to repent. By lowering me through illness, *He grants me salvation*, physical salvation and spiritual salvation. Therefore, *return, o' my soul, to your resting places*, do not be upset that you are sick, *for it is Hashem Who has dealt kindly with you* — your suffering has been granted to you as a גמול, a present from Hashem for your own welfare, either according to your deeds, or according to the love which He has for you and His personal concern for you.

The Psalmist turns to address God and says, *But when You*

Name of Hashem: "I beseech You, o' Hashem, deliver my soul." Then Hashem deals graciously [with me] and is just, and our God takes pity. Hashem protects the unaware; I had been brought low, but He grants me salvation. Return, o' my soul, to your resting places, for it is Hashem Who has dealt kindly with you. But when You delivered my soul from death, my eye from tears and my foot from stumbling. Then I shall walk on before Hashem in the lands of the living. I am convinced when I say that I was greatly afflicted when I said in my haste: "All mankind is deluded" (*ibid.* 116:1-11).

delivered my soul from death even though my death had been divinely decreed, and when You delivered *my eye from tears* when I cried before You from my suffering[79], You thereby saved *my foot from stumbling* away from the path of goodness and righteousness. For now *I shall walk on before Hashem in the lands of the living*, for as long as I live I will walk always before Hashem as the righteous ones do, as God said to Avraham, "Walk before me and be perfect" (Bereishis 17:1), and I will not stumble in sin.

האמנתי כי אדבר *I am convinced when I say that I was greatly afflicted when I said in my haste, "All mankind is deluded".* I firmly assert that I was greatly afflicted when I said that all

---

79. Cf. Melachim II 20:3, *And Chizkiya wept a great weeping.*

מָה אָשִׁיב לַיהוה כָּל תַּגְמוּלֹהִי עָלָי: כּוֹס
יְשׁוּעוֹת אֶשָּׂא וּבְשֵׁם יהוה אֶקְרָא: נְדָרַי לַיהוה
אֲשַׁלֵּם נֶגְדָה נָּא לְכָל־עַמּוֹ: יָקָר בְּעֵינֵי יהוה הַמָּוְתָה
לַחֲסִידָיו: אָנָּא יהוה כִּי אֲנִי עַבְדֶּךָ אֲנִי עַבְדְּךָ בֶּן

mankind is deluded. At that moment of despair, I said it in haste without calmness of mind, that all mankind is deluded, that the existence of man is purposeless, all that he does is futile, he walks in vanity all the days of his life and in his death his name is covered in darkness. Such is what I said in haste without contemplation. And now I assert that I said it at a time when I *was greatly afflicted*; I was downtrodden and plunging into hopelessness. Now I recognize that there is hope, that there is reward for man's deeds, that man is not deluded.

What shall I do for Hashem in return for all His kindness to me, for reviving me from my immense despair. What was the great goodness which God granted me? His gift is not that He merely gave me life, but that He gave me the opportunity to praise and thank Him[80], to raise the cup of salvations and call in the name of Hashem. Thus, *what shall I do for Hashem in return* for enabling me to *raise the cup of salvations and call in the name of Hashem*, to praise Him and publicize His greatness, and to *fulfill my vows to Hashem in the presence of*

---

80. See *Chovos HaLevavos, Shaar Avodas Elokim*, ch. 6.

What shall I do for Hashem in return for all His kindness to me? I shall raise the cup of salvations and call in the Name of Hashem. I will fulfill my vows to Hashem in the presence of all His people. Difficult in the eyes of Hashem is the death of his devoted ones. Please, Hashem, since I am Your servant, the son of Your handmaid, loosen my

all His people — for this opportunity is the greatest gift which God has given me.

The Psalmist now concludes with the idea with which he introduced his personal saga — God's desire for the lives of the righteous so that they should sing praises to Him, for the dead cannot praise God. Therefore, *difficult in the eys of Hashem is the death of his devoted one*; the death of his devout ones is dreaded, for only in their lives can they praise Him.

The Psalmist now begins an appeal to God to save him from his enemies who rise up against him, specifically the king of Ashur and his legions. *Please, Hashem, since I am Your servant,* then it is not proper that You allow me to be defeated and given over in servitude to another master. I am not like a slave who can be bought and sold, whose ownership can be transferred, because *I am Your servant, the son of Your handmaid,* I was born into Your household and, according to the law, I cannot be sold. Therefore, it is only fitting that you now loosen my bonds and free me from the threat of the king of Ashur.

אֲמָתֵךְ פְּתַחְתָּ לְמוֹסֵרָי: לְךָ אֶזְבַּח זֶבַח תּוֹדָה וּבְשֵׁם יהוה אֶקְרָא: נְדָרַי לַיהוה אֲשַׁלֵּם נֶגְדָה נָּא לְכָל עַמּוֹ: בְּחַצְרוֹת בֵּית יהוה בְּתוֹכֵכִי יְרוּשָׁלָיִם הַלְלוּיָהּ:

הַלְלוּ אֶת יהוה כָּל גּוֹיִם שַׁבְּחוּהוּ כָּל הָאֻמִּים: כִּי גָבַר עָלֵינוּ חַסְדּוֹ וֶאֱמֶת יהוה לְעוֹלָם הַלְלוּיָהּ:

לך אזבח זבח תודה ובשם ה׳ אקרא *I will bring you offerings to acknowledge my debt of gratitude* for the miraculous defeat of Sancheriv and I will *call in the Name of Hashem*, further publicizing His greatness. *I will fulfill my vows to Hashem* on behalf of two recipients of His kindness: first, *in the presence of all His people* — that is, in appreciation for the kindness He has bestowed upon the Jewish community; second, *in the courts of the House of Hashem, in your midst, o' Yerushalayim* — that is, in appreciation for the kindness He has bestowed upon the city of Yerushalayim and the Holy Temple, that He protects it from any adversary that attempts to destroy it. For all of Your benevolence do I vow offerings of thanksgiving — for Your salvation of the people of Israel, the city of Yerusha-layim, and the Holy Temple.

הללי את ה׳ כל גוים *Praise Hashem, all you nations* (Tehillim

bonds. I will bring You offerings to acknowledge my debt of gratitude, and call in the Name of Hashem. I will fulfill my vows to Hashem in the presence of all His people. In the courts of the House of Hashem, in your midst, o' Yerushalayim, Halleluyah! (*ibid.*, 12-19).

Praise Hashem, all you nations; laud Him, all you tribes of mankind. For His lovingkindness was mighty over us, and the faithfulness of Hashem endures forever, Halleluyah! (*ibid.*, 117).

117). After describing how God fulfilled his request and saved the people of Israel from the army of Sancheriv, the Psalmist explains why the gentiles must also praise Him. *Praise Hashem, all you nations* — nations which Sancheriv captured and brought to the outskirts of Jerusalem when he prepared to conquer the holy city, and which were freed as a result of God's salvation of Israel. *For His lovingkindness was mighty over us* — the other nations were saved merely as a result of God's kindness to *us* when He conquered Sancheriv. Because they were also saved, they are also obligated to thank Him.

In the three phrases that follow, the Psalmist refers back to his prayer in לא לנו. *Praise Hashem* refers to *to Your own name give honor*; *for His lovingkindness was mighty over us* refers to *for the sake of Your lovingkindness*; and *the faithfulness* (אמת) *of Hashem endures forever* refers to *for the sake of*

*If there are at least three participants at the Seder, the
leader chants each of the following four verses aloud,
and the others respond by repeating the first verse each
time, followed by the succeeding verse, just as it is
recited in shul.*

הוֹדוּ לַיהוה כִּי טוֹב   כִּי לְעוֹלָם חַסְדּוֹ:

יֹאמַר נָא יִשְׂרָאֵל   כִּי לְעוֹלָם חַסְדּוֹ:

יֹאמְרוּ נָא בֵית אַהֲרֹן   כִּי לְעוֹלָם חַסְדּוֹ:

יֹאמְרוּ נָא יִרְאֵי יהוה   כִּי לְעוֹלָם חַסְדּוֹ:

your truth (אמתך), and means that His promise to save us
remains eternal.

הודו לה׳ כי טוב *Give thanks to Hashem, for He is good.* The
Psalmist commands all of the nations to give thanks to God
because of His kindness and generosity to them, while *say it
now, o' Israel* — Israel has a special obligation to thank God,
because He has given us a much greater measure of kindness.
But even more, *say it now, o' House of Aharon,* to whom God
has been even more gracious by giving them a lofty spiritual
status, and so, too, *say it now, o' those that fear Hashem* —
they have an even greater obligation to thank Him; every
person's obligation to thank God is directly proportional to the
kindness which God has given him[81].

---

81. See *Malbim* on Tehillim 63:4.

255

*If there are at least three participants at the Seder, the
leader chants each of the following four verses aloud,
and the others respond by repeating the first verse each
time, followed by the succeeding verse, just as it is
recited in shul.*

Give thanks to Hashem, for He is good,
for His lovingkindness endures forever.
Say it now, o' Yisrael,
for His lovingkindness endures forever.
Say it now, o' House of Aharon,
for His lovingkindness endures forever.
Say it now, o' those that fear Hashem,
for His lovingkindness endures forever

מן המצר קראתי י-ה *From out of the straits* — the Psalmist
recounts his personal experience in detail — *I called upon
God,* from the straits of mortal illness. *He answered me through
the breadth of Divine relief.* God could have revived me from
my illness and, once the danger had passed, let me live on as
normal, giving me no assurance that He would again help me.
But in His infinite kindness, He continued to communicate
with me and assured me that He would again save me from
mortal danger, which indeed He did when the king of Ashur
rose up against me[82]. When He continued to communicate with
me I knew then that *Hashem was for me; therefore I did not
fear.* Had God only saved me from the grips of death, I would

---

82. Cf. Melachim II 20:6, *And from the hand of the king of Ashur I will deliver
you.*

מִן הַמֵּצַר קָרָאתִי יָּה עָנָנִי בַמֶּרְחַב יָה: יהוה לִי
לֹא אִירָא מַה יַּעֲשֶׂה לִי אָדָם: יהוה לִי בְּעֹזְרָי וַאֲנִי
אֶרְאֶה בְשֹׂנְאָי: טוֹב לַחֲסוֹת בַּיהוה מִבְּטֹחַ בָּאָדָם:
טוֹב לַחֲסוֹת בַּיהוה מִבְּטֹחַ בִּנְדִיבִים: כָּל גּוֹיִם
סְבָבוּנִי בְּשֵׁם יהוה כִּי אֲמִילַם: סַבּוּנִי גַם סְבָבוּנִי

have still feared that — although the decree of death had been
lifted — I was still not fully absolved. But when God answered
me *through the breadth of Divine relief,* I knew that just as He
had listened to my prayers and performed a miracle to save
me from my illness, so, too, would He listen to my prayers and
save me from Sancheriv, and *therefore I did not fear.*

The Psalmist expresses His new faith in God on two levels.
First, *what can man do to me?*, I know that God will protect
me from my enemies. Second, *I shall calmly look upon those
who hate me;* I will look at their downfall. Not only will God
protect me from them, but He will help me defeat them.

טוב לחסות בה׳ מבטח באדם It is obvious, then, that *it is better
to trust in Hashem than to rely on man.* One can rely on man
all one wants, but doing so will assure no refuge, מחסה, in
times of trouble. But one who *trusts* in God, on the other hand,

From out of the straits I called upon God; He answered me through the breadth of Divine relief. Hashem was for me; therefore I did not fear; what can man do to me? If Hashem is for me through my helpers, I shall calmly look upon those who hate me. It is better to trust in Hashem than to rely on man. It is better to trust in Hashem than to rely on noblemen. All the nations surrounded me; it was with the Name of Hashem that I cut them down. They surrounded me; indeed, they closed in about

is not only assured refuge in times of trouble, but his very trust in God becomes a refuge and source of strength. The Psalmist expresses this idea in his use of the word, לחסות, which has two meanings: (1) *to trust,* (2) *to find shelter.* Trusting in God in itself provides shelter.

טוב לחסות בה׳ מבטח בנדיבים *It is better to trust in Hashem than to rely on noblemen.* The Psalmist explains that trust in man is ineffective for two reasons. First, one has no guarantee that the man in whom he trusts will agree to satisfy his needs; he may not want to help. Second, even if he trusts *in noblemen,* נדיבים, so called because they unselfishly offer their generous assistance, he is still not guaranteed that he will be helped, for his needs may be beyond their ability; they may want to help, but are unable.

כל גוים סבבוני *All the nations surrounded me;* that is, I realize that when all the nations surrounded me, *it was with*

בְּשֵׁם יהוה כִּי אֲמִילַם: סַבּוּנִי כִדְבוֹרִים דֹּעֲכוּ כְּאֵשׁ
קוֹצִים בְּשֵׁם יהוה כִּי אֲמִילַם: דָּחֹה דְחִיתַנִי לִנְפּוֹל
וַיהוה עֲזָרָנִי: עָזִּי וְזִמְרָת יָהּ וַיְהִי לִי לִישׁוּעָה: קוֹל

the Name of Hashem — it was upon God's command. God
providentially arranged, סבב, that all of the nations should
come lay siege to Yerushalayim in order for Him to vanquish
them there. *They surrounded me; indeed, they closed in about
me* — even though they came upon Yerushalayim time after
time (Sancheriv invaded the land of Yehudah three times), it
was all *with the name of Hashem* — divinely ordained to ensure
that *I cut them down.*

Even the third time, when *they surrounded me like bees;
they were put out as a fire of thorns.* This, too, was *with the
name of Hashem* — it was divinely planned in order that *I cut
them down.*

Even when *you have pushed me again and again that I
might fall,* and the natural course determined that I should
indeed fall for I had no strength to stand up against my
enemies, nevertheless, והי עזרני, *Hashem helped me.* עזר, help,
is merely the protection from enemies' harm, but not their
defeat (which is referred to as ישועה, salvation). However,
עזי וזמרת י-ה ויהי לי לישועה, *Hashem's might and the praise of*

me; it was with the Name of Hashem that I cut them down. They surrounded me like bees; they were put out as a fire of thorns; it was with the Name of Hashem that I cut them down. True, you have pushed me again and again that I might fall, but Hashem helped me. Hashem's might and the praise of His strength became a salvation for me. Therefore

His strength became a salvation for me. Not only did He save me from enemies' harm, but he defeated my enemies as well.

The Psalmist confidently describes the king of Israel walking from his home to the Holy Temple, hearing on the way, *the voice of rejoicing and salvation in the tents of the righteous*[83], as they proclaim, ימין ה' עשה חיל *"The right hand of Hashem does valiantly"*; first, they describe God preparing His forces, חיל, to fight and defeat Ashur. Then, they proclaim, ימין ה' עשה חיל, *"The right hand of Hashem has ever proven exalted"*; His hand is exalted above the forces of the enemy, and, therefore, again, ימין ה' עשה חיל *"The right hand of Hashem does valiantly"*, His all-powerful forces, חיל, completely confound the enemy camp.

After his perilous ordeals, the Psalmist says with certainty,

---

83. The *Malbim* refers to his commentary on Yeshayahu 30:29, and points out that this verse alludes to the course of events which occurred when the king of Ashur was defeated: when the people of Jerusalem began to sing the traditional festival song on the day before Pesach, God began His conquest of the army of Ashur. At the moment that the song pinnacled at the slaughtering of the Pesach sacrifice, outside the city God crushed the army of Ashur. Thus, at the time of the *voice of rejoicing* came the *salvation.*

רָנָּה וִישׁוּעָה בְּאָהֳלֵי צַדִּיקִים יְמִין יהוה עֹשָׂה חָיִל:
יְמִין יהוה רוֹמֵמָה יְמִין יהוה עֹשָׂה חָיִל: לֹא אָמוּת
כִּי אֶחְיֶה וַאֲסַפֵּר מַעֲשֵׂי יָהּ: יַסֹּר יִסְּרַנִי יָּהּ וְלַמָּוֶת
לֹא נְתָנָנִי: פִּתְחוּ לִי שַׁעֲרֵי צֶדֶק אָבֹא בָם אוֹדֶה יָהּ:
זֶה הַשַּׁעַר לַיהוה צַדִּיקִים יָבֹאוּ בוֹ:

(Each of the following verses is repeated:)

אוֹדְךָ כִּי עֲנִיתָנִי וַתְּהִי לִי לִישׁוּעָה: אודך אֶבֶן

I shall not die on two grounds. First, I know that God revived
me from my illness in order that *I shall live and recount the
works of God,* for it is not the dead that proclaim God's might.
Second, I know that I shall not die because *God has chastised
me heavily* with afflictions, *but He has not turned me over to
death* — my afflictions took the place of death. That is, my
sins were atoned for by the afflictions which I suffered and I
need not die for them. *I shall not die* because I must live and
recount the works of God, and I have already suffered
afflictions which atoned for my sins.

The Psalmist continues to describe the king's walk. The
king, accompanied by the righteous men, arrives at the

261

let the voice of rejoicing and salvation be in the tents of the righteous: "The right hand of Hashem does valiantly. The right hand of Hashem has ever proven exalted. The right hand of Hashem does valiantly still." I shall not die, but I shall live and recount the works of God. God has chastised me heavily, but He has not turned me over to death. Open for me the gates of justice; I will enter into them and give thanks to God. This is the gate to Hashem, the righteous shall enter into it.

(Each of the following verses is repeated:)

I will thank You for having afflicted me, thereby becoming my salvation. I... The stone which the

entrance to the Holy Temple to praise God and to present thanksgiving offerings and the day's sacrifices to Him. The king commands the gatekeepers, *Open for me the gates of justice; I will enter into them and give thanks to God.* He calls them the gates of *justice*, שערי צדק, because God acted within the limits of righteous justice when He brought salvation by way of afflictions in accordance with the Psalmist's deeds, and not by way of undeserved compassion.

זה השער לה' *This is the gate to Hashem*, the gate leading to the Holy Temple. The king had his own gate leading to the Holy Temple (as described in the Book of Yechezkel, chapters 44 and 46). The king, on this occasion, allows the righteous

262

מָאֲסוּ הַבּוֹנִים הָיְתָה לְרֹאשׁ פִּנָּה: אבן מֵאֵת יהוה
הָיְתָה זֹּאת הִיא נִפְלָאת בְּעֵינֵינוּ: מאת זֶה הַיּוֹם עָשָׂה
יהוה נָגִילָה וְנִשְׂמְחָה בוֹ: זה

*If there are at least three participants at the Seder, the
leader chants each of the following four verses aloud,
and the others repeat after him:*

אָנָּא יהוה הוֹשִׁיעָה נָּא:
אָנָּא יהוה הוֹשִׁיעָה נָּא:
אָנָּא יהוה הַצְלִיחָה נָּא:
אָנָּא יהוה הַצְלִיחָה נָּא:

men to enter through his special gate and so says to them, *The
righteous shall enter into it.*

אודך *I will thank you.* The king begins to sing praises of
thanksgiving to God from inside the gateway he has just
entered. He gives thanks for the afflictions which he suffered,
because through them God granted him *salvation* (cf.
Yeshayahu 12:1).

אבן מאסו הבונים *The stone* — the kingdom of Israel is
compared to a building and the king to a building's foundation
(cf. Yeshayahu 28:16). Thus, the king declares, *The stone which
the builders disdained* — this refers to the attempt of Shevna
and his men to oust the king from his throne (cf. *Sanhedrin
26a*); *has become the chief cornerstone* — the king emerged

builders disdained has become the chief cornerstone. The... This is Hashem's doing; it is marvelous in our eyes. This... Hashem has made this day; we will rejoice in Him and delight. Hashem.... (*ibid.*, 5-24).

If there are at least three participants at the Seder, the leader chants each of the following four verses aloud, and the others repeat after him:

We beseech You, o' Hashem, save us.
We beseech You, o' Hashem, save us.
We beseech You, o' Hashem, cause us to prosper.
We beseech You, o' Hashem, cause us to prosper.

victorious over the rebels. The king's triumph was not due to natural forces; rather, *this is Hashem's doing*, and because it came about through miracles and wonders, *it is marvelous in our own eyes*. Therefore it is *Hashem* Who *has made this day*, and no other force, and therefore *we will rejoice in Him and delight*; we will rejoice in God, and not merely in the salvation which He brought us. The primary joy is not that we were saved, but that God showed us that He cares for us and gave us His banner to proudly display to the rest of the world.

אנא ה' After the king praises God, all of the people join in to pray, *We beseech You, o' Hashem, save us* from adversity, and *cause us to prosper* by granting success to all of our endeavors, from now and forever.

בָּרוּךְ הַבָּא בְּשֵׁם יהוה בֵּרַכְנוּכֶם מִבֵּית יהוה:
ברוך אֵל יהוה וַיָּאֶר לָנוּ אִסְרוּ חַג בַּעֲבֹתִים עַד
קַרְנוֹת הַמִּזְבֵּחַ: אל אֵלִי אַתָּה וְאוֹדֶךָ אֱלֹהַי אֲרוֹמְמֶךָ:
אלי הוֹדוּ לַיהוה כִּי טוֹב כִּי לְעוֹלָם חַסְדּוֹ: הודו

When the people finish their prayer, the *kohanim* who
serve in the Holy Temple come to greet the king. They bless
the king with the Priestly Blessing and they add, *Blessed be he
who comes with the name of Hashem*, echoing the Torah's
words, *And they will put my name upon the Children of Israel,
and I will bless them* (Bamidbar 6:27). The name of Hashem
had already been placed upon the people, and in His name
they all came to the Holy Temple. The *kohanim* continue, *We
have blessed you out of the House of Hashem*, for the blessing
emanates forth from His House, from the One Who dwells
there and Who blesses the people. (This verse corresponds to
the first phrase of the Priestly Blessing, *May Hashem bless you
and protect you* (Bamidbar 6:24).)

Hashem is God, may He shine His light upon us. As they
go out to greet the king with beacons of light, he proclaims
that through this light do they glorify God (cf. Yeshayahu
24:15), and may He in return bless us with His light. (This

265

Blessed be he who comes with the Name of Hashem; we have blessed you out of the House of Hashem. Let... Hashem is God, may He shine His light upon us; keep the festival offering bound with cords until you reach the high corners of the altar. Hashem... You are my God; I shall acknowledge You; o' my God, I will exalt You. You... Give thanks to Hashem, for He is good, for His lovingkindness endures forever. Give thanks... (*ibid.*, 26-29).

phrase corresponds to the second phrase of the Priestly Blessing, *May Hashem illuminate His countenance towards you* (Bamidbar 6:25).)

The king responds to the *kohanim* and commands, *Keep the festival offering bound with cords until you reach the high corners of the altar*; he commands them to perform the specific sacrificial services of binding the offering and bringing it to the altar. He blesses them that God should turn His countenance to them and accept their offering, for the acceptance of an offering is sure sign that God is pleased with them (cf. Malachi 1:8). (This phrase corresponds to the third and final phrase of the Priestly Blessing, *May Hashem turn His countenance towards you* (Bamidbar 6:26).)

You are my God; I shall acknowledge You for the goodness which You grant us; *o' my God, I will exalt You* and relate praises of your all-encompassing glory. The king concludes

יְהַלְלוּךָ יהוה אֱלֹהֵינוּ כָּל מַעֲשֶׂיךָ וַחֲסִידֶיךָ
צַדִּיקִים עוֹשֵׂי רְצוֹנֶךָ וְכָל עַמְּךָ בֵּית יִשְׂרָאֵל בְּרִנָּה
יוֹדוּ וִיבָרְכוּ וִישַׁבְּחוּ וִיפָאֲרוּ וִירוֹמְמוּ וְיַעֲרִיצוּ
וְיַקְדִּישׁוּ וְיַמְלִיכוּ אֶת שִׁמְךָ מַלְכֵּנוּ כִּי לְךָ טוֹב
לְהוֹדוֹת וּלְשִׁמְךָ נָאֶה לְזַמֵּר כִּי מֵעוֹלָם וְעַד עוֹלָם
אַתָּה אֵל:

כִּי לְעוֹלָם חַסְדּוֹ:	הוֹדוּ לַיהוה כִּי טוֹב
כִּי לְעוֹלָם חַסְדּוֹ:	הוֹדוּ לֵאלֹהֵי הָאֱלֹהִים
כִּי לְעוֹלָם חַסְדּוֹ:	הוֹדוּ לַאֲדֹנֵי הָאֲדֹנִים
כִּי לְעוֹלָם חַסְדּוֹ:	לְעֹשֵׂה נִפְלָאוֹת גְּדֹלוֹת לְבַדּוֹ
כִּי לְעוֹלָם חַסְדּוֹ:	לְעֹשֵׂה הַשָּׁמַיִם בִּתְבוּנָה

with a command to all of the people, *Give thanks to Hashem,
for He is good, that His lovingkindness endures forever.*

הודו לה׳ כי טוב *Give thanks to Hashem, for He is good*
(Tehillim 136). After commanding the people to praise and
bless God, the Psalmist commands them to give thanks for all
of the kindness they received from Him, from His attributes of

All Your works shall proclaim Your praise, o' Hashem our God, and let Your devoted ones, the righteous who do Your will, and all Your people, the House of Yisrael, render homage with jubilation and bless and laud and extol and exalt, praise and sanctify and glorify Your Name, o' our King. For it is good to render You homage and it is pleasant to sing to Your Name, for from eternity to eternity You are God.

Give thanks to Hashem that He is good,
    for His lovingkindness endures forever.
Give thanks to the God of gods,
    for His lovingkindness endures forever.
Give thanks to the Master of masters,
    for His lovingkindness endures forever.
To Him Who alone does great wonders,
    for His lovingkindness endures forever.
To Him Who shapes the heavens with understanding,
    for His lovingkindness endures forever.

lovingkindness and generosity even to those who are unworthy. His acts of kindness take on two forms — those within the bounds of natural law and those that are supernatural.

For the acts of kindness He does within the laws of nature, the Psalmist says, *Give thanks to the God of gods* and *to the Master of masters*. The ancient nations attributed the acts of

לְרוֹקַע הָאָרֶץ עַל הַמָּיִם   כִּי לְעוֹלָם חַסְדּוֹ:

לְעֹשֵׂה אוֹרִים גְּדֹלִים   כִּי לְעוֹלָם חַסְדּוֹ:

אֶת הַשֶּׁמֶשׁ לְמֶמְשֶׁלֶת בַּיּוֹם   כִּי לְעוֹלָם חַסְדּוֹ:

אֶת הַיָּרֵחַ וְכוֹכָבִים לְמֶמְשְׁלוֹת
בַּלָּיְלָה   כִּי לְעוֹלָם חַסְדּוֹ:

לְמַכֵּה מִצְרַיִם בִּבְכוֹרֵיהֶם   כִּי לְעוֹלָם חַסְדּוֹ:

וַיּוֹצֵא יִשְׂרָאֵל מִתּוֹכָם   כִּי לְעוֹלָם חַסְדּוֹ:

בְּיָד חֲזָקָה וּבִזְרוֹעַ נְטוּיָה   כִּי לְעוֹלָם חַסְדּוֹ:

לְגֹזֵר יַם סוּף לִגְזָרִים   כִּי לְעוֹלָם חַסְדּוֹ:

וְהֶעֱבִיר יִשְׂרָאֵל בְּתוֹכוֹ   כִּי לְעוֹלָם חַסְדּוֹ:

וְנִעֵר פַּרְעֹה וְחֵילוֹ בְיַם סוּף   כִּי לְעוֹלָם חַסְדּוֹ:

לְמוֹלִיךְ עַמּוֹ בַּמִּדְבָּר   כִּי לְעוֹלָם חַסְדּוֹ:

לְמַכֵּה מְלָכִים גְּדֹלִים   כִּי לְעוֹלָם חַסְדּוֹ:

וַיַּהֲרֹג מְלָכִים אַדִּירִים   כִּי לְעוֹלָם חַסְדּוֹ:

לְסִיחוֹן מֶלֶךְ הָאֱמֹרִי   כִּי לְעוֹלָם חַסְדּוֹ:

וּלְעוֹג מֶלֶךְ הַבָּשָׁן   כִּי לְעוֹלָם חַסְדּוֹ:

To Him Who firmly establishes the earth upon the waters, for His lovingkindness endures forever.

To Him Who fashions great lights, for His lovingkindness endures forever.

The sun for dominion by day, for His lovingkindness endures forever.

The moon and the stars for dominions at night, for His lovingkindness endures forever.

To Him Who slays Egypt through their firstborn, for His lovingkindness endures forever.

And brought Yisrael out from their midst, for His lovingkindness endures forever.

With a strong hand and with an outstretched arm, for His lovingkindness endures forever.

To Him Who divides the Sea of Reeds into parts, for His lovingkindness endures forever.

And made Yisrael pass through the midst of it, for His lovingkindness endures forever.

And poured out Pharaoh and his host into the Sea of Reeds, for His lovingkindness endures forever.

To Him Who leads His people through the wilderness, for His lovingkindness endures forever.

To Him Who smites great kings, for His lovingkindness endures forever.

And killed mighty kings, for His lovingkindness endures forever.

Sichon, the king of the Amorites, for His lovingkindness endures forever.

And Og, the king of Bashan, for His lovingkindness endures forever.

וְנָתַן אַרְצָם לְנַחֲלָה   כִּי לְעוֹלָם חַסְדּוֹ:
נַחֲלָה לְיִשְׂרָאֵל עַבְדּוֹ   כִּי לְעוֹלָם חַסְדּוֹ:
שֶׁבְּשִׁפְלֵנוּ זָכַר לָנוּ   כִּי לְעוֹלָם חַסְדּוֹ:
וַיִּפְרְקֵנוּ מִצָּרֵינוּ   כִּי לְעוֹלָם חַסְדּוֹ:
נֹתֵן לֶחֶם לְכָל בָּשָׂר   כִּי לְעוֹלָם חַסְדּוֹ:
הוֹדוּ לְאֵל הַשָּׁמָיִם   כִּי לְעוֹלָם חַסְדּוֹ:

nature to gods and masters such as the stars and constellations, who, they believed, ruled the earth, and the heavenly angels who ruled the stars and constellations. The Psalmist rejoins that it is God Who is the source of all.

For the acts of kindness He does above and beyond the laws of nature, the Psalmist says, *To Him Who alone does great wonders.* Whereas the acts of kindness within nature come about via the laws which He established and are, therefore, not directly from His hand, the acts of kindness which are not within the laws of nature are directly performed by Him while He temporarily represses the laws of nature.

The Psalmist returns to the praises for His kindnesses within nature and says, *To Him Who shapes the heavens with understanding... To Him who firmly establishes the earth upon the waters.* We are obligated to constantly thank the Creator Who constantly renews the works of creation. We must thank

And gave their land as an inheritance, for His lovingkindness endures forever.

As an inheritance to Yisrael His servant, for His lovingkindness endures forever.

Who remembered us in our lowly state, because His lovingkindness endures forever.

And freed us from our oppressors, because His lovingkindness endures forever.

Who gives food to all flesh, since His lovingkindness endures forever.

Give thanks to the God of Heaven, for His lovingkindness endures forever.

Him when we consider the details of His creation, how He *firmly establishes the earth upon the waters* and prevents the waters from engulfing the earth. Furthermore, the Psalmist tells us that we owe thanks to *Him Who fashions great lights*, causing the sun to give forth light during the day and the moon to reflect light at night.

The Psalmist now describes the miraculous acts of kindness. *To Him Who slays Egypt through their firstborn*, for through the deaths of the Egyptian firstborn did He bring Israel forth from Egypt with a mighty hand. The wonders He performed were for the sake of Israel's redemption, so that the most tragic disaster that occurred to Egypt was the greatest good that could occur to Israel, for through it He *brought Israel out from their midst*. Then, *To Him Who divides the Sea of Reeds into parts... And made Israel pass through the midst of it*, the

נִשְׁמַת כָּל חַי תְּבָרֵךְ אֶת שִׁמְךָ
יהוה אֱלֹהֵינוּ וְרוּחַ כָּל
בָּשָׂר תְּפָאֵר וּתְרוֹמֵם זִכְרְךָ מַלְכֵּנוּ תָּמִיד. מִן
הָעוֹלָם וְעַד הָעוֹלָם אַתָּה אֵל וּמִבַּלְעָדֶיךָ אֵין
לָנוּ מֶלֶךְ גּוֹאֵל וּמוֹשִׁיעַ פּוֹדֶה וּמַצִּיל וּמְפַרְנֵס
וּמְרַחֵם. בְּכָל עֵת צָרָה וְצוּקָה אֵין לָנוּ מֶלֶךְ
אֶלָּא אָתָּה. אֱלֹהֵי הָרִאשׁוֹנִים וְהָאַחֲרוֹנִים
אֱלוֹהַּ כָּל בְּרִיּוֹת אֲדוֹן כָּל תּוֹלָדוֹת הַמְהֻלָּל
בְּרוֹב הַתִּשְׁבָּחוֹת הַמְנַהֵג עוֹלָמוֹ בְּחֶסֶד
וּבְרִיּוֹתָיו בְּרַחֲמִים. וַיהוה לֹא יָנוּם וְלֹא יִישָׁן

purpose of this miracle was for the destruction of the Egyptians, *And poured out Pharaoh and his host into the Sea of Reeds*, for God could have saved Israel in some other manner.

The Psalmist adds to the list of God's kindnesses, *To Him Who leads His people through the wildnerness*. The kindness is not merely that God protected His people in the desert, but that He gave them the opportunity to study the ways of God and His Torah, and to cast away from their hearts the corrupt conceptions they had absorbed from the Egyptians. In reward for the difficulties they suffered from the journey through the wilderness, God *killed mighty kings...Sichon, the king of the Amorites...And Og, the king of Bashan... And gave their land as an*

$\mathbf{THE}$ soul of every living thing shall bless Your Name, o' Hashem our God, and the spirit of all flesh shall ever glorify and exalt Your remembrance, o' our King. From the remotest past to the most distant future, You are God, and beside You we have no King, Who redeems, and saves, delivers and rescues, sustains and has compassion; in all times of trouble and distress we have no King but You. God of the first and of the last, God of all creatures, Master of all that is begotten, proclaimed in an abundance of praises, Who guides His world with lovingkindness and His creatures

inheritance. These are great examples of His kindness, for although the journey through the wildnerness itself was an act of kindness, He bestowed greater kindness upon the people by rewarding them for the difficulties incurred during the journey.

The Psalmist now expresses gratitude for a fundamental principle. All of the miracles that God performed for us in the past set the foundation for the miracles He will perform in the future. Since He *remembered us in our lowly state,* we can be assured that He will yet remember us whenever we fall low, and He will remember the miracles He wrought for us in the past.

נתן לחם לכל בשר *Who gives food to all flesh.* Although it

הַמְעוֹרֵר יְשֵׁנִים וְהַמֵּקִיץ נִרְדָּמִים וְהַמֵּשִׂיחַ
אִלְּמִים וְהַמַּתִּיר אֲסוּרִים וְהַסּוֹמֵךְ נוֹפְלִים
וְהַזּוֹקֵף כְּפוּפִים. לְךָ לְבַדְּךָ אֲנַחְנוּ מוֹדִים. אִלּוּ
פִינוּ מָלֵא שִׁירָה כַּיָּם וּלְשׁוֹנֵנוּ רִנָּה כַּהֲמוֹן גַּלָּיו
וְשִׂפְתוֹתֵינוּ שֶׁבַח כְּמֶרְחֲבֵי רָקִיעַ וְעֵינֵינוּ
מְאִירוֹת כַּשֶּׁמֶשׁ וְכַיָּרֵחַ וְיָדֵינוּ פְרוּשׂוֹת כְּנִשְׁרֵי
שָׁמַיִם וְרַגְלֵינוּ קַלּוֹת כָּאַיָּלוֹת אֵין אֲנַחְנוּ
מַסְפִּיקִים לְהוֹדוֹת לְךָ יהוה אֱלֹהֵינוּ וֵאלֹהֵי
אֲבוֹתֵינוּ וּלְבָרֵךְ אֶת שְׁמֶךָ עַל אַחַת מֵאָלֶף אֶלֶף
אַלְפֵי אֲלָפִים וְרִבֵּי רְבָבוֹת פְּעָמִים הַטּוֹבוֹת

appears to us that sustenance comes through natural means to
every living creature, nevertheless it is God Who controls the
forces of nature which distribute food. He is the source of all
sustenance, of all life, for everything on earth emanates from
His kindness.

with compassion. And Hashem neither slumbers nor sleeps; it is He, rather, Who awakens those who sleep, Who rouses those that are stunned, Who gives speech to the mute, Who sets free those that are bound, supports the falling and raises up those that are bowed down. To You and to You alone do we give thanks. Were our mouths full with song as the sea, and our tongues with joy's outpouring as the swell of its waves, and our lips with praise as the expanse of heaven, and though our eyes were brilliant like the sun and moon, our hands spread out like the eagles of the heavens, and our feet as light as the deer — we would still be unable to thank You sufficiently, Hashem our God and God of our fathers, and to bless Your Name for even one of the thousand thousand, thousands of thousands and and myriad of myriads of favors which You have bestowed upon our fathers and upon us. You have

שֶׁעָשִׂיתָ עִם אֲבוֹתֵינוּ וְעִמָּנוּ. מִמִּצְרַיִם גְּאַלְתָּנוּ יהוה אֱלֹהֵינוּ וּמִבֵּית עֲבָדִים פְּדִיתָנוּ בְּרָעָב זַנְתָּנוּ וּבְשָׂבָע כִּלְכַּלְתָּנוּ מֵחֶרֶב הִצַּלְתָּנוּ וּמִדֶּבֶר מִלַּטְתָּנוּ וּמֵחֳלָיִם רָעִים וְנֶאֱמָנִים דִּלִּיתָנוּ. עַד הֵנָּה עֲזָרוּנוּ רַחֲמֶיךָ וְלֹא עֲזָבוּנוּ חֲסָדֶיךָ וְאַל תִּטְּשֵׁנוּ יהוה אֱלֹהֵינוּ לָנֶצַח. עַל כֵּן אֵבָרִים שֶׁפִּלַּגְתָּ בָּנוּ וְרוּחַ וּנְשָׁמָה שֶׁנָּפַחְתָּ בְּאַפֵּינוּ וְלָשׁוֹן אֲשֶׁר שַׂמְתָּ בְּפִינוּ הֵן הֵם יוֹדוּ וִיבָרְכוּ וִישַׁבְּחוּ וִיפָאֲרוּ וִירוֹמְמוּ וְיַעֲרִיצוּ וְיַקְדִּישׁוּ וְיַמְלִיכוּ אֶת שִׁמְךָ מַלְכֵּנוּ. כִּי כָל פֶּה לְךָ יוֹדֶה וְכָל לָשׁוֹן לְךָ תִשָּׁבַע וְכָל בֶּרֶךְ לְךָ תִכְרַע וְכָל קוֹמָה לְפָנֶיךָ תִשְׁתַּחֲוֶה. וְכָל לְבָבוֹת יִירָאוּךָ וְכָל קֶרֶב וּכְלָיוֹת יְזַמְּרוּ לִשְׁמֶךָ. כַּדָּבָר שֶׁכָּתוּב כָּל עַצְמֹתַי תֹּאמַרְנָה יהוה מִי כָמוֹךָ מַצִּיל עָנִי מֵחָזָק מִמֶּנּוּ וְעָנִי וְאֶבְיוֹן מִגֹּזְלוֹ. מִי יִדְמֶה לָּךְ וּמִי יִשְׁוֶה לָּךְ וּמִי יַעֲרָךְ לָךְ הָאֵל הַגָּדוֹל הַגִּבּוֹר וְהַנּוֹרָא אֵל עֶלְיוֹן קוֹנֵה שָׁמַיִם וָאָרֶץ.

redeemed us from Egypt, o' Hashem our God, and freed us from the house of slavery; You have fed us in famine and satisfied us in plenty. You have delivered us from the sword, freed us from pestilence, and relieved us from severe and lasting diseases. Until now Your compassion has helped us, and Your kindnesses have not forsaken us, so Hashem our God, forsake us never. Therefore the limbs which You have apportioned for us, the spirit and soul which You have breathed into our nostrils and the tongue which You have put into our mouth, shall all render homage, bless, praise, glorify, exalt and declare the power, the holiness and dominion of Your Name, o' our King. For every mouth shall render You homage, every tongue shall swear You allegiance, every knee shall bend before You, and all that stands upright shall fall down before You; all hearts shall fear You, and all the inmost passions shall sing praises to Your Name, even as it is written, "All my limbs shall say, 'O' Hashem, who is like You, Who delivers the poor from one that is stronger than him, the poor and the defenseless from one who would rob him?' " Who is like You, who is equal to You, and who can be compared to You, o' great,

נְהַלֵּלְךָ וּנְשַׁבֵּחֲךָ וּנְפָאֶרְךָ וּנְבָרֵךְ אֶת שֵׁם קָדְשֶׁךָ כָּאָמוּר לְדָוִד בָּרְכִי נַפְשִׁי אֶת יהוה וְכָל קְרָבַי אֶת שֵׁם קָדְשׁוֹ:

הָאֵל בְּתַעֲצֻמוֹת עֻזֶּךָ הַגָּדוֹל בִּכְבוֹד שְׁמֶךָ הַגִּבּוֹר לָנֶצַח וְהַנּוֹרָא בְּנוֹרְאוֹתֶיךָ הַמֶּלֶךְ הַיּוֹשֵׁב עַל כִּסֵּא רָם וְנִשָּׂא:

שׁוֹכֵן עַד מָרוֹם וְקָדוֹשׁ שְׁמוֹ. וְכָתוּב רַנְּנוּ צַדִּיקִים בַּיהוה לַיְשָׁרִים נָאוָה תְהִלָּה: בְּפִי יְשָׁרִים תִּתְהַלָּל וּבְדִבְרֵי צַדִּיקִים תִּתְבָּרַךְ וּבִלְשׁוֹן חֲסִידִים תִּתְרוֹמָם וּבְקֶרֶב קְדוֹשִׁים תִּתְקַדָּשׁ:

וּבְמַקְהֲלוֹת רִבְבוֹת עַמְּךָ בֵּית יִשְׂרָאֵל בְּרָנָּה יִתְפָּאֵר שִׁמְךָ מַלְכֵּנוּ בְּכָל דּוֹר וָדוֹר. שֶׁכֵּן חוֹבַת כָּל הַיְצוּרִים לְפָנֶיךָ יהוה אֱלֹהֵינוּ וֵאלֹהֵי אֲבוֹתֵינוּ לְהוֹדוֹת לְהַלֵּל לְשַׁבֵּחַ לְפָאֵר לְרוֹמֵם לְהַדֵּר לְבָרֵךְ לְעַלֵּה וּלְקַלֵּס עַל כָּל דִּבְרֵי שִׁירוֹת וְתִשְׁבָּחוֹת דָּוִד בֶּן יִשַׁי עַבְדְּךָ מְשִׁיחֶךָ:

strong, and awesome God, the Most High God, the Owner of heaven and earth? We shall proclaim Your praise, laud You, glorify You and bless Your Holy Name, even as it is said: "By David. Bless Hashem, o' my soul, and all that is within me, bless His holy Name."

O' God, in the abundance of Your might, great in the glory of Your Name, almighty in eternity and feared for Your awesome acts, the King Who, highly exalted, is seated upon a throne.

Dwelling in eternity, His Name is exalted and holy. And it is written: "Exult, o' righteous ones, in beholding Hashem; it behooves the upright to sing praises of the acts that reveal His might." By the mouth of the upright there is song in Your praise, by the words of the righteous You are blessed, by the tongue of Your devoted ones You are extolled, and in the midst of the holy Your are sanctified.

And in the assemblies of the tens of thousands of Your people Yisrael, Your Name, o' our King, is glorified in every generation with fervent emotion. For it is the duty of all creatures to give thanks before You, o' Hashem our God and God of our fathers, and to praise Your mighty acts, to laud, glorify, exalt and

יִשְׁתַּבַּח שִׁמְךָ לָעַד מַלְכֵּנוּ הָאֵל הַמֶּלֶךְ הַגָּדוֹל
וְהַקָּדוֹשׁ בַּשָּׁמַיִם וּבָאָרֶץ כִּי לְךָ נָאֶה יהוה אֱלֹהֵינוּ
וֵאלֹהֵי אֲבוֹתֵינוּ שִׁיר וּשְׁבָחָה הַלֵּל וְזִמְרָה עֹז
וּמֶמְשָׁלָה נֶצַח גְּדֻלָּה וּגְבוּרָה תְּהִלָּה וְתִפְאֶרֶת קְדֻשָּׁה
וּמַלְכוּת בְּרָכוֹת וְהוֹדָאוֹת מֵעַתָּה וְעַד־עוֹלָם. בָּרוּךְ
אַתָּה יהוה אֵל מֶלֶךְ גָּדוֹל בַּתִּשְׁבָּחוֹת אֵל הַהוֹדָאוֹת
אֲדוֹן הַנִּפְלָאוֹת הַבּוֹחֵר בְּשִׁירֵי זִמְרָה מֶלֶךְ אֵל חֵי
הָעוֹלָמִים:

*In most homes the fourth cup is drunk immediately
after Hallel, followed by nirtzah and then, the
Haggadah songs. In some Ashkenzic communities,
however, the songs are now sung until after ki lo naeh,
(page 296) and then the wine is drunk, followed by
nirtzah and the remainder of the songs.*

*One should have in mind that it is his intention to
fulfill the requirement of drinking the fourth of the
four cups of wine.*

בָּרוּךְ אַתָּה יהוה אֱלֹהֵינוּ מֶלֶךְ הָעוֹלָם
בּוֹרֵא פְּרִי הַגָּפֶן:

281

proclaim Your might, to bless, to extol You and to praise You in keeping with all the words and songs of praise by Your servant David, the son of Yishai, Your Anointed.

Praised be Your Name forever, o' our King, God, the King Who is great and holy in Heaven and on earth. For to You, o' Hashem our God and God of our fathers, pertain song and laud, praise and hymn, strength and dominion, victory, greatness, and might, renown and glory, holiness and kingship, blessings and [utterances of] thanksgiving henceforth and unto eternity. Blessed be You Hashem, God and King, great in hymns of praise, God of thanksgivings, Master of wonders, Who takes pleasure in hymns, King, God, the Life of all times.

In most homes the fourth cup is drunk immediately after Hallel, followed by nirtzah and then, the Haggadah songs. In some Ashkenzic communities, however, the songs are now sung until after ki lo naeh, (page 296) and then the wine is drunk, followed by nirtzah and the remainder of the songs.

One should have in mind that it is his intention to fulfill the requirement of drinking the fourth of the four cups of wine.

Blessed be you, Hashem our God, King of the universe, Who creates the fruit of the vine.

The entire amount of the fourth cup is drunk (to enable one to recite the berachah after drinking wine), within the required period of time, while reclining to the left.

בָּרוּךְ אַתָּה יהוה אֱלֹהֵינוּ מֶלֶךְ הָעוֹלָם עַל הַגֶּפֶן וְעַל פְּרִי הַגֶּפֶן וְעַל תְּנוּבַת הַשָּׂדֶה וְעַל אֶרֶץ חֶמְדָּה טוֹבָה וּרְחָבָה שֶׁרָצִיתָ וְהִנְחַלְתָּ לַאֲבוֹתֵינוּ לֶאֱכוֹל מִפִּרְיָהּ וְלִשְׂבּוֹעַ מִטּוּבָהּ. רַחֵם נָא יהוה אֱלֹהֵינוּ עַל יִשְׂרָאֵל עַמֶּךָ וְעַל יְרוּשָׁלַיִם עִירֶךָ וְעַל צִיּוֹן מִשְׁכַּן כְּבוֹדֶךָ וְעַל מִזְבַּחֶךָ וְעַל הֵיכָלֶךָ וּבְנֵה יְרוּשָׁלַיִם עִיר הַקּוֹדֶשׁ בִּמְהֵרָה בְיָמֵינוּ וְהַעֲלֵנוּ לְתוֹכָהּ וְשַׂמְּחֵנוּ בְּבִנְיָנָהּ וְנֹאכַל מִפִּרְיָהּ וְנִשְׂבַּע מִטּוּבָהּ וּנְבָרֶכְךָ עָלֶיהָ בִּקְדֻשָּׁה וּבְטָהֳרָה (בשבת וּרְצֵה וְהַחֲלִיצֵנוּ בְּיוֹם הַשַּׁבָּת הַזֶּה) וְשַׂמְּחֵנוּ בְּיוֹם חַג הַמַּצּוֹת הַזֶּה כִּי אַתָּה יהוה טוֹב וּמֵטִיב לַכֹּל וְנוֹדֶה לְךָ עַל הָאָרֶץ וְעַל פְּרִי הַגֶּפֶן: בָּרוּךְ אַתָּה יהוה עַל הָאָרֶץ וְעַל פְּרִי הַגֶּפֶן:

The entire amount of the fourth cup is drunk (to enable one to recite the berachah after drinking wine), within the required period of time, while reclining to the left.

Blessed be You, Hashem our God, King of the universe, for the vine and the fruit of the vine; for the produce of the field and for the desirable, good and spacious land which You have given to our fathers as an inheritance in favor, that they might eat of its fruit and be satisfied with its goodness. Have compassion, Hashem our God, upon Your people Yisrael, upon Yerushalayim, Your City, and upon Tzion, the Abode of Your glory, upon Your altar and upon Your Temple, and rebuild Yerushalayim, the city of holiness, speedily in our days; bring us up in it and make us rejoice in its rebuilding. May we eat of its fruit and be satisfied with its goodness so that we may bless You for it in holiness and purity.

(On Shabbos add: *And be pleased to fortify us on this Shabbos day.*) And gladden us on this day of the Festival of Unleavened Bread, for You, Hashem, are good and do good to all. To You we give thanks for the land and for the fruit of the vine. Blessed be You, Hashem, for the land and for the fruit of the vine.

נִרְצָה

חֲסַל סִדּוּר פֶּסַח כְּהִלְכָתוֹ. כְּכָל מִשְׁפָּטוֹ וְחֻקָּתוֹ. כַּאֲשֶׁר זָכִינוּ לְסַדֵּר אוֹתוֹ. כֵּן נִזְכֶּה לַעֲשׂוֹתוֹ: זָךְ שׁוֹכֵן מְעוֹנָה. קוֹמֵם קְהַל עֲדַת מִי מָנָה. בְּקָרוֹב נַהֵל נִטְעֵי כַנָּה. פְּדוּיִם לְצִיּוֹן בְּרִנָּה:

לַשָׁנָה הַבָּאָה בִּירוּשָׁלָיִם:

Those who live in Eretz Yisrael say both the following songs on the night of the Pesach Seder. Those who live in chutz la'aretz say the following song only on the first night and then proceed to Ki Lo Naeh (page 296). On the second night, they skip this song and proceed to Va'amartem Zevach Pesach (page 258).

Nirtzah

THE order of the Pesach is complete, according to its laws, all of its ordinances and statutes. Just as we merited to perform it, so may we merit to offer the sacrifice in deed. O' Pure One, Who abides on high, uplift the assembly of the community who cannot be counted (Israel). Soon, and in joy, may You lead the offshoots of the stock which You have planted, redeemed, to Tzion.

Next Year May We Be in Yerushalayim!

Those who live in Eretz Yisrael say both the following songs on the night of the Pesach Seder. Those who live in chutz la'aretz say the following song only on the first night and then proceed to Ki Lo Naeh (page 296). On the second night, they skip this song and proceed to Va'amartem Zevach Pesach (page 258).

וּבְכֵן וַיְהִי בַּחֲצִי הַלַּיְלָה

אָז רוֹב נִסִּים הִפְלֵאתָ   בַּלַּיְלָה.
בְּרֹאשׁ אַשְׁמוּרֶת זֶה   הַלַּיְלָה.
גֵּר צֶדֶק נִצַּחְתּוֹ כְּנֶחֱלַק לוֹ   לַיְלָה.
וַיְהִי בַּחֲצִי הַלַּיְלָה:

דַּנְתָּ מֶלֶךְ גְּרָר בַּחֲלוֹם   הַלַּיְלָה.
הִפְחַדְתָּ אֲרַמִּי בְּאֶמֶשׁ   לַיְלָה.
וַיָּשַׂר יִשְׂרָאֵל לְמַלְאָךְ וַיּוּכַל לוֹ   לַיְלָה.
וַיְהִי בַּחֲצִי הַלַּיְלָה:

זֶרַע בְּכוֹרֵי פַתְרוֹס מָחַצְתָּ בַּחֲצִי   הַלַּיְלָה.
חֵילָם לֹא מָצְאוּ בְּקוּמָם   בַּלַּיְלָה.
טִיסַת נְגִיד חֲרוֹשֶׁת סִלִּיתָ בְּכוֹכְבֵי   לַיְלָה.
וַיְהִי בַּחֲצִי הַלַּיְלָה:

יָעַץ מְחָרֵף לְנוֹפֵף אִוּוּי הוֹבַשְׁתָּ פְגָרָיו   בַּלַּיְלָה.
כָּרַע בֵּל וּמַצָּבוֹ בְּאִישׁוֹן   לַיְלָה.
לְאִישׁ חֲמוּדוֹת נִגְלָה רָז חֲזוֹת   לַיְלָה.
וַיְהִי בַּחֲצִי הַלַּיְלָה:

Vayehi Bachatzi Halaylah

And It Came To Pass at Midnight

Of old You worked so many miracles   at night;
At the start of the watches,   this very night;
To the righteous convert [Avraham] You gave
       victory when [his army] divided for him   in the night;
And it came to pass at midnight.

You judged the King of Gerar in a dream   in the night;
Frightened [Laban] the Aramean the preceding   night;
And Yisrael [Yaakov] fought an angel and
       overcame him   in the night;
And it came to pass at midnight.

The firstborn sons of Pasros [Egypt] You
       crushed   at midnight;
Their host they never found as they arose   in the night;
The soaring flight of [Sisra] the prince of
       Charoshes You trampled by the stars   of night;
And it came to pass at midnight.

Blaspheming [Sancheriv] schemed to raise his
       hand against [Yerushalayim] the cherished
       Abode; You let his [soldiers] carcasses rot   in the night;
Bel [Babylon's god] and its pedestal fell
       prostrate in the dark   of the night;
To [Daniel] the man of [Your] delight was
       revealed the secret of the [king's] vision   of night;
And it came to pass at midnight.

מִשְׁתַּכֵּר בִּכְלֵי קֹדֶשׁ נֶהֱרַג בּוֹ   בַּלַּיְלָה.

נוֹשַׁע מִבּוֹר אֲרָיוֹת פּוֹתֵר בְּעִתּוּתֵי   לַיְלָה.

שִׂנְאָה נָטַר אֲגָגִי וְכָתַב סְפָרִים   בַּלַּיְלָה.

וַיְהִי בַּחֲצִי הַלַּיְלָה:

עוֹרַרְתָּ נִצְחֲךָ עָלָיו בְּנֶדֶד שְׁנַת   לַיְלָה.

פּוּרָה תִדְרוֹךְ לְשׁוֹמֵר מַה   מִלַּיְלָה.

צָרַח כַּשּׁוֹמֵר וְשָׂח אָתָא בֹקֶר וְגַם   לַיְלָה.

וַיְהִי בַּחֲצִי הַלַּיְלָה:

קָרֵב יוֹם אֲשֶׁר הוּא לֹא יוֹם וְלֹא   לַיְלָה.

רָם הוֹדַע כִּי לְךָ הַיּוֹם אַף לְךָ   הַלַּיְלָה

שׁוֹמְרִים הַפְקֵד לְעִירְךָ כָּל הַיּוֹם וְכָל   הַלַּיְלָה.

תָּאִיר כְּאוֹר יוֹם חֶשְׁכַּת   לַיְלָה.

וַיְהִי בַּחֲצִי הַלַּיְלָה:

289

[Belshatzar] drank himself drunk with the
    sacred [Temple] vessels, was slain   that very night;
[Daniel] saved from the lion's den, interpreted
    the fearful phantasms   of night;
[Haman] the Agagi nursed hatred in his heart
    and wrote [lethal] edicts   in the night;
        And it came to pass at midnight.

You aroused Your victory over him by
    disturbing [Achashverosh's] sleep   at night;
The wine-press [of our enemies' destruction]
    You will tread for [Jewry that asks]
    "Watchman! What will be   of the night?"
[God] will exclaim like the watchman and say,
    "Morning has come [for Jewry] and also [for
    Esav]   the night";
        And it came to pass at midnight.

O' bring the [Mashiach's] day [of Redemption]
    which is neither day nor   night;
Make it known, exalted God, that Yours is the
    day and even Yours   the night;
Appoint sentries for Your city, for all the day
    and all   the night;
    Brighten as with the light of the day the
    darkness of   night;
        And it came to pass at midnight.

290

וּבְכֵן וַאֲמַרְתֶּם זֶבַח פֶּסַח

בַּפֶּסַח.   אֹמֶץ גְּבוּרוֹתֶיךָ הִפְלֵאתָ

פֶּסַח.   בְּרֹאשׁ כָּל מוֹעֲדוֹת נִשֵּׂאתָ

פֶּסַח.   גִּלִּיתָ לְאֶזְרָחִי חֲצוֹת לֵיל

וַאֲמַרְתֶּם זֶבַח פֶּסַח

בַּפֶּסַח.   דְּלָתָיו דָּפַקְתָּ כְּחוֹם הַיּוֹם

בַּפֶּסַח.   הִסְעִיד נוֹצְצִים עֲגוֹת מַצּוֹת

פֶּסַח.   וְאֶל הַבָּקָר רָץ זֵכֶר לְשׁוֹר עֵרֶךְ

וַאֲמַרְתֶּם זֶבַח פֶּסַח

בַּפֶּסַח.   זֹעֲמוּ סְדוֹמִים וְלוֹהֲטוּ בָּאֵשׁ

פֶּסַח.   חֻלַּץ לוֹט מֵהֶם וּמַצּוֹת אָפָה בְּקֵץ

בַּפֶּסַח.   טֵאטֵאתָ אַדְמַת מוֹף וְנוֹף בְּעָבְרְךָ

וַאֲמַרְתֶּם זֶבַח פֶּסַח

פֶּסַח.   יָהּ רֹאשׁ כָּל אוֹן מָחַצְתָּ בְּלֵיל שִׁמּוּר

פֶּסַח.   כַּבִּיר עַל בֵּן בְּכוֹר פָּסַחְתָּ בְּדַם

Va'amartem Zevach Pesach

Say Then: It Is the Feast of Pesach

The power of Your mighty deeds You	
wondrously displayed	on Pesach;
Above all festivals did You elevate	Pesach;
To the oriental [Avraham] You revealed the	
[miraculous exodus at] midnight	of Pesach;

Say then: It is the feast of Pesach.

At his door You knocked in the heat of midday	on Pesach;
He served the sparkling angels cakes of matzah	on Pesach;
And ran to the cattle, a harbinger of the ox,	
[the festive offering] related	to Pesach;

Say then: It is the feast of Pesach.

The men of Sedom kindled Your wrath, and	
were set aflame with fire	on Pesach;
Lot was saved from their midst, and baked	
matzos at the close	of Pesach;
You swept clean the ground of Moph and	
Noph [Egypt] when You passed through	on Pesach;

Say then: It is the feast of Pesach.

God, You crushed every firstborn's head on	
the watchnight	of Pesach;
O' Great One, yet over Your firstborn You	
skipped by [to spare him] because of the	
blood [marking the doors]	of the Pesach;

לְבִלְתִּי תֵּת מַשְׁחִית לָבֹא בִפְתָחַי   בַּפֶּסַח.

וַאֲמַרְתֶּם זֶבַח פֶּסַח

מִסְגֶּרֶת סֻגְּרָה בְּעִתּוֹתֵי   פֶּסַח.

נִשְׁמְדָה מִדְיָן בִּצְלִיל שְׂעוֹרֵי עֹמֶר   פֶּסַח.

שׂוֹרְפוּ מִשְׁמַנֵּי פוּל וְלוּד בִּיקַד יְקוֹד   פֶּסַח.

וַאֲמַרְתֶּם זֶבַח פֶּסַח

עוֹד הַיּוֹם בְּנֹב לַעֲמוֹד עַד גָּעָה עוֹנַת   פֶּסַח.

פַּס יַד כָּתְבָה לְקַעֲקֵעַ צוּל   בַּפֶּסַח.

צָפֹה הַצָּפִית עָרוֹךְ הַשֻּׁלְחָן   בַּפֶּסַח.

וַאֲמַרְתֶּם זֶבַח פֶּסַח

קָהָל כִּנְּסָה הֲדַסָּה צוֹם לְשַׁלֵּשׁ   בַּפֶּסַח.

רֹאשׁ מִבֵּית רָשָׁע מָחַצְתָּ בְּעֵץ חֲמִשִּׁים   בַּפֶּסַח.

שְׁתֵּי אֵלֶּה רֶגַע תָּבִיא לְעוּצִית   בַּפֶּסַח.

תָּעֹז יָדְךָ וְתָרוּם יְמִינְךָ כְּלֵיל הִתְקַדֶּשׁ חַג   פֶּסַח.

וַאֲמַרְתֶּם זֶבַח פֶּסַח

293

So as not to let the destroyer enter my
  doorways   on Pesach;
  Say then: It is the feast of Pesach.

The locked shut [city of Yericho] fell at the time   of Pesach;
Midyan was wiped out through a barley cake,
  the omer offering   of Pesach;
The stalwart men of Pul and Lud [Ashur] were
  burned in a great blaze   on Pesach;
  Say then: It is the feast of Pesach.

"Yet today" [Sancheriv planned] to arrive at
  Nov [and besiege Yerushalayim] till [he had
  his downfall when] came the time   of Pesach;
An unseen hand wrote to prophesy the
  destruction of Tzul [Babylon]   on Pesach;
While they set the watch, prepared the table,   on Pesach;
  Say then: It is the feast of Pesach.

Hadassah [Esther] assembled the [Jewish]
  community for a three-day fast   on Pesach;
The head of the wicked house [Haman] You
  destroyed on a fifty-foot gallows   on Pesach;
Double misfortune o' bring instantly on Utzis
  [Edom]   on Pesach;
May Your Hand be strengthened, and Your
  right Hand exalted, as on that night when
  You sanctified the Festival   of Pesach;
  Say then: It is the feast of Pesach.

כִּי לוֹ נָאֶה. כִּי לוֹ יָאֶה:

אַדִּיר בִּמְלוּכָה. בָּחוּר כַּהֲלָכָה. גְּדוּדָיו יֹאמְרוּ לוֹ. לְךָ וּלְךָ. לְךָ כִּי לְךָ. לְךָ אַף לְךָ. לְךָ יהוה הַמַּמְלָכָה. כִּי לוֹ נָאֶה. כִּי לוֹ יָאֶה:

דָּגוּל בִּמְלוּכָה. הָדוּר כַּהֲלָכָה. וָתִיקָיו יֹאמְרוּ לוֹ. לְךָ ולך וכו'.

זַכַּאי בִּמְלוּכָה חָסִין כַּהֲלָכָה טַפְסְרָיו יֹאמְרוּ לוֹ לך ולך וכו'.

יָחִיד בִּמְלוּכָה כַּבִּיר כַּהֲלָכָה לִמּוּדָיו יֹאמְרוּ לוֹ לך ולך וכו'.

מֶלֶךְ בִּמְלוּכָה נוֹרָא כַּהֲלָכָה סְבִיבָיו יֹאמְרוּ לוֹ לך ולך וכו'.

עָנָו בִּמְלוּכָה פּוֹדֶה כַּהֲלָכָה צַדִּיקָיו יֹאמְרוּ לוֹ לך ולך וכו'.

קָדוֹשׁ בִּמְלוּכָה רַחוּם כַּהֲלָכָה שִׁנְאַנָּיו יֹאמְרוּ לוֹ לך ולך וכו'.

תַּקִּיף בִּמְלוּכָה תּוֹמֵךְ כַּהֲלָכָה תְּמִימָיו יֹאמְרוּ לוֹ לך ולך וכו'.

Those who do not drink the fourth cup until this point, do so now, according to the instructions on page 282. They then say the berachah after drinking wine and continue to recite "The order of the Pesach service," etc., until "Next year in Yerushalayim!" and then continue from here.

Ki Lo Na'eh, Ki Lo Ya'eh

For To Him It Is Becoming; For To Him It Is Fitting

Mighty in majesty, truly supreme, His
companies [of angels] say to Him: To You,
again to You; to You, for to You; to You,
indeed to You; to You, Hashem, belongs
all sovereignty. For to Him it is becoming;
for to Him it is fitting.

Excelling in majesty, truly resplendent, His
faithful [in Jewry] say to Him: To You etc.

Pristine in majesty, truly powerful, His [angelic]
princes say to Him: To You etc.

Unique in majesty, truly omnipotent, His
disciples [in Jewry] say to Him: To You etc.

Ruling in majesty, truly held in awe, His surrounding [Heavenly] companions say to Him: To You etc.

Humble in majesty, truly a Redeemer, His
righteous ones [in Jewry] say to Him: To You etc.

Holy in majesty, truly compassionate, His
chorus of angels say to Him: To You etc.

Forceful in majesty, truly all-sustaining, His
perfect ones say to Him: To You etc.

Those who do not drink the fourth cup until this point, do
so now, according to the instructions on page 282. They
then say the berachah after drinking wine and continue
to recite "The order of the Pesach service," etc., until "Next
year in Yerushalayim!" and then continue from here.

אַדִּיר הוּא

אַדִּיר הוּא יִבְנֶה בֵיתוֹ בְּקָרוֹב בִּמְהֵרָה בִּמְהֵרָה בְּיָמֵנוּ בְּקָרוֹב אֵל בְּנֵה אֵל בְּנֵה בְּנֵה בֵיתְךָ בְּקָרוֹב.

בָּחוּר הוּא גָּדוֹל הוּא דָּגוּל הוּא הָדוּר הוּא וָתִיק הוּא זַכַּאי הוּא חָסִיד הוּא יִבְנֶה בֵיתוֹ בְּקָרוֹב. בִּמְהֵרָה בִּמְהֵרָה בְּיָמֵינוּ בְּקָרוֹב. אֵל בְּנֵה אֵל בְּנֵה. בְּנֵה בֵיתְךָ בְּקָרוֹב:

טָהוֹר הוּא יָחִיד הוּא כַּבִּיר הוּא לָמוּד הוּא מֶלֶךְ הוּא נוֹרָא הוּא סַגִּיב הוּא עִזּוּז הוּא פּוֹדֶה הוּא צַדִּיק הוּא יִבְנֶה בֵיתוֹ בְּקָרוֹב. בִּמְהֵרָה בִּמְהֵרָה בְּיָמֵינוּ בְּקָרוֹב. אֵל בְּנֵה אֵל בְּנֵה. בְּנֵה בֵיתְךָ בְּקָרוֹב.

קָדוֹשׁ הוּא רַחוּם הוּא שַׁדַּי הוּא תַּקִּיף הוּא יִבְנֶה בֵיתוֹ בְּקָרוֹב. בִּמְהֵרָה בִּמְהֵרָה בְּיָמֵינוּ בְּקָרוֹב. אֵל בְּנֵה אֵל בְּנֵה. בְּנֵה בֵיתְךָ בְּקָרוֹב:

Adir Hu

Mighty Is He

May He build His House soon! Speedily, yes
  speedily, in our days, soon! Build, o' God;
  build, o' God; build Your House soon!
Foremost is He, great is He, supreme is He
May He build...

Resplendent is He, faithful is He, worthy is He,
  kindly is He
May He build...

Pure is He, unique is He, omnipotent is He,
  learned is He, sovereign is He, awesome is
  He, sublime is He, powerful is He, the
  Redeemer is He, righteous is He
May He build...

Holy is He, compassionate is He, the Almighty
  is He, puissant is He
May He build...

*Those who live in chutz la'aretz and have not yet
counted the Omer after maariv on the second night of
Pesach do so now.*

בָּרוּךְ אַתָּה יהוה אֱלֹהֵינוּ מֶלֶךְ הָעוֹלָם אֲשֶׁר
קִדְּשָׁנוּ בְּמִצְוֹתָיו וְצִוָּנוּ עַל סְפִירַת הָעוֹמֶר:
הַיּוֹם יוֹם אֶחָד לָעֹמֶר:

יְהִי רָצוֹן מִלְּפָנֶיךָ יְיָ אֱלֹהֵינוּ וֵאלֹהֵי אֲבוֹתֵינוּ שֶׁיִּבָּנֶה בֵּית
הַמִּקְדָּשׁ בִּמְהֵרָה בְיָמֵינוּ וְתֵן חֶלְקֵנוּ בְּתוֹרָתֶךָ. וְשָׁם נַעֲבָדְךָ בְּיִרְאָה
כִּימֵי עוֹלָם וּכְשָׁנִים קַדְמוֹנִיּוֹת:

אֶחָד מִי יוֹדֵעַ

אֶחָד מִי יוֹדֵעַ. אֶחָד אֲנִי יוֹדֵעַ. אֶחָד אֱלֹהֵינוּ שֶׁבַּשָּׁמַיִם וּבָאָרֶץ:
שְׁנַיִם מִי יוֹדֵעַ. שְׁנַיִם אֲנִי יוֹדֵעַ. שְׁנֵי לֻחוֹת הַבְּרִית. אֶחָד אֱלֹהֵינוּ
שֶׁבַּשָּׁמַיִם וּבָאָרֶץ:
שְׁלֹשָׁה מִי יוֹדֵעַ. שְׁלֹשָׁה אֲנִי יוֹדֵעַ. שְׁלֹשָׁה אָבוֹת. שְׁנֵי לֻחוֹת הַבְּרִית.
אֶחָד אֱלֹהֵינוּ שֶׁבַּשָּׁמַיִם וּבָאָרֶץ:

299

Those who live in chutz la'aretz and have not yet counted the Omer after maariv on the second night of Pesach do so now.

Blessed be You, Hashem our God, King of the universe, Who has sanctified us by His commandments and commanded us concerning the counting of the Omer.

Today is the first day of the Omer.

May it be Your will, Hashem, our God and God of our fathers, that the Temple be speedily rebuilt in our days, and give us our portion in your Torah, so that we may serve You there with awe as in the days of old and as in former years.

Echad Mi Yodei'a

Who Knows One?

Who knows one? I know one. Our God is One, in heaven and on the earth.

Who knows two? I know two. The tablets of the covenant are two, our God is One, in heaven and on the earth.

Who knows three? I know three. The Patriarchs are three, the tablets of the covenant are two, our God is One, in heaven and on the earth.

אַרְבַּע מִי יוֹדֵעַ. אַרְבַּע אֲנִי יוֹדֵעַ. אַרְבַּע אִמָּהוֹת. שְׁלֹשָׁה אָבוֹת. שְׁנֵי לֻחוֹת הַבְּרִית. אֶחָד אֱלֹהֵינוּ שֶׁבַּשָּׁמַיִם וּבָאָרֶץ:

חֲמִשָּׁה מִי יוֹדֵעַ. חֲמִשָּׁה אֲנִי יוֹדֵעַ. חֲמִשָּׁה חֻמְשֵׁי תוֹרָה. אַרְבַּע אִמָּהוֹת. שְׁלֹשָׁה אָבוֹת. שְׁנֵי לֻחוֹת הַבְּרִית. אֶחָד אֱלֹהֵינוּ שֶׁבַּשָּׁמַיִם וּבָאָרֶץ:

שִׁשָּׁה מִי יוֹדֵעַ. שִׁשָּׁה אֲנִי יוֹדֵעַ. שִׁשָּׁה סִדְרֵי מִשְׁנָה. חֲמִשָּׁה חֻמְשֵׁי תוֹרָה. אַרְבַּע אִמָּהוֹת. שְׁלֹשָׁה אָבוֹת. שְׁנֵי לֻחוֹת הַבְּרִית. אֶחָד אֱלֹהֵינוּ שֶׁבַּשָּׁמַיִם וּבָאָרֶץ:

שִׁבְעָה מִי יוֹדֵעַ. שִׁבְעָה אֲנִי יוֹדֵעַ. שִׁבְעָה יְמֵי שַׁבַּתָּא. שִׁשָּׁה סִדְרֵי מִשְׁנָה. חֲמִשָּׁה חֻמְשֵׁי תוֹרָה. אַרְבַּע אִמָּהוֹת. שְׁלֹשָׁה אָבוֹת. שְׁנֵי לֻחוֹת הַבְּרִית. אֶחָד אֱלֹהֵינוּ שֶׁבַּשָּׁמַיִם וּבָאָרֶץ:

שְׁמוֹנָה מִי יוֹדֵעַ. שְׁמוֹנָה אֲנִי יוֹדֵעַ. שְׁמוֹנָה יְמֵי מִילָה. שִׁבְעָה יְמֵי שַׁבַּתָּא. שִׁשָּׁה סִדְרֵי מִשְׁנָה. חֲמִשָּׁה חֻמְשֵׁי תוֹרָה. אַרְבַּע אִמָּהוֹת. שְׁלֹשָׁה אָבוֹת. שְׁנֵי לֻחוֹת הַבְּרִית. אֶחָד אֱלֹהֵינוּ שֶׁבַּשָּׁמַיִם וּבָאָרֶץ:

תִּשְׁעָה מִי יוֹדֵעַ. תִּשְׁעָה אֲנִי יוֹדֵעַ. תִּשְׁעָה יַרְחֵי לֵדָה. שְׁמוֹנָה יְמֵי מִילָה. שִׁבְעָה יְמֵי שַׁבַּתָּא. שִׁשָּׁה סִדְרֵי מִשְׁנָה. חֲמִשָּׁה חֻמְשֵׁי תוֹרָה. אַרְבַּע אִמָּהוֹת. שְׁלֹשָׁה אָבוֹת. שְׁנֵי לֻחוֹת הַבְּרִית. אֶחָד אֱלֹהֵינוּ שֶׁבַּשָּׁמַיִם וּבָאָרֶץ:

Who knows four? I know four. The Matriarchs are four, the Patriarchs are three, the tablets of the covenant are two, our God is One, in heaven and on the earth.

Who knows five? I know five. The books of the Torah are five, the Matriarchs are four, the Patriarchs are three, the tablets of the covenant are two, our God is One, in heaven and on the earth.

Who knows six? I know six. The Mishnah sections are six, the books of the Torah are five, the Matriarchs are four, the Patriarchs are three, the tablets of the covenant are two, our God is One, in heaven and on the earth.

Who knows seven? I know seven. The days of the week are seven, the Mishnah sections are six, the books of the Torah are five, the Matriarchs are four, the Patriarchs are three, the tablets of the covenant are two, our God is One, in heaven and on the earth.

Who knows eight? I know eight. The days of circumcision are eight, the days of the week are seven, the Mishnah sections are six, the books of the Torah are five, the Matriarchs are four, the Patriarchs are three, the tablets of the covenant are two, our God is One, in heaven and on the earth.

Who knows nine? I know nine. The months of childbirth are nine, the days of circumcision are eight, the days of the week are seven, the Mishnah sections are six, the books of the Torah are five, the Matriarchs are four, the Patriarchs are three, the tablets of the covenant are two, our God is One, in heaven and on the earth.

עֲשָׂרָה מִי יוֹדֵעַ. עֲשָׂרָה אֲנִי יוֹדֵעַ. עֲשָׂרָה דִבְּרַיָּא. תִּשְׁעָה יַרְחֵי לֵדָה. שְׁמוֹנָה יְמֵי מִילָה. שִׁבְעָה יְמֵי שַׁבַּתָּא. שִׁשָּׁה סִדְרֵי מִשְׁנָה. חֲמִשָּׁה חֻמְשֵׁי תוֹרָה. אַרְבַּע אִמָּהוֹת. שְׁלֹשָׁה אָבוֹת. שְׁנֵי לֻחוֹת הַבְּרִית. אֶחָד אֱלֹהֵינוּ שֶׁבַּשָּׁמַיִם וּבָאָרֶץ:

אַחַד עָשָׂר מִי יוֹדֵעַ. אַחַד עָשָׂר אֲנִי יוֹדֵעַ. אַחַד עָשָׂר כּוֹכְבַיָּא. עֲשָׂרָה דִבְּרַיָּא. תִּשְׁעָה יַרְחֵי לֵדָה. שְׁמוֹנָה יְמֵי מִילָה. שִׁבְעָה יְמֵי שַׁבַּתָּא. שִׁשָּׁה סִדְרֵי מִשְׁנָה. חֲמִשָּׁה חֻמְשֵׁי תוֹרָה. אַרְבַּע אִמָּהוֹת. שְׁלֹשָׁה אָבוֹת. שְׁנֵי לֻחוֹת הַבְּרִית. אֶחָד אֱלֹהֵינוּ שֶׁבַּשָּׁמַיִם וּבָאָרֶץ:

שְׁנֵים עָשָׂר מִי יוֹדֵעַ. שְׁנֵים עָשָׂר אֲנִי יוֹדֵעַ. שְׁנֵים עָשָׂר שִׁבְטַיָּא. אַחַד עָשָׂר כּוֹכְבַיָּא. עֲשָׂרָה דִבְּרַיָּא. תִּשְׁעָה יַרְחֵי לֵדָה. שְׁמוֹנָה יְמֵי מִילָה. שִׁבְעָה יְמֵי שַׁבַּתָּא. שִׁשָּׁה סִדְרֵי מִשְׁנָה. חֲמִשָּׁה חֻמְשֵׁי תוֹרָה. אַרְבַּע אִמָּהוֹת. שְׁלֹשָׁה אָבוֹת. שְׁנֵי לֻחוֹת הַבְּרִית. אֶחָד אֱלֹהֵינוּ שֶׁבַּשָּׁמַיִם וּבָאָרֶץ:

שְׁלֹשָׁה עָשָׂר מִי יוֹדֵעַ. שְׁלֹשָׁה עָשָׂר אֲנִי יוֹדֵעַ. שְׁלֹשָׁה עָשָׂר מִדַּיָּא. שְׁנֵים עָשָׂר שִׁבְטַיָּא. אַחַד עָשָׂר כּוֹכְבַיָּא. עֲשָׂרָה דִבְּרַיָּא. תִּשְׁעָה יַרְחֵי לֵדָה. שְׁמוֹנָה יְמֵי מִילָה. שִׁבְעָה יְמֵי שַׁבַּתָּא. שִׁשָּׁה סִדְרֵי מִשְׁנָה. חֲמִשָּׁה חֻמְשֵׁי תוֹרָה. אַרְבַּע אִמָּהוֹת. שְׁלֹשָׁה אָבוֹת. שְׁנֵי לֻחוֹת הַבְּרִית. אֶחָד אֱלֹהֵינוּ שֶׁבַּשָּׁמַיִם וּבָאָרֶץ:

Who knows ten? I know ten. The Ten Commandments are ten, the months of childbirth are nine, the days of circumcision are eight, the days of the week are seven, the Mishnah sections are six, the books of the Torah are five, the Matriarchs are four, the Patriarchs are three, the tablets of the covenant are two, our God is One, in heaven and on the earth.

Who knows eleven? I know eleven. The stars [in Joseph's dream] are eleven, the Ten Commandments are ten, the months of childbirth are nine, the days of circumcision are eight, the days of the week are seven, the Mishnah sections are six, the books of the Torah are five, the Matriarchs are four, the Patriarchs are three, the tablets of the covenant are two, our God is One, in heaven and on the earth.

Who knows twelve? I know twelve. Twelve are the tribes of Yisrael, the stars are eleven, the Ten Commandments are ten, the months of childbirth are nine, the days of circumcision are eight, the days of the week are seven, the Mishnah sections are six, the books of the Torah are five, the Matriarchs are four, the Patriarchs are three, the tablets of the covenant are two, our God is One, in heaven and on the earth.

Who knows thirteen? I know thirteen. God's attributes are thirteen, the tribes of Yisrael are twelve, the stars are eleven, the Ten Commandments are ten, the months of childbirth are nine, the days of circumcision are eight, the days of the week are seven, the Mishnah sections are six, the books of the Torah are five, the Matriarchs are four, the Patriarchs are three, the tablets of the covenant are two, our God is One, in heaven and on the earth.

חַד גַּדְיָא

חַד גַּדְיָא. חַד גַּדְיָא. דְזַבִּין אַבָּא בִּתְרֵי זוּזֵי. חַד גַּדְיָא חַד גַּדְיָא:

וְאָתָא שׁוּנְרָא וְאָכְלָא לְגַדְיָא דְזַבִּין אַבָּא בִּתְרֵי זוּזֵי. חַד גַּדְיָא חַד גַּדְיָא:

וְאָתָא כַלְבָּא וְנָשַׁךְ לְשׁוּנְרָא. דְאָכְלָא לְגַדְיָא. דְזַבִּין אַבָּא בִּתְרֵי זוּזֵי. חַד גַּדְיָא חַד גַּדְיָא:

וְאָתָא ווּטְרָא וְהִכָּא לְכַלְבָּא. דְנָשַׁךְ לְשׁוּנְרָא. דְאָכְלָא לְגַדְיָא. דְזַבִּין אַבָּא בִּתְרֵי זוּזֵי. חַד גַּדְיָא חַד גַּדְיָא:

וְאָתָא נוּרָא וְשָׂרַף לְחוּטְרָא. דְהִכָּה לְכַלְבָּא. דְנָשַׁךְ לְשׁוּנְרָא. דְאָכְלָא לְגַדְיָא. דְזַבִּין אַבָּא בִּתְרֵי זוּזֵי. חַד גַּדְיָא חַד גַּדְיָא:

וְאָתָא מַיָּא וְכָבָה לְנוּרָא. דְשָׂרַף לְחוּטְרָא. דְהִכָּה לְכַלְבָּא. דְנָשַׁךְ לְשׁוּנְרָא. דְאָכְלָא לְגַדְיָא. דְזַבִּין אַבָּא בִּתְרֵי זוּזֵי. חַד גַּדְיָא חַד גַּדְיָא:

וְאָתָא תוֹרָא וְשָׁתָה לְמַיָּא. דְכָבָה לְנוּרָא. דְשָׂרַף לְחוּטְרָא. דְהִכָּה לְכַלְבָּא. דְנָשַׁךְ לְשׁוּנְרָא. דְאָכְלָא לְגַדְיָא. דְזַבִּין אַבָּא בִּתְרֵי זוּזֵי. חַד גַּדְיָא חַד גַּדְיָא:

וְאָתָא הַשּׁוֹחֵט וְשָׁחַט לְתוֹרָא. דְשָׁתָה לְמַיָּא. דְכָבָה לְנוּרָא. דְשָׂרַף לְחוּטְרָא. דְהִכָּה לְכַלְבָּא. דְנָשַׁךְ לְשׁוּנְרָא. דְאָכְלָא לְגַדְיָא. דְזַבִּין אַבָּא בִּתְרֵי זוּזֵי. חַד גַּדְיָא חַד גַּדְיָא:

Chad Gadya

An Only Kid

An only kid, an only kid, which my father bought for two zuzim. An only kid, an only kid.

And the cat came, and ate the kid, which my father bought for two zuzim. An only kid, an only kid.

And the dog came, and bit the cat, that ate the kid, which my father bought for two zuzim. An only kid, an only kid.

And the stick came, and beat the dog, that bit the cat, that ate the kid, which my father bought for two zuzim. An only kid, an only kid.

And the fire came, and burned the stick, that beat the dog, that bit the cat, that ate the kid, which my father bought for two zuzim. An only kid, an only kid.

And the water came, and extinguished the fire, that burned the stick, beat the dog, that bit the cat, that ate the kid, which my father bought for two zuzim. An only kid, an only kid.

And the ox came, and drank the water, that extinguished the fire, that burned the stick, that beat the dog, that bit the cat, that ate the kid, which my father bought for two zuzim. An only kid, an only kid.

And the slaughterer came, and killed the ox, that drank the water, that extinguished the fire, that burned the stick, that beat the dog, that bit the cat, that ate the kid, which my father bought for two zuzim. An only kid, an only kid.

וְאָתָא מַלְאַךְ הַמָּוֶת וְשָׁחַט לְשׁוֹחֵט. דְּשָׁחַט לְתוֹרָא. דְּשָׁתָה לְמַיָּא.
דְּכָבָה לְנוּרָא. דְּשָׂרַף לְחוּטְרָא. דְּהִכָּה לְכַלְבָּא. דְּנָשַׁךְ לְשׁוּנְרָא.
דְּאָכְלָא לְגַדְיָא. דְּזַבִּין אַבָּא בִּתְרֵי זוּזֵי. חַד גַּדְיָא חַד גַּדְיָא:
וְאָתָא הַקָּדוֹשׁ בָּרוּךְ הוּא וְשָׁחַט לְמַלְאַךְ הַמָּוֶת. דְּשָׁחַט לְשׁוֹחֵט.
דְּשָׁחַט לְתוֹרָא. דְּשָׁתָה לְמַיָּא. דְּכָבָה לְנוּרָא. דְּשָׂרַף לְחוּטְרָא.
דְּהִכָּה לְכַלְבָּא. דְּנָשַׁךְ לְשׁוּנְרָא. דְּאָכְלָא לְגַדְיָא. דְּזַבִּין אַבָּא
בִּתְרֵי זוּזֵי. חַד גַּדְיָא חַד גַּדְיָא:

*One should continue to occupy himself with the story
of the Exodus and the laws of Pesach until sleep
overtakes him.*

*Many recite Shir Hashirim which expresses the
overwhelming love between Hashem and His chosen
people, Yisrael.*

And the Angel of Death came, and slew the slaughterer, who killed the ox, that drank the water, that extinguished the fire, that burned the stick, that beat the dog, that bit the cat, that ate the kid, which my father bought for two zuzim. An only kid, an only kid.

And then came the Holy One, Blessed be He, and smote the Angel of Death, who slew the slaughterer, who killed the ox, that drank the water, that extinguished the fire, that burned the stick, that beat the dog, that bit the cat, that ate the kid, which my father bought for two zuzim. An only kid, an only kid.

*One should continue to occupy himself with the story
of the Exodus and the laws of Pesach until sleep
overtakes him.*

*Many recite Shir Hashirim which expresses the
overwhelming love between Hashem and His chosen
people, Yisrael.*

APPENDIX

Who wrote the Malbim Haggadah?

The *Malbim Haggadah*, as it is commonly called, was first published in Warsaw in 5643/1883, and again in 5654/1894. The 5643/1883 edition was reprinted and distributed several times by various printers in Israel and the United States during the past four decades. The 5654/1894 edition, however, was reprinted once in 5665/1905 in Warsaw and was not reprinted again until 5751/1991 in Jerusalem.

The few words on the cover of the 5751/1991 edition express the prevalent, unquestioned assumption about the authorship of this work. The title reads (translated from Hebrew), *Haggadah of Pesach with commentary by the Gaon Malbim.*

At first glance, the original title pages (which, for the first printings, were also used for the covers) of both the 5643/1883 and 5654/1894 editions imply that the commentary, entitled *Medrash Haggadah*, was written by the *Malbim*, and that the ten short paragraphs, referred to as *Asarah Maamaros*, addenda in footnote form to the commentary, was written by Rav Naftali Maskil LeAison.

A closer examination of the text of the title page of the

5654/1894 edition, however, tells a different story. The title page of that edition says that this commentary on the Haggadah "paves the way in the depths of meaning, explains the order and connection of the paragraphs, and proves that all of the teachings of the sages which were derived from verses of the Torah have a firm basis in the verses themselves and are solidly grounded in the language of the text according to the established rules of style and order, [this commentary having been written] in the way of explaining the teachings of our sages (בדרך באורי דרשות חז"ל) of the honorable rabbi (מאת כבוד הרב), the great Gaon, the renowned Tzaddik, Our teacher, Rabbi Meir Leibush Malbim, ztvk'l, with notes entitled 'Ten Essays' explaining the sayings of our Sages of blessed memory, by Naftali, son of the Gaon our teacher Avraham ztvk'l Maskil LeAison."

The wording of this paragraph suggests that the commentary was conceived in the method of and written in the style of the *Malbim* — "in the way of explaining... of the *Malbim*" — that is, in the *Malbim*'s method, but that it was not actually written by the *Malbim*, but by Rav Naftali Maskil LeAison, who followed the style and explanatory approach of the *Malbim*. Particular phrases in the footnotes by Rav Naftali also suggest that he wrote the commentary[1].

Of course, this wording of the title page and the phrases in the footnotes by no means point conclusively to Rav Naftali as the author of the commentary[2], but they nevertheless provide a strong argument for the case.

On the other hand, the title page of the 5643/1883 edition, unlike that of the 5654/1894 edition, almost clearly states that

this commentary is the work of the *Malbim*. But it, too, can be read otherwise. The title page of the earlier edition states that the commentary "proves that all of the teachings of the sages which were derived from verses of the Torah have a firm basis in the verses themselves and are solidly grounded in the language of the text according to the established rules of style and order, the derived teachings and the straightforward meaning of the verse complementing one another, this being the path which ascends to the House of God in understanding the teachings of our sages of blessed memory, the holy way shall it be called, by the honorable rabbi, the great Gaon, the renowned Tzaddik..., Our teacher, Rabbi Meir Leibush Malbim, *ztvk'l*, with 'Ten Essays' comprising notes of explanation of the sayings of our Sages of blessed memory, by Naftali, son of the Gaon our teacher Avraham ztvk'l Maskil LeAison."

This elegant description of the commentary suggests that it was written by the *Malbim*[3]. Here, too, however, the text can be interpreted to mean that the approach is that of the *Malbim*.

Further evidence suggests that the *Malbim* did not write this commentary. The *Malbim* passed away in 5639/1879, four years before this commentary was first published. This alone does not necessarily prove that it was not written by the *Malbim*; after all, it may have merely been published posthumously (although it begs one's curiousity that two editions came out, and both were published after the supposed author's death). However, none of the biographers of the *Malbim* mention the commentary on the Haggadah in the lists of his works (Rosenbloom, 5748/1988; Rottenberg, 5739/1979;

Schaechter, 5743/1983; Yashar, 5736/1976).

Furthermore, several sources state explicitly that the *Malbim* did not write this commentary but that it was written in the style of the *Malbim* by Rav Naftali Maskil LeAison, such as *Bet Eked Sepharim* (Friedberg, 5711/1951)[4], *HaGaon Malbim* (Yashar, 5736/1976), and the publisher's introduction to the *Otzer Perushim* version of the *Malbim*'s commentary on the Torah[5].

Additional proof can be deduced from other sources. In 5643/1882, a Haggadah was published in Vilna with commentaries from fifteen great Sages, including the *Malbim*. The commentary by the *Malbim* appeared only on the section of the Four Sons. This is significant for several reasons.

First, the commentary is completely different from the commentary which appears in the Haggadah attributed to the *Malbim*. If the *Malbim* was the author, then when he compiled his commentary on the Haggadah, why did he ignore what he had written about the Four Sons? Of course, since his Haggadah was published after his death, it could be that its compiler — Rav Naftali — was unaware of what the *Malbim* had written about the Four Sons elsewhere. However, where does this elsewhere happen to be? It is the *Malbim*'s own commentary on the Torah to Shmos 13:12, published long before Rav Naftali compiled the Haggadah. It is impossible that Rav Naftali was unaware of it. Perhaps he was aware of it but opted to omit it from the commentary on the Haggadah. But why would he ignore such an important exposition?

Second, did the publishers of this 5643/1882 Haggadah not know that in a few months time, the *Malbim*'s own Haggadah

would be published? Did Rav Naftali have a monopoly on the rest of the *Malbim*'s writings on the Haggadah so that the Vilna publishers could only use the *Malbim*'s essay on the Four Sons? Or did Rav Naftali know about the *Malbim*'s unpublished manuscripts on the Haggadah, and the Vilna publishers did not? It is no wonder that Rabbi M. M. Yashar, of blessed memory, a respected *talmid chacham* and Rav who wrote a comprehensive book about the *Malbim* and his teachings, cites the essay on the Four Sons in his biography (pp.116-119) and writes in his list of works by the *Malbim*, "20. Haggadah of Pesach according to the style of the *Malbim*, compiled by Rav Naftali Maskil LeAison, Warsaw, 5643/1883" (p. 290).

However, perhaps clarification may come from comparing the commentary in *Medrash Haggadah* to the commentary of the *Malbim* in other places. For example, if we compare the commentary on the verses in the Haggadah cited from the Torah with the *Malbim*'s commentary on those verses in their original places and we find them to be identical, we could argue that this would be proof that the *Malbim* wrote the commentary on the Haggadah. Of course, we have already shown that there is absolutely no similarity between the *Malbim*'s elucidation of the Four Sons in his commentary on the Torah and the explanation found in the commentary on the Haggadah. That does not necessarily dismiss the possibility that the *Malbim* wrote the commentary on the Haggadah; it could easily be that the *Malbim*, when writing commentary on the Haggadah, preferred to adhere to the simple meaning of the text relevant to understanding the Haggadah at the Pesach Seder, and saved his homiletical harangue against the destroy-

ers of the Jewish faith of his time for a different literary location.

However, there appears to be no overwhelming similarity between the two commentaries. Some differ dramatically, even diametrically (for example, *Medrash Haggadah* on Psalm 113 and the *Malbim* on Psalm 113), while others are identical (for example, *Medrash Haggadah* on the word ורב, *and numerous*, and the *Malbim*'s commentary on Devarim 26:5), and some have nothing to do with each other (see the two commentaries on Devarim 26:8). Although very few of the differing explanations are exclusive — that is, the different explanations of the two sources on the same verse or word can both be true at the same time — this is not so much proof that the *Malbim* wrote the commentary on the Haggadah as it is proof that God's Torah is profoundly rich in truth and meaning.

In conclusion, from a comparison of the commentary on the Haggadah with the *Malbim*'s commentary on the Torah, no proof can be deduced as to the authorship of the *Medrash Haggadah*.

In view of the likelihood that Rav Naftali Maskil LeAison authored this commentary, it is difficult to understand how this commentary has come to be known, in the relatively short span of one hundred years, as the *Malbim Haggadah* by lay persons and Torah sages alike. Although the original title page was misleading, contemporaries of the author should have known who wrote it.[6] Nevertheless, the misconception is certainly a praise to the scholarship of the true author, and it must be emphasized that the apparent possibility that the *Malbim* may not have authored it in no way diminishes its outstanding contribution to Torah literature.

Who was
Rav Naftali Maskil LeAison?

Rav Naftali Maskil LeAison was born in 5589/1829 in Radoshkovich, Belorussia, near Minsk, to a family of illustrious Torah scholars. He studied under his father, the great Rav Avraham Maskil LeAison, so named after his book *Maskil LeAison*, a collection of Talmudic novellae. His father wrote several books of commentary and novellae on the Talmud, the *Sifri*, the *Mishneh Torah*, and the *Shulchan Aruch*, and is commonly known by his notes which appear in the back of the popular Vilna edition of the Talmud under the title, *Mitzpeh Aison*.

Rav Naftali was the most well known of three sons, all of whom were exceptional Torah scholars. He worked as a book dealer and a scribe, and was an admired and respected poet, bibliographer, and bibliophile. He wrote a number of books, edited, corrected, and reprinted older books, and published several of his father's manuscripts during his father's life as well as after his death.

In the Torah world, Rav Naftali's name is well known and recognized for one particular outstanding contribution — the book *Seder HaDoros*, a voluminous work listing the names and giving brief biographical sketches of the prominent personalities of Jewish history. First printed in circa 5485/1725, *Seder HaDoros* became almost useless due to the printing errors and omissions of subsequent printings. For twenty years Rav Naftali researched and clarified every unclear detail, and organized and revised the entire text of the book. He finally published

Seder HaDoros anew in 5637/1877 (volume one) and 5642/1882 (volumes two and three). It has been reprinted several times since Rav Naftali's death.

Rav Naftali received wide acclaim for his work on *Seder HaDoros*. The approbations of the great sages of his generation which appear at the beginning of the volume, including the *Beis HaLevi*, the *Netziv*, HaGaon HaRav Yitzchok Elchonon Spector, and HaGaon HaRav Yom Tov Lipman HaKohen reveal the great homage his scholarship earned him.

It is interesting to note that Rav Naftali was not only admired by the Torah sages, but by the Haskalists as well, especially for his research and poetry. Some Haskalists were under the impression that Rav Naftali himself was of their camp[7]. Although his business required him to deal with Haskalists and he may have frequently come into contact with them, his writings clearly show that he had nothing to do with their "enlightened" ways of thinking, and nor did his philosophy ever veer from the truth of the Torah. Furthermore, the words which the great Torah leaders of his generation wrote about him indicate that they knew him personally and clearly attest to his upright character, his *Yiras Shamayim*, and his devotion to Torah.

Rav Naftali fought against the Haskalah movement in a subtle, non-confrontational way (unlike other great Torah champions of that generation, such as the *Malbim*). Particular sections of his commentary on the Haggadah are subtle refutations in response to some of the beliefs of the Haskalists.

HaGaon HaRav Baruch HaLevi Epstein, the author of *Torah Temimah*, includes in his memoirs a brief sketch of Rav Naftali.

He calls Rav Naftali "one of the most distinguished residents of Minsk" and "a wonderful man whom I was privileged to know quite well." He writes the following about Rav Naftali:

> Although Rav Naftali associated with a number of *maskilim* and others whose loyalty to Judaism was suspect, he nonetheless enjoyed a close relationship with many Torah leaders of the generation who still respected him, seeing in him a man of pure faith and Torah scholarship. They were sure that he used his haskalah knowledge as a tailor uses his needle or a shoemaker uses his strap.... Rav Naftali's relationship with the maskilim of his generation could be compared to a person with a thick scarf wrapped half-way around his head: he knew them more than they knew him. His attitude was "see but don't be seen." Whenever he was brought to public discussion with them he tried to hide his true identity, very often using a pseudonym....
>
> *(Mekor Baruch*, vol. 4, pp. 1712-1714)

From the *Torah Temimah's* description of Rav Naftali (ibid.,) it is evident that a love and admiration for Torah and Torah scholars was part and parcel of his personality. The *Torah Temimah* records how Rav Naftali visibly rejoiced with genuine delight when he stood in the presence of and heard words of Torah from the great sage, the *Beis HaLevi.*

Rav Naftali died in 5658/1897 in Minsk.

Notes

1. For example, see the second footnote in the 5654/1894 edition in which Rav Naftali refers to a certain explanation in the commentary as "according to our approach in explaining the teaching of Ben Zoma".

2. The indicative words on the title page can alternatively be read, "... [this commentary having been written] in the way of explaining the teachings of our sages, [this commentary having been written] by... the *Malbim*." And the words "by Naftali... Maskil LeAison" could be referring only to the ten footnotes, and not to the entire commentary.

As for the words "according to our approach" that Rav Naftali writes in the footnotes, he could merely be referring to the commentary which "we" are discussing (the same way a teacher will say to his students, "according to our text...").

3. This may be the reason why so many people know this commentary as the *Malbim*'s. The 5643/1883 edition, the title page of which seems to suggest rather clearly that the *Malbim* was the author, was reprinted several times. The 5654/1894 edition, on the other hand, the title page of which more clearly implies that Rav Naftali was the author, remained in obscurity until 5751/1991, perhaps because of the very few editions in existence.

4. Although the editor lists the first printing of the commentary on the Haggadah as 5603/1843, this is a mistake, and should read 5643/1883.

A second lexicon, called *Bet Eked Sepharim He'Chadash*, was written in 5736/1976 updating the list of literature from 5711 until 5736, by M. Moriah, published by Zion Institute in Safed. This lexicon mentions three printings of the *Malbim Haggadah*: one in 5699/1939 in Lodz, another in 5720/1960 in Bnai Brak, and the Warsaw 5643/1883 edition (it is interesting to note that Moriah lists them in that order), and attributes its authorship to the *Malbim*. The author's research and results are unclear, because he was apparently unaware of the 5654/1894 edition (the 5699/1939 and 5720/1960 editions were both reprints of the 5643/1883 edition), while the original *Bet Eked Sepharim* not only lists it, but lists it — as well as the first edition — under Rav Naphtali's authorship.

5. In *Mishpachas Maskil LeAison* by Tzvi Harkavi (5713/1953, p. 11), the biographer lists the Haggadah as one of the works of Rav Naftali, but

parenthetically inserts "with the *Malbim*" under the 5643/1883 edition. The intention of the author is unclear, and his parenthetical statement may merely be his understanding of the ambiguity of the original title page which appeared on the 5643/1883 edition.

6. Rav Naftali published several books and articles anonymously, and, therefore, it is not inconceivable to suggest that he did not mind if he not be known as the author of this book.

7. For example, *The Jewish Encyclopedia*, published by one of the leaders of "enlightened" American Jewry at the turn of the century.

References

Friedberg, Ch. B. (5711/1951). *Bet Eked Sepharim — Bibliophraphical Lexicon.* Tel Aviv: Hotzaat Bar-Yuda, v. I, p. 267.

Rosenbloom, N. H. (5748/1988). *HaMalbim.* Jerusalem: Mosad HaRav Kook.

Rottenberg, Y. (5739/1979). *Sefer HaMalbim.* Bnai Brak: Hotzaat Netzach, p. 80.

Schaechter, Sh. Z. (5743/1983). *The Malbim, his literary work and thought — a doctoral dissertation.* Jerusalem: Hebrew University.

Yaari, A. (1960). *Bibliography of the Passover Haggadah, from Earliest Printed Edition to 1960.* Jerusalem: Bamberger & Wahrman.

Yashar, M.M. (5736/1976). *HaGaon Malbim.* Jerusalem: Hotzaat Hod, p. 290.

Otzer HaPerushim al Tanach. Tel Aviv: Hotzaat Miphorshei HaTanach

Tzfunot Torah Quarterly (Tammuz 5751/Summer 1991). Bnai Brak.

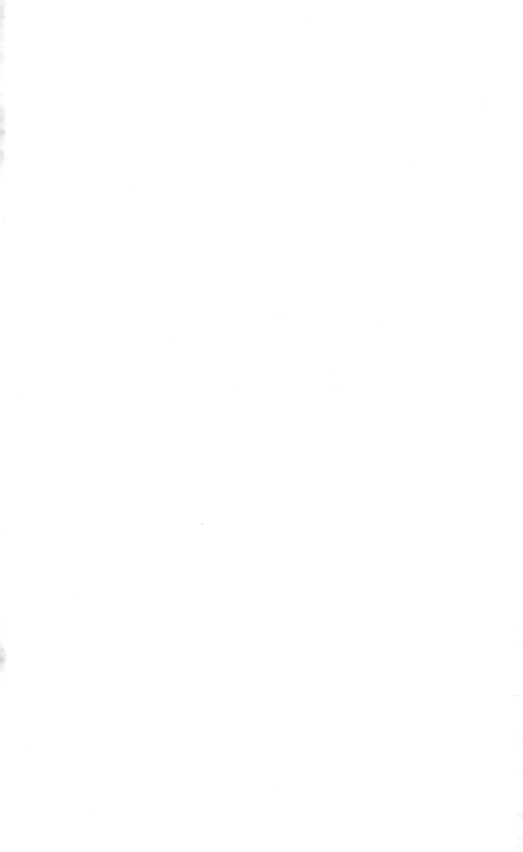

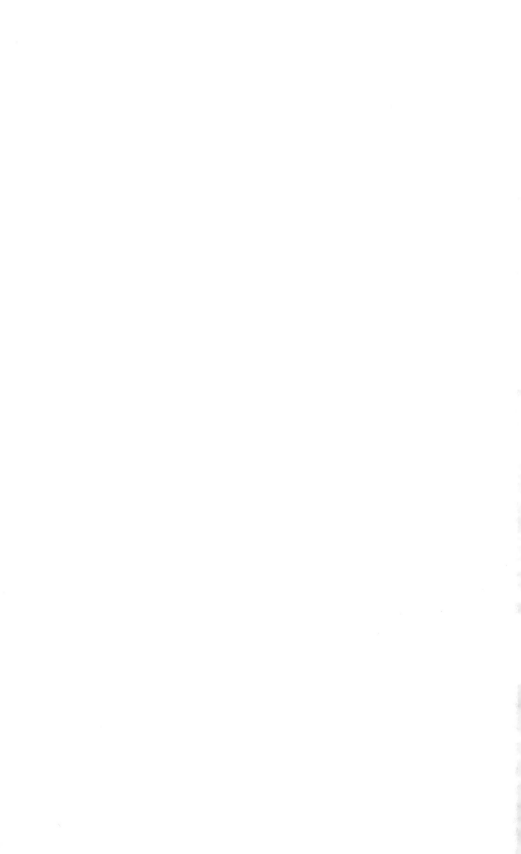